M000159955

Trauma and the
Teaching of Writing

Trauma and the Teaching of Writing

edited by

Shane Borrowman

STATE UNIVERSITY OF NEW YORK PRESS

Published by
State University of New York Press, Albany

© 2006 State University of New York

All rights reserved

Printed in the United States of America

No part of this book may be used or reproduced in any manner whatsoever without
written permission. No part of this book may be stored in a retrieval system or
transmitted in any form or by any means including electronic, electrostatic, magnetic
tape, mechanical, photocopying, recording, or otherwise without the prior permission
in writing of the publisher.

For information, address State University of New York Press,
90 State Street, Suite 700, Albany, NY 12207

Production by Christine L. Hamel
Marketing by Anne M. Valentine

Library of Congress Cataloging-in-Publication Data

Borrowman, Shane.
  Trauma and the teaching of writing / edited by Shane Borrowman.
    p. cm.
  Includes bibliographical references and index.
    ISBN 0-7914-6277-3 (alk. paper) — ISBN 0-7914-6278-1 (pbk. : alk. paper)
    1. English language—Rhetoric—Study and teaching—Psychological aspects. 2. English
language—Composition and exercises—Study and teaching—Psychological aspects. 3.
English language—Composition and exercises—Study and teaching—United States. 4.
English language—Rhetoric—Study and teaching—United States. 5. Psychic trauma—United
States—History—20th century. 6. Creative writing—Therapeutic use. 7.
Autobiography—Therapeutic use. I. Title.

PE1404.B665 2005
808'.042'071—dc22
                                                                              2004058877

10 9 8 7 6 5 4 3 2 1

for Elizabeth

Contents

Introduction

Shane Borrowman

"The place where you came from ain't there any more, and where
you had in mind to go is cancelled out."
—Joyce Carol Oates, "Where Are You Going,
Where Have You Been?"

OF ALL THE possible emotions that could be associated with the morning of
September 11, 2001, I never expected to feel personal shame, yet I am unable
to arrive on any term that seems more accurate. In the years since that day, as
I have replayed my own actions and inactions in the classroom, I am left with
an unshakeable feeling that I failed my students in some simple, fundamental
way. Like many post-secondary instructors, I cancelled class rather than pro-
ceeding with business as usual discussing the events that were unfolding. On
the morning of September 11, 2001, I watched the towers fall and saw the
immediate pictures of the aftermath at the Pentagon. When I left for my office,
I took with me the portable television purchased years before so my wife could
watch the impeachment hearings of William Jefferson Clinton from her office.
It still sits in a drawer in my filing cabinet, against unfortunate future need; as
I revised this work, in fact, I pulled my television from its desk drawer once
more to watch the news about a shooting at a local high school. Parents were
being asked to pick up their children, and two members of my department
immediately left on this errand. Only the gunman was injured, and the event
was over before I became aware of it. Earlier in the year, on Saturday, February
1, 2003, I graded papers at my desk and used this television to listen to updates
about the Space Shuttle Columbia. But on September 11, 2001, I used this

1

television to watch the live feed from New York and decided to cancel my business writing classes for the day. The university was not cancelling classes officially, but the unofficial closure was nearly complete. My business students, I assumed, would be in no better condition to learn than I was to teach.

When I entered the classroom, the television hanging in the corner was on, playing the same coverage I had been watching, and the students sat quietly. No one spoke above a whisper. As I finished my explanation of the homework, work we would have done during class time that day, Mollie L. entered the room and took her seat in the front. She is a small, studious woman who rarely spoke in class but enjoyed discussing her experiences studying abroad in Florence. Her hands often had specks of off-white paint on them, proof of the work she was doing for her landlord to offset the cost of rent. Mollie worked all night doing inventory at a local video store, had slept as late as possible, and had not watched the news that morning.

Before I could answer her question about why class was cancelled, there was a rush among the students to see who could share the incredible news. It was my first experience of the terrible glee with which horror is shared, and I was as stunned as Mollie. She struggled to process the news, removed her glasses as she neared tears, and focused her attention on the television, which continued to run its live footage from the scene of the destruction. I mumbled some final words I no longer remember and returned to my office, *retreated* to my office, I think now, where other members of the English department were still gathered around my tiny television.

Maybe this was a teachable moment—that label applied to so many classroom failures or near-failures. Maybe. But it shames me now that I didn't do more; I can find no point in the story of my memories on which to hang my image of myself as a strong, capable instructor, an instructor able to take his students in hand and to help them understand the world of which our classroom is a part. My failure that day was not unique, but company does not lessen my belated misery, although now, more than two years after the fact, I understand why I acted as I did. Why many of us acted as we did.

My failure that September morning, on the simplest possible level, came about because of a lack of preparation. There have been other traumas in my life as a teacher and student—the seizing of the American embassy in Iran, the attempted assassination of Ronald Reagan, the Shuttle disasters, the bombing of the federal building in Oklahoma City, the list could go on—but there has never, ever been anything like the terrorist attacks on September 11, 2001. Not in my experience. Not in anyone's experience. Those attacks were, as Tim O'Brien writes of a much smaller atrocity, "a new wrinkle . . . [a sin that is] real fresh and original." That morning, as the attacks and their aftermath unfolded, "We . . . witnessed something essential, something brand-new and profound, a piece of the world so startling there was not yet a name for it" (86). I was at a loss in class that day because it had never entered my mind that I might have to be prepared for such an occurrence.

On one level, then, this collection of essays on teaching in times of trauma exists in the hope that others will not be caught flat-footed, as I was, for we are not alone as teachers in a traumatic time, and while the trauma of September 11 is at present unique in its scope, it is not entirely unique. There have been shared traumas in the past, as there will be others in the future, and teachers have always faced these traumas concurrently with their students.

The idea for this collection predates the events of September 2001, however. As early as the fall of 1996, I was exploring the idea of a collection of essays focused on the experience of teaching English at the post-secondary level in American universities during the Vietnam War. Various contributors—some of them represented in this volume—responded positively to the idea, but their responses were more favorable than those of any publisher. This lack of interest was, logically enough, based in an understanding of market forces: A book for such a narrow audience—professionals in rhetoric and composition—on such a narrowly focused topic—teaching and the Vietnam War—simply would not, it was thought at the time, sell enough copies to be worth the publisher's investment of time and resources. That collection exists only as notes in a manila folder, slowly shuffling to the back of a file drawer.

That Vietnam-oriented collection is the parent of this book, and a number of essays in these pages would have fit comfortably within its pages. In important ways, this is that book, for the focus on the Vietnam War was, I think now, a misrepresentation of the focus I had in mind. It wasn't Vietnam that was important; rather, it was the act of teaching in a world operating under the weight of that ongoing trauma.

In the preface to *Teaching Hearts and Minds*, a very fine reflection on the experience of teaching Vietnam War literature to the post-war generations, Barry M. Kroll sets forth his book's purpose primarily by describing what the book is not:

> Although this is a book about teaching and learning, it is not, strictly speaking, a pedagogical work. . . . Nor is it primarily a theoretical book. That is not to say that pedagogical and theoretical issues were unimportant to my project or that they will be ignored in the following pages. [. . .] But readers who are looking either for explicit pedagogical advice or for detailed theoretical argument will be disappointed. Instead, they will find a book based on my investigations of college students' processes of reflective inquiry. (vii)

The same is true, with minor changes, of this collection of essays. It is not, primarily, a pedagogical work on the healing effects of writing in times of trauma, nor is it primarily a theoretical work on a new field in composition that could aptly be named "trauma studies." Yet pedagogy and theory feature prominently in some of the essays that follow. This collection is not, primarily, about the reflections of students, in writing, following shared traumas, but the voices of students in such times do appear. Instead, this is a collection of reflective essays by both new and established scholars and teachers in rhetoric and composition, reflections on the work we do in the world we share. And in this present time, it is impossible to ignore the past as we reflect on circumstances. This is the thread that connects the essays that follow.

The essays in this collection defy easy categorization, for even the most analytical is personal—just as the most personal is analytical. Most exist, instead, within a tapestry of understanding and experience, where history, memory, and trauma cross with pedagogy and rhetoric/composition theory. It is a tapestry where there are as many—or more—questions as there are answers, questions both posed and tentatively answered by the contributors to this collection. Richard Miller, in *Composition Studies in the New Millennium: Rereading the Past, Rewriting the Future*, asks, "Where were you when the planes hit the towers?" (252). Many contributors to this collection answer this explicit question and its implicit follow-up: "As a teacher and scholar, what did you do then?" Some extend this line of questioning even further, particularly into the past, asking "As a teacher and scholar, what did you do then and what have you, or others, done before?"

When I solicited the essays for this collection, I asked an open-ended question; I asked teachers and scholars to reflect on their experiences in the writing classroom during moments of shared national trauma and tragedy. This general question produced a wide range of responses, most falling into a general category defined by Stephanie Dyer and Dana C. Elder as "suasive" essays, "persuasion [that] reinforces the values of the community for the benefit of the community" (137). Rather than arguing the inherent rightness of a given response to moments of trauma, the essays in this collection support a range of responses, all meant to deepen and broaden our understanding of what it means to teach in times of trauma. Within this general category, the essays that follow range from historical analysis through reflective narrative, and nearly all rely on a foundation in the personal responses of the writers.

The definition of *trauma* within this volume is not fixed, not codified; instead, many writers define the term, explicitly or implicitly, as they reflect. The baseline definition, perhaps the cultural definition, of trauma that exists behind the definitions offered here is well articulated by Marian MacCurdy in "From Trauma to Writing: A Theoretical Model for Practical Use":

> "Trauma" to many connotes mental "unhealth" if not outright illness. Yet trauma does not only refer to catastrophic moments. Dictionaries define trauma as a bodily injury produced by some act of violence or some agency outside the body; the condition resulting from the injury; or a startling experience that has a lasting effect on mental life. Trauma can be a single inci-

dent or a series of incidents. . . . In popular language we speak of one who
has been "traumatized" by some terrible experience, but in point of fact no
one can reach adulthood without some moments of trauma. (161)

While she is defining personal trauma, such as rape, MacCurdy's definition
does articulate the general understanding of trauma held by teachers. The definitions offered by the contributors to this volume are based upon this understanding, but they are also refutations of MacCurdy's qualifier, specifically that
trauma "does not only refer to catastrophic moments." The definitions of
trauma put forth here are all about trauma that is a direct result of shared
moments of horror—personal trauma that transcends the personal, shared
traumas affecting the national (and international) community, historical
approaches to trauma that inform current practices.

Darin Payne, in "The World Wide Agora: Negotiating Citizenship and
Ownership of Response Online," explicates a range of possible understandings of trauma, particularly situated in an historical and cultural context. His
explication begins with a begged question and the situating of his own definition: "The very idea of September 11th as a 'national' event—a national
trauma—begs the question: Whose event, or trauma, was it? (Whose is it
still?) Such ownership needs to be as contingent and variable as other events
in America's history have finally become." To understand trauma—particularly those considered to be "our" shared national traumas—in the writing
classroom, he argues, "we must work to redefine *national* with a sense of *inter-*
or even *trans*-national." Only through such a repositioning of our understanding of shared trauma can we, as students, teachers, and citizens, avoid
"the general tendency . . . towards homogenous reductivism rather than heterogeneous complexity."

Further complicating the range of possible definitions of *national
trauma*, Peter N. Goggin and Maureen Daly Goggin, in "Presence in
Absence: Discourses and Teaching (In, On, and About) Trauma," explore a
trinity of definitions of *trauma*—national, natural, and personal—with the
intention of "conceptualizing trauma and ways of understanding the discourses both generated by and surrounding it." Their analysis covers both
"*metadiscourse on writing* (about trauma) and *writing during trauma*," con-
cluding with a description and analysis of their own pedagogical work in the
writing classroom after September 11. "For those who teach writing," they
argue, "the terrorist attacks [of 9/11] and the aftermath of grief, retribution,
and reconstruction on a national scale have challenged us to re-examine and
reconsider scholarly theories on and pedagogical assumptions about the
teaching of writing."

Building upon Payne's argument against reduction and homogenization
and Goggins' analysis of the writing classroom and trauma, Richard Marback,
in "Here and Now: Remediating National Tragedy and the Purposes for

Teaching Writing," argues that the trauma of September 11 "should lead compositionists to take a hard evaluative look at the purposes of teaching first-year writing." As teachers and scholars of composition, we must, he argues, consider the ways in which we "direct the attention of students to the audiences, contexts, and purposes of their making of meaning here and now." This is particularly true, given that most of our students did not experience the immediate tragedies in New York City, rural Pennsylvania, and at the Pentagon; instead, "They experienced images of wreck and rubble, reports of death and destruction, and representations of despair and heroism, again, and again, and again." The composition classroom, for Marback, is a place where these images can be reimaged, reinterpreted, and reframed. A place where meaning about past events can be meaningfully formed.

Patricia Murphy, Ryan Muckerheide, and Duane Roen continue this analysis of and reflection on the writing classroom, particularly after September 11, through a focus on Abraham Maslow's hierarchy of needs. They write of students' needs changing as the events of September 11 played out on that Tuesday and into its aftermath: "[We] quickly understood that the events of 9/11 made it necessary for us to shift attention from students' esteem needs and self-actualization needs—the standard focus of much university teaching—to safety needs." Forcing students to remain focused on business-as-usual "would not result in much learning," they felt, while investing "a modest amount of time addressing safety" allowed students to come to terms with the trauma and then return meaningfully to the work of their education in rhetoric and writing. Murphy, Muckerheide, and Roen broaden the scope of their reflection by beginning with a focus on an English 101 instructor's reaction to the events of September 11 as they unfolded, moving to the reflection of an instructor adapting his syllabus for Spring 2002 to address students' needs, and ending with the reflections of a campus administrator who trains new teachers.

In "Teaching Writing in Hawaii after Pearl Harbor and 9/11: How to 'Make Meaning' and 'Heal' Despite National Propaganda," Daphne Desser further complicates the rhetorical situation of teaching writing in times of shared trauma through a localized, situated analysis of both the present and the past. She argues that often the drive to reframe and reinterpret ongoing trauma falls into a trap wherein "interpretation, analysis, and argumentation . . . make the 'seemingly incomprehensible' safe for consumption by transforming it into material that is manageable, orderly, civilized, and palatable"— a transformation that "[ignores] trauma's inevitable inability to be fully defined, processed, or understood." Arguing that the composition classroom is a site where the master narratives of a culture can be explored—explored in a way that allows "the mystery of trauma [to] remain in [students'] writing"— Desser supports "a redefinition of healing that emphasizes our disciplinary knowledge of rhetorical analysis and production" while arguing against the superficial image/narrative of the "'writing teacher as healer'" that can unwittingly support a superficial sense of closure.

Exploring another angle on the master narratives by which trauma is defined, Theresa Enos, Joseph Jones, Lonni Pearce, and Kenneth Vorndran, in "Consumerism and the Coopting of National Trauma," argue that the writing classroom, particularly in times of trauma, "presents opportunities . . . for both self-reflection and cultural critique." They focus their analysis specifically on "citizenship and consumerism [. . . and] on the reactions of [their] students to a call [by the media after 9/11] that intimately links citizenship with consumption." Like Desser, their analysis of the present is situated in an historical context—particularly the modern call to consume against the "call to conserve" during the traumas of two world wars. Between these two "calls," though, the authors analyze another: "The Call to Question," the call answered by instructors who wanted to "ensure that [their] students [have] a space to participate in civil discourse" in the writing classroom.

While Enos, Jones, Pearce, and Vorndran write of recent coopting of national discourse, Keith Miller and Kathleen Weinkauf write of the wholesale coopting of the past, particularly within the Civil Rights movement of the 1960s. Specifically, they argue that "in order to teach the rhetoric of the civil rights movement effectively, faculty must recognize its female pioneers, the sexism that these women faced and often overcame, and the wholesale erasure of their efforts by the news media." While their analysis is focused solely on teaching the misappropriated texts of the past, Miller and Weinkauf's message for writing teachers serves as a cautionary note. The cultural appropriation machine that drives the production and reproduction of the dominant American ideology functions in both the present and past. The present is the product of the past, and this product is defective and dysfunctional if understanding of the past is itself fundamentally flawed and incomplete.

Examining the present through the production of a specific product, Lynn Z. Bloom argues in "Writing Textbooks in/for Times of Trauma" that "in a changed world, a collection of readings intended to stimulate students' reasoned discussion and critical thinking and writing [must] respond to" the cataclysmic events of a day such as September 11. Analyzing her own experiences as she revised the seventh edition of *The Essay Connection,* Bloom argues that readings on international terrorism—allowing for an in-depth focus on this topic in English composition classes—must be included in a reader such as this "not because of morbid reasons, or a sentimental desire to memorialize a past that will never come again, but as an ethical response to a world [the students] did not ask for but will nevertheless have to live in."

Focusing on another genre of writing common to the composition classroom, Wendy Bishop and Amy Hodges, in "Loss and Letter Writing," argue that as writers "we use letters to investigate the conditions of daily life [and concurrently] make meaning of our worlds via the written word." Drawing from the saved letters that have meaning in their own lives, Bishop and Hodges argue that letter writing, used in the composition classroom, "created a space where classroom authors could rehearse and revise, could investigate place and personas." Like Desser, they worry over the issue of teacher-as-healer and make suggestions about assignments "that will tap issues of importance and interest to . . . a first-year writer" through letter writing—while still allowing for some distance between teacher, writer, and the sometimes-intimate subject under discussion.

Continuing the discussion of student engagement, Dana Elder, in "How Little We Knew: Spring 1970 at the University of Washington," reflects on the seemingly apathetic students he now teaches by contrasting them with the students who surrounded his own educational experience, arguing that this disinterestedness may be a natural result of lessons that were hard-learned by his generation of first-year college students. "I think this should be an easy story to tell," he writes. "It is not because it is a tale of the end of innocence, reflected in the lives and attitudes of college students and colleagues today." He writes of student protests, often met with violence; student demands, largely ignored; and, ultimately, student efforts to effect cultural change, efforts that remain "largely unfinished."

Writing in a similar mode to Elder, Richard Leo Enos in "'This rhetoric paper almost killed me!'" reflects on his experiences as a visiting scholar at the American School of Classical Studies at Athens in the spring of 1974—and expounds on the lessons he learned then "that bear on our own discipline." Specifically, he argues that "In a country such as ours, where we take for granted not only the availability of information but also access to various sites, the constraints of governmental control are not taken seriously." Elaborating on this aspect of the American scholar's attitude, he writes, "We assume a natural peace and tranquil environment for study."

In "Are You Now, or Have You Ever Been, an Academic?" Edward M. White and I explore this American attitude to which Richard Leo Enos points—reflecting on the traumas of academe, from FBI investigations of students and the censoring of great books to the post-9/11 world for exchange students and the often murky popular understanding of academic freedom. Ultimately, we argue that as teachers and professionals in rhetoric and composition in the new millennium, "we may be facing trauma as a permanent state, rather than an occasional anomaly. We may have always faced trauma in this way, in fact—trauma as an ongoing condition—without fully realizing it."

The final essay in this collection, "'We have common cause against the night,'" presents responses from the writing program administrators listserv (wpa-l) hosted by David Schwalm and Barry Maid at Arizona State University East. Unlike the previous essays, this work presents the ongoing responses of a diverse group of academics to the events of September 11, 2001. That difference aside, the posts to the wpa-l show the same depth of caring—for students and for one another—clearly articulated throughout all of these works.

In the end, the suasive essays in this collection are reflective inquiries, as Kroll defines that activity in *Hearts and Minds;* they are "connected as well as critical, responsive as well as reflective, an activity of heart as well as mind" (156). Contributors to this volume situate their analyses historically, pedagogically, and theoretically within the field of rhetoric and composition; they also situate them personally, situate them in the individual experience of shared trauma. At the end of *Hearts and Minds,* Kroll shares one of his most personal, and illuminating, reflections:

> When I got off that plane in Oakland in July 1970, I never imagined that I would teach a class about the Vietnam War, an experience I was determined to put behind me. As a soldier, I had seen firsthand the hollow rhetoric of that slogan about winning "hearts and minds." As a teacher, I have tried to reclaim and redeem that phrase, using it to describe a course that fosters personal connection and critical reflection—a course that stirs students' hearts and challenges their minds. (166)

The essays in this volume are stirring testimonies by pedagogues and theorists on their own experiences within and beyond the writing classroom during times of trauma. My own motivation for editing this collection is similar to that motive suggested by Kroll, although I came to this knowledge very late in the process of writing and editing the work. In the introduction to *Writing and Healing: Toward an Informed Practice,* Charles Anderson and Marian MacCurdy write, speaking of all who survive the traumas of the past and seek to understand them in the present, "As trauma survivors, we share one very important characteristic: We feel powerless, taken over by alien experiences we could not anticipate and did not choose. Healing depends upon gaining control over that which has engulfed us. We cannot go back and change the past" (5).

With this collection, I want to help future teachers take an early hold on the shared traumas they will face with their students—a hold solidified by a better understanding of the traumas of the present and the past. But this is also an act of atonement, if not of redemption. On the morning of September 11, 2001, I failed 48 business writing students on a simple, fundamental, human level; this is my attempt to reclaim and redeem the part of myself that did not act on that day, or that wishes to have acted differently.

WORKS CITED

Dyer, Stephanie and Dana C. Elder. "Suasive Narrative and the Habit of Reflection." *The Subject is Story: Essays for Writers and Readers.* Ed. Wendy Bishop and Hans Ostrom. Portsmouth, NH: Boynton/Cook, 2003. 136–46.

Kroll, Barry M. *Teaching Hearts and Minds: College Students Reflect on the Vietnam War in Literature*. Carbondale: Southern Illinois U P, 1992.

MacCurdy, Marian M. "From Trauma to Writing: A Theoretical Model for Practical Use." *Writing and Healing: Toward an Informed Practice*. Ed. Charles M. Anderson and Marian M. MacCurdy. Urbana, IL: NCTE, 2000. 158–200.

Miller, Richard E. "Teaching after September 11." *Composition Studies in the New Millennium: Rereading the Past, Rewriting the Future*. Eds. Lynn Z. Bloom, Donald A. Daiker, Edward M. White. Carbondale: Southern Illinois U P, 2003. 252–55.

Oates, Joyce Carol. "Where Are You Going, Where Have You Been?" Celestial Timepiece: A Joyce Carol Oates Home Page. 26 Sept. 2003. <*http://www.usfca. edu/~southerr/wgoing2.html*>.

O'Brien, Tim. "How to Tell a True War Story." *The Things They Carried*. New York: Penguin, 1990. 73–91.

The World Wide Agora

Negotiating Citizenship and
Ownership of Response Online

Darin Payne

IN THE APRIL 2002 issue of *Harper's Magazine,* Thomas de Zengotita argued pessimistically that, six months after the terrorist attacks on the World Trade Center and the Pentagon, much of the American public was "over it." That is, the citizens of this country had allegedly moved on and, in the process, absorbed the events of September 11 just as they do any other major media event: by accepting them as part of the surface-level flow of information and images that comprises most, if not all, of America's contemporary social existence. This was supposedly the United State's eventual "national" response. In many respects, de Zengotita's argument is a rehash of Baudrillard's articulations of the *simulacra* and the depthlessness of postmodern life, even though de Zengotita never references Baudrillard or his work. The problem with that argument as both writers tend to present it is that it assumes a level of homogenization among the American public so as to efface the very differences in identities, life experiences, and material and discursive conditions that would create a wide range of responses beyond mere "absorption." Simply put, the meaning of an event like September 11th cannot be reductively divorced from the readers of the event and their attendant subjective contexts, histories, and forms of identification.

The very idea of September 11 as a "national" event—a national *trauma*—begs the question: whose event, or trauma, was it? (Whose is it still?) Such ownership needs to be as contingent and variable as other events in America's history have finally become in these postmodern, politically responsible times. October 12, 1492, was long regarded, after all, as a national event worthy of a common response among U.S. citizens alike. So was December 7, 1941. But the meanings affixed to Columbus's "discovery" of America and to the bombing of Pearl Harbor now range widely: just ask Native Americans or Japanese Americans if they are "over" those events.

If we are to enact a primary agenda currently driving composition studies—namely the construction of students as "agents of social change" through rhetorical practices informed by social and cultural diversity and an explicit recognition of the contingent nature of meaning—and if we are to make productive use in our classrooms of events that might otherwise be deemed "national trauma," then we must in good conscience actively work against reductive generalizations. Instead, we must work to redefine "national" to mean something more akin to the complex, shifting term that, divorced from major media events, we usually understand it to be. Moreover, we need to infuse the term "national" with a sense of the *inter-* or even *trans-*national; our present historical moment, as Manuel Castells characterizes it, is marked by continuous flows of information, identities, and goods and services within a globalized political economy and across traditional geopolitical boundaries. Almost any *national* event is inevitably enmeshed in global formations.

In the ideal writing classroom, the process of redefining national events in such ways—and, in the process, developing the kind of discourse aptly suited to current pedagogical goals—would occur through "contact zone dialogics": conversations shot through with the social, cultural, and national differences embodied in and enacted by a diverse group of student-participants. Indeed, such hope is more or less central to much work of leading composition scholars such as Trimbur, Cooper, Halasek, and numerous others building on Mary Louise Pratt and Mikhail Bakhtin.[1] Unfortunately, the utopic vision of self-reflexive, self-conscious discourse in response to and recognition of diverse subject positionality is necessarily cut short by countless conditions of time and place. The geographics and socioeconomics determining institutional demographics; the constructed reality offered up by mainstream American media and so prevalent in our students' lives; the ideological work of the university as one of Althusser's "state apparatuses": all work to both reduce and/or discourage expressions of difference in the writing classroom. As a result, the opportunity to redefine *national trauma* in appropriately complex ways is severely hindered. The classroom, like the evening news, can become a forum for a homogenized response that does indeed begin to look like that analyzed by De Zengotita. At best, students may give or receive one or two "alternative" perspectives and incorporate them into their own intellectual and emotional understandings of the event. At worst, everyone shares temporary grief for an artificially common loss.

Yet, significant opportunities for more complex interchanges—some more akin to what Pratt and Bakhtin wish for and more in accord with what I describe above as necessary in composition studies—*do* exist. They are present in the discursive space of the World Wide Web (hereafter the Web) and accessible from within the networked classroom. I argue in this essay that the Web offers writing teachers a dynamic forum for engaging students in dialogues about national events that are more informed by social and cultural diversity and more infused with a sense of the global than most classrooms in higher education usually are. At the same time—and before readers dismiss the rest of this essay as a replay of the technophilic global village narrative—I argue that the Web has its own set of homogenizing tendencies that can deceptively undermine those opportunities. By understanding such tendencies, and by utilizing the Web as more than a set of readings made accessible through hypertext (as is too often the case in English studies), writing teachers can productively exploit and explicate the tensions among irreducibly diverse responses to (inter)national events like September 11.

THE GLOBAL VILLAGE:
THE PROMISE OF CIVIC DISCOURSE ONLINE

The "global village narrative" referenced above is almost always saturated with technophilic optimism; as Selfe and Hawisher show, that narrative is at the heart of arguments by such Web proponents as Howard Rheingold and Nicholas Negroponte, each of whom sees the Web as both the mechanism for and site of social connection and democratic action in an inevitably global world ("Introduction" 8). Such scholars often draw on work by Marshall McLuhan, whose vision of twenty-first century electronic media (as a human-made and human-making system of meaning and communication) involves an interconnected world of simultaneous visual and audile communication unencumbered by bounds of time and space.

That vision—at least as it plays out in much of the apologists' literature about the Web—has the look and feel of Bakhtinian dialogue and the promise of contact zone potentiality. As McLuhan argues in both *Understanding Media* and especially *The Global Village,* new electronic communications technology will bring into conflict irreducibly diverse cultures, each of which will find the need to respond to the other—and, importantly, to the self-as-other—if they are to escape violence. As McLuhan's co-author Bruce Powers writes, East and West are now coming together in a new "acoustic" space, one "built on holism, the idea that there is no cardinal center, just many centers floating in a cosmic system which honors only diversity. The acoustic mode rejects hierarchy; but, should hierarchy exist, knows intuitively that hierarchy is exceedingly transitory" *(Global Village x).* As an "extension of our senses and our selves," then, new electronic media situate us *relationally* in much the way that discourse does for Bakhtin. Ideally, for Bakhtin, discourse becomes the medium in which the self, the other, and the relations among them are played out and laid bare; in which hierarchies are understood as arbitrary rather than natural; and in which difference is an end unto itself rather than a problem to be solved through rational ordering.[2] Such is the general vision of Bakhtinian dialogue central to Pratt's conception of the contact zone and so often invoked (implicitly or explicitly) as a means of democratization in composition studies. It is also the general vision articulated in appropriations of McLuhan's "global village" metaphor.[3]

If we look to the Web—which for all intents and purposes did not even exist at the time *The Global Village* was printed in 1989 (a significant year that many mark as the end of the Cold War and communism and the beginning of a newly interdependent global market economy[4]), we find seeds of promise for such democratization. In countless configurations online—in chatrooms, personal Web pages, Weblogs, discussion boards, and Webzines—people whom members of dominant cultural America might regard as "cultural others" represent and enact their subject positions, engage in practices of what Pratt calls *transculturation* and *autoethnography* as forms of power negotiation, and offer by counterexample opportunities for recognition of the self as "other." Such practices are demonstrated in Selfe and Hawisher's *Global Literacies and the World Wide Web,* an anthology devoted to illustrations of online discourses in/from Hungary, Greece, Australia, Palau, Norway, Japan, Scotland, Mexico, Cuba, and South Africa. Each chapter explores the ways in which particular, usually nondominant, social groups use the Web to make their positions (both their subject positions and their positions on social issues) better known, to gather support, and to foster collective will at regional, national, and international levels.

The organized resistances to international trade that have occurred during the past few years—demonstrated so aptly by the 1999 World Trade Organization (WTO) protests in Seattle and the 2001 Free Trade Area of the Americas (FTAA) protests in Quebec City—provide further examples of democratic discourse online that, of necessity, transcends national boundaries. As Douglas Kellner argues in *Theorizing Globalization,* recent forms of resistance to the WTO would no doubt never have occurred (and indeed did not) before the Web made possible democratic dialogue and social organization. Of the protests in Seattle, he writes,

> Many websites contained anti-WTO material and numerous mailing lists used the Internet to distribute critical material and to organize the protest. The result was the mobilization of caravans from throughout the United States to take protestors to Seattle, many of whom had never met and were recruited through the Internet. There were also significant numbers of inter-

national participants in Seattle which exhibited labor, environmentalist, feminist, anti-capitalist, animal rights, anarchist, and other groups organized to protest aspects of globalization and form new alliances and solidarities for future struggles. In addition, protests occurred throughout the world, and a proliferation of anti-WTO material against the extremely secret group spread throughout the Internet.

Furthermore, the Internet provided critical coverage of the event, documentation of the various groups' protests, and debate over the WTO and globalization. Whereas the mainstream media presented the protests as "anti-trade," featured the incidents of anarchist violence against property, while minimizing police violence against demonstrators, the Internet provided pictures, eyewitness accounts, and reports of police brutality and the generally peaceful and non-violent nature of the protests. While the mainstream media framed the protests negatively and privileged suspect spokespeople like Patrick Buchanan as critics of globalization, the Internet provided multiple representations of the demonstrations, advanced reflective discussion of the WTO and globalization, and presented a diversity of critical perspectives.

Kellner cites numerous other examples of oppositional organizations' rhetorical work facilitated—enabled even—by the Web; he discusses, for instance, the plight of the Zapatistas in Mexico, Jody Williams's Nobel Prize–winning work on eradicating land mines, and Dutch women's Clean Clothes Campaign against exploited labor in the garment industry.

The examples Kellner offers are more than just supportive illustrations of my contentions that we have become global citizens in the information age and that civic discourse in response to national events should be infused with a sense of the international. These examples demonstrate the extent to which global networked structures are now in place both for those in power (transnational authorities) and for those unwillingly oppressed (transnational resistance). The discourse that produces and is a product of that dynamic contributes to the "heteroglossia" idealized in contact zone pedagogies; in the networked classroom, such textual richness, such discursive potential, is available in virtually limitless supply, particularly within and across networks of multiple-linked documents— the function of which George Landow describes as "the hypertextual dissolution of centrality." According to Landow, this dissolution, "which makes the [hypertext] medium such a potentially democratic one, also makes it a model of a society of conversations in which no one conversation, no one discipline or ideology, dominates or founds the others" (89). By its very design, Landow argues, hypertext emphasizes marginality and "Otherness" and creates shifting, self-conscious vantage points from which to engage in discourse.

Certainly in the traditional classroom, a teacher and/or his/her students can bring to the table a wide range of published responses to an event like the

WTO protests in Seattle, responses that perhaps embody much of the diversity in subject positions that would create a kind of contact zone or dissolution of centrality in reading experiences. But the teachers and students are constrained by time and by access to material resources. As Kellner notes, the Web offers publishing opportunities to the countercultural and otherwise marginalized that normally available mainstream publications simply do not. A student or an entire class following a trail of links through numerous different online responses to the WTO protests in Seattle is far more likely to produce something in the way of "irreducible diversity" in discourse since the numbers and kinds of available responses are exponentially greater, as are the sociocultural and geopolitical locations from which they originate.

Moreover, the networked environment offers students unmatched opportunities to move from being relatively private readers to public writers of such diverse discourses. The Web is growing increasingly interactive, as dynamic hypertext facilitates and routinely encourages immediate responses to writing: many Webzine articles, like those found in *Salon.com*, often include their author's hyperlinked e-mail address for contact; public discussion boards, such as those of *YahooGroups*, usually enable and invite readers' responses to threaded conversations; linked forms for letters to editors of online newspapers or Webzines are usually prominently accessible along the margins or frames of standardized interfaces; and server space for students' own Web productions on commercial sites like *Hotmail* is free.[5] What the Web offers, then, are direct and immediate possibilities for engagement in public dialogues about (inter)national events—dialogues that transcend traditional boundaries imposed by time, space, and access to the means of production.

The reading and writing classroom that uses the Web for such student engagement begins to resemble what Iris Marion Young would call a site for postmodern democracy, one that includes "real participatory structures in which actual people, with their geographical, ethnic, gender, and occupational differences, assert their perspectives on social issues within institutions that encourage the representation of their distinct voices" (116). While particular institutions in higher education may often function to *dis*courage distinct voices in the ways referenced in my introduction, some of those functions may be countered through networked interactions on the Web. In *A Rhetoric of Electronic Communities*, Tharon Howard summarizes that hope when he writes that wide-area networking systems like the Web, "can open us to a polyphony so diverse and centrifugal that it sometimes appears to lead to sheer anarchy" (21). While Howard does not explicitly reference the inter- or transnational dialogue that the Web enables, such subject positions can only increase the "polyphony" he celebrates. Moreover, that increase is both unavoidable and necessary for the "democratization of composition studies" in the post-1990s era of global political economies.

Like many others contributing to this volume and no doubt many reading it, I was teaching composition during the fall of 2001. By coincidence I happened to be teaching an advanced writing course in a networked classroom titled "Rhetoric, Composition, and Computers," a course focused on online discourse and writing for the Web. In the wake of September 11, the class direction shifted slightly—away from our planned "normal" real-world projects (primarily online publications in response to an array of self-selected local political issues) to reading and writing about the terrorist attacks, U.S. foreign policy, and the implications of war. The shift was not one I imposed but one encouraged by the ever-present large-scale rhetorical situation, the national trauma that was neither to be ignored nor set aside for later.

In class over the following few months, my students and I moved through Web-based position statements—both reading them and writing them—on September 11's unfolding circumstances and subsequent deliberations, calls for and against war, critiques of the Bush Administration and of the terrorists' motivations, and impassioned narratives of individuals affected by the event and its repercussions. The discourses we read came from mainstream, alternative, and radical online presses; they came from personal Web pages and discussion boards; they came from our home state of Hawai'i, as well as from the U.S. mainland, England, Canada, India, Israel, Ireland, and numerous other countries; and they were intertwined in a much larger network of linked heteroglossic discourse. What all this helped to destabilize was the general dichotomy artificially constructed in mainstream American media and rightly critiqued by Edward Said, namely that of the West and Islam, or more accurately, the West and the Rest[6]—or, to put it in terms of dialogism, the Self and the Other.

Yet before I become too self-congratulatory, as is often the case in teacher reflections and hopeful "how-to" panegyrics, I need to acknowledge here that the Web, while in many of these ways a more dialogic environment than the face-to-face classroom, has its limitations, its restrictions, even its own hegemonic functions that counter the potential for truly representative democratic discourse. In the following section, I wish to temper the technophilia that is emerging in my own narrative: I offer below, then, some reminders of the centripetal technological structures of the Web that mitigate the alleged centrifugal polyphony of voices that Howard, cited above, hopes for.

THE GLOBAL COLONY:
LIMITATIONS OF CIVIC DISCOURSE ONLINE

Kellner, cited in the preceding section, draws on examples of anti-global–capitalism movements to illustrate what he calls a form of "globalization-from-below," the contestation and reconfiguration of ideology and power by those oppressed by dominant capitalist forces—processes not unlike transculturation and autoethnography at work in Pratt's idealized contact zone. However, Kellner also argues for a serious recognition of globalization-from-above, what many critics of capitalism and technology see as the routine impositions of ideology, material culture, and sociopolitical identification that are both byproducts of and necessary grounds for the growth of global capitalism. For such critics technologies like the Web have facilitated a "globalized hegemony of market capitalism, where capital creates a homogenous world culture of commercialization, commodification, administration, and domination" (Kellner). Although Kellner does not wish to accept only such skeptical and determinist positions, the evidence for them is also evidence for the need to look carefully at the ways in which the Web is integral to the evolving relations of technology, capitalism, and culture on a global scale.

To begin, teachers using the networked classroom need to recognize what Selfe and Selfe call "the politics of the interface." They argue convincingly that the standardized interfaces between users and personal computers are hegemonic by design; the vast majority of us using PCs or Macs routinely access the contents of our computers via a system of metaphors: we go to the computer's *desktop* and open *folders*, which may be stored in *briefcases* or *file cabinets*. Representations of a universalized corporate American culture dominate the personal computer's interface—representations which privilege particular forms of what Bourdieu would call cultural capital and which embody what Althusser and countless others would call dominant ideologies. The browser-interfaces for the Web—particularly Internet Explorer and Netscape's Navigator—are similarly laden with the values of white, middle-class America (though less restricted to corporate culture and more normative of consumerism). Both browsers are, without question, near monopolies and as such contribute to the exclusion of alternative interfaces, ones that perhaps would embody other metaphorical means of differently defining social identifications and relationships.

Add to this the increasing standardization of online discourse; the abundance of Websites and technical manuals offering guidelines for writing the Web are a mere part of a large system of constraints on the production of discourse. The principles of writing for the Web are driven, first and foremost, by commercial interests and Western capitalist ideology. Readers are regularly defined as consumers (of information, entertainment, and material goods) who skim Web pages at best, who need to be "sold" on the "product" instantly, and who operate in the discursive realm of sound-bites. Such advice comes from Web design leaders such as Jakob Nielson, popular guidebooks and sites such as "Web Pages that Suck," and even textbooks developed for composition studies, our allegedly enlightened discipline that professes to work against hegemonic discourse and cultural homogenization.[7]

Defenders of such advice will argue that they are merely working *within* the system, that they are offering guidelines based on principles of classical rhetoric. Indeed, Nielson's advice comes from his studies of how people read online; he wishes simply to capitalize on that knowledge of audience to empower writers.[8] But that defense is akin to perpetuating the privileging of the literary canon and standardized academic discourse in order to appeal to established reading expectations of the academy. Even worse in this case, however, is that established norms, which then translate into expectations, are being set by large-scale corporate conglomerates like Time-Warner/AOL. The discourse that is coming to dominate the Web, then, is a function of both the technology itself and its integral relationship with Americanized global capitalism. At the time of this writing, I am reviewing the possible models for a class Webzine that have been brought forth by the students in my advanced "Writing for Electronic Media" class. Without exception, they all look very similar in layout, design, and discursive style, and they are all modeled on the "My X" template, in which X can be replaced by such institutional identities such as "CNN," "NRA," "Yahoo," or even "Blackboard" or "WebCT" (the two leading course management applications driving curricula in higher education worldwide). Interestingly, the presence of commercial advertising in the layout and design helps to further such sites' legitimacy, according to my students. These are the normative designs that have gained legitimacy and are the new forms of cultural capital online.

Beyond interface designs, the technology of the Web is less inherently democratic than hypertext apologists like Richard Lanham and George Landow would have us believe. Numerous scholars have demonstrated the ways in which routinized access to the Internet—via certain commercial desktop machines, standard browsers, and search engines—is primarily oriented toward information storage and retrieval rather than discussion (Burns; Hawisher; Selfe and Selfe; Knapp). Moreover, as Dave Healy shows, virtual forums themselves tend to construct a public sphere that encourages homogeneity in discourse. Such anti-democratic tendencies—when combined with the domination of standardized Web discourse described above—help to shape literate practices on the Web as hegemonic *by design*. To send students into cyberspace is to subject them to practices of dominant cultural power that seriously constrain what and how they read and write.

Built into the very design of the Web are additional technical codes of power and domination that work even further against the potentially democratizing discourse I described in the preceding section. Consider, for example, the panoptic surveillance functions enabled by individual and network IP addresses through which users must access the Web. Such functions serve corporate interests, of course. Software loosely termed "adware" and "spyware" is routinely downloaded to computers without users' knowledge; Web reading habits are then analyzed and sent back to corporations, who can in turn target individual users with product-specific advertisements. Further, enough stories of government Internet surveillance in the wake of 9/11 have become commonplace in the news; given such knowledge, how likely is it that individuals or groups positioned on the margins of mainstream American culture are going to voice critique, dissent, or anything outside the realm of "acceptable" mainstream discourse? Noam Chomsky and Barbara Kingsolver could get away with being voices of dissent in the aftermath of 9/11, but how can one expect a student from the Middle East, either visiting on a visa or even "naturalized," to express any positioned statements that might be construed as a threat to national security? Such statements—which would help to redefine national trauma in the appropriately complex and dialogic ways referenced in my introduction—would in fact be a threat to the students' civil rights. The same needs to be said for writing *teachers;* I am a lawful permanent resident, not a citizen, and I have grown increasingly aware of my own position as a foreigner whose allegiance to the United States is potentially suspect. A fellow faculty member from Turkey, who teaches international relations in the Political Science Department at my university, exemplifies the point even further; he tells me that he has recently "toned down" his critiques of U.S. foreign policy because of his ethnogeographic origins, that he is insecure about his own voice in the classroom in the wake of September 11, and that he has taken the path of least resistance for the sake of personal and professional security.

Finally, any use of technology—including pedagogical applications of the Web—must be situated in what Robert Johnson calls "a complex of use." Johnson argues that, like rhetoric, technology is subject to (and contributes to) the contingencies of social and material existence. The use of the Web in higher education is inevitably shaped by the centripetal forces mentioned in my introduction: the demographic, institutional, economic, and sociocultural practices and formations that often encourage homogeneity in discourse. Students in a networked composition classroom, if they are involved in now-standard practices of collaboration upon which composition pedagogies are often built, are subject to the tendencies toward consensus and "groupthink" articulated over a decade ago by John Trimbur and Greg Myers in response to collaborative learning. Such forces, normalized and unavoidable, serve as rhetorical constraints on both the reading and writing of online discourse in the networked classroom, despite the capabilities of the Web's global reach and its seeming facilitation of unencumbered self-publication.

The list of ways in which participation on the Web is technically and socially determined (and determining) is far longer than what I have room for here. I've simply scratched the surface of that list in the hopes of tempering the blind faith in its democratizing potential too often expressed in the literatures of our field. I've also done so to illustrate the tension that exists between what Kellner calls globalization-from-above and globalization-from-below— what amounts to a tension between the reproduction and the transformation of dominant cultural ideologies in America and beyond. This is a relatively new and broader dimension of the dynamic that has defined English studies during the past 30 years, one comprised of the reproduction of privilege in the discursive and disciplinary practices of academia and the necessary challenges to that reproduction. We can hardly step outside that dynamic; even those who espouse liberatory pedagogies and who believe in the radical politicization of composition studies must to a considerable degree work from within. The same needs to be acknowledged in relation to the Web and its facilitation of globalization; it is a new agora[9] that invites irreducible diversity inclusive of international perspectives and simultaneously works to assert the opposite.

Working from within, then, what we can do as teachers is make that dynamic visible to our students and to ourselves on a regular basis. Doing so around a national event—a large-scale rhetorical exigence that demands response and definition borne out of and representative of multiple perspectives—is simply necessary if we are to be faithful to professed goals of contact zone dialogue. Helping students negotiate that dynamic on the Web is also a means of actively working "from below" against the hegemonic forces shaping the event "from above," and it is as much a democratically responsible move in the specific moment as it is a general pedagogical move to make over time. In the next and final section, I briefly articulate some practical ways to involve students online in response to national trauma, ways that I hope will help them productively explicate and negotiate some of the tensions between "national" definitions and international ones, between domination and marginalization, and ultimately between the Self and the Other.

CONCLUSION: SOME SUGGESTIONS
FOR PEDAGOGY AND PRAXIS

Even though it is a product of only the last decade or so, and despite the rapidity of technological invention and obsolescence, the Web is clearly here for awhile. Moreover, it has matured to a point at which certain online discursive practices and social formations have become established and will likely still be in place when this anthology is on the shelves. With that in mind, I offer here guidelines, grounded in those practices and formations, for pedagogical uses of the Web, specifically uses that will facilitate the explication and negotiation of competing definitions of (inter)national events.

Making use of the Web as a reading resource has already been sketched above; exposing students to diverse responses to events like September 11, the WTO protests, or other (inter)national events has the potential to create for them a dialogue much broader than that made available through CNN, cable, and network news. Given the potential for even Web discourse to be hegemonic, however, it is useful for teachers to be aware of avenues for dialogue marginalized from the mainstream. Beyond sending students into cyberspace via search engines or directories (which will often yield hierarchically ordered sites of dominant cultural discourse), teachers can direct them to specific Web forums, which can range from *The New York Times*'s online discussion forum to a wide variety of newsgroups and discussion boards labeled ".alt"—a domain indicator of *alternative* discourse. Alternative newsgroups and discussion boards tend often to demand lower-end technologies (they are usually text-based and can be accessed through simple telnet functions available on even pre-Pentium PCs), in part because those running such forums are attempting to counter the exclusionary functions inherent in the digital divide. The participants in such forums regularly reference other forums, Websites, or alternative presses and are thus a good starting point for students seeking voices not usually heard on ABC's *Nightline* or Fox News. None of which is to suggest that students be kept away from those sources of information; *juxtaposing* mainstream media and alternative presses opens the door to demystifying the normative work of dominant cultural productions and to inquiries into the ways in which events are framed according to socially contingent networks of identification and knowledge construction.

Beyond alternative and mainstream online presses, teachers can direct students to Websites or Webzines from other countries—which can easily be located through their domain names. Servers located outside America usually include an identifying suffix as part of their URLs: ".au" for Australia, ".ca" for Canada, ".uk" for the United Kingdom, and so on. Indeed, many of the articles my students read in the aftermath of September 11 were from England's online editions of *The Guardian,* a press well known for its dissenting, counter-cultural views.

Finally, students can be directed to *Webrings*—related Websites that are linked together through special HTML coding and are overseen by a Webring master. The sites in Webrings often (but not always) express shared political positions or philosophies. By analyzing the common grounds of specific Webrings, students can begin to see more clearly how responses to events are developed within definable discourse communities and how, in turn, the meanings of those events are ultimately bound to those communities. Such intellectual practices can locate students more explicitly and reflectively within what Gilles Deleuze calls *nomadic centers* of knowledge construction: "provisional structures that are never permanent, always straying from one set of information to another" (Said 374, qtd. in Landow 95). It is the simultaneous access to competing, shifting structures of knowledge that is most promising here, for students gathering information from differing, perhaps even opposing, Webrings are denied the stability of singular, normative responses—those of which I referenced in my introduction as artificially "national" and inevitably reductive.

In addition to being active Web readers, from within most of the above forums students can usually participate as writers. They can often respond directly to open, unmoderated newsgroups and discussion boards, adding their voices to both national and international conversations. *Moderated* forums—which also include newsgroups and discussion boards, as well as letters to editors of Webzines and other online presses—will prove less accessible for student writers. Nonetheless, submissions to such forums are usually as easy as submissions to unmoderated forums; through simple online forms or e-mail links, students can send in their responses, learning in the process the rhetorical strategies needed for most civic discourse—namely that filtered through various gatekeeping constraints and screened through particular ideological frameworks.

If they wish to bypass editorial gatekeeping functions, students can publish their own Webzines, either as individuals, in groups, or as a class. HTML editors such as Frontpage and Dreamweaver have made writing for the Web almost as simple as writing for print in word processing programs. By publishing their own Webzines, teachers and students can develop responses to national events in formats and lengths not constrained by normal discussion board or newsgroup netiquette. Moreover, they can in turn situate their writing within larger discursive formations—by linking directly to other online responses to the same event, by participating in Webrings, and by advertising their sites on various open forums.

Assuming such writing is located within, and in concert with, the kinds of reading practices referenced above, it will of necessity be an act of negotiation, one in which students must account for and respond to diverse, global perspectives. It will also be an act of negotiation in that writing demands attention to rhetorical conventions; if students are to produce complex artifacts such as Webzines, they will need to study them, to rhetorically analyze their discursive patterns and the attendant political positions at work within them. Indeed, much of the Web's colonizing tendencies articulated in the preceding section can become a subject of critique in the classroom, one made necessary as a prelude to civic discourse online and an integral part of laying bare the tensions between the reproduction and tranformation of dominant cultural power.

Additional publication opportunities beyond those mentioned here will no doubt be common by the time this essay is in print. A growing trend at the time of this writing, for example, is the *Weblog,* or *blog* for short. *Blogging* has become a popular form of online writing that is analogous to public journal writing; individuals write daily political rants, poems, reflections, or whatever suits them, posting them to a single page that is updated each day. The technical means for blogging simplifies writing for the Web even further than HTML editors and file-transfer programs. To introduce, set up, and begin writing a blog demands only a single class session—perhaps two at most.

What is most important, however, is not so much the technical avenues for reading and writing the Web—be they blogs, Webzines, or moderated and unmoderated forums. Rather, what is important is the recognition of the Web's capacity for discursive practices less hegemonic and more dialogic than those allowed for in traditional print-based arenas. The accessibility of the Web to groups marginalized from mainstream America and to groups outside America's geopolitical, national boundaries is central to that capacity. While there are enough tendencies in the design and ownership of the Web to significantly reduce that capacity, it is not likely to be eliminated any time soon.

Finding international and alternative discursive spaces online can take some work, but it is work worth doing—especially in times of national trauma, when the mechanisms for the production of dominant cultural ideology are brought out in full force and the general tendency is toward homogenous reductivism rather than heterogeneous complexity. I offer the suggestions here for reading, writing, and analyzing the Web during times of national trauma as forms of both pedagogy and praxis: they are educational and rhetorical actions informed by disciplinary knowledge and values communally constructed and maintained. The democratic values that give rise to the practices sketched here are those referenced in my introduction as central to current rhetorical theory and composition pedagogy, the convergence of which is often articulated as a shared project in composing critical agents of social change, adept in the kinds of literacy needed to participate in a world of increasing diversity and decreasing space. When traumatic national events hit, that project needs to come to the fore, especially given the ways in which mainstream media affix meanings and shape public responses to such events. Civic participation needs to be realized in structures that facilitate negotiations of homogeneous and exclusionary definitions of "national trauma" with other alternatives. As a new agora far more inclusive of difference and far less determined by geographic space than has ever been possible, the Web can, at least with some cautionary measures, serve as one such structure.

NOTES

1. See, for example, Trimbur's "Consensus and Difference," Cooper's "Postmodern Possibilities," and Halasek's *Pedagogy of Possibility.*

2. This is the central utopic vision of Bakhtin's theory of discourse evident in his essays in *The Dialogic Imagination* and summarized by Michael Holquist.

3. It is important to point out that McLuhan's vision was not in and of itself as technophilic or utopic as the positions of many who now appropriate it. In *The Global Village,* the chapter outlining advantages of a globally connected world is eight pages long; the chapter outlining disadvantages is 37 pages.

4. See, for example, Robert Gilpin's *The Challenge of Global Capitalism:The World Economy in the 21st Century.*

5. Of course nothing is truly free; commercial sites that allow space for self-publication infiltrate that space with advertising. Such infiltration exemplifies, on a minor scale, the integral relations among capitalism, technology, and the current era of globalization. The notion of the Web as a "free" space is akin to the notion of "free" markets; both are shot through with conditions and constraints that produce and are products of Western capitalist ideologies.

6. Said makes these specific claims in "The Clash of Ignorance," published in October 2001. He also makes these claims in his book *Covering Islam: How the Media and the Experts Determine How We See the Rest of the World,* printed before the events of September 11, 2001.

7. See, for example, Jennifer Hamada's "Designing the Web," a hypertext analyzing current handbooks in composition that specifically address writing for the Web; Hamada demonstrates the ways in which several handbooks tend to reproduce a reductive, mainstream, consumer-oriented understanding of what Web writing means. Available at the time of this writing at *http://www2.hawaii.edu/~jhamada/comprhet/prelim.htm.*

8. To be fair, Neilson has contributed to an international project in creating "cultural user-interfaces" (CUIs), which are designed to be more representative and appropriate to specific cultures outside America. However, work in this area remains essentially marginalized and, in Neilson's case, overshadowed by work that contributes to standardization and homogenization in accord with dominant cultural American representations. For further information, see *http://www.acm.org/sigchi/bulletin/1996.3/international.html.*

9. The *agora* in Ancient Greece was the meeting ground, the assembly, where citizens would gather to debate matters of civic concern; training in rhetoric was to a large degree training for civic participation in the agora.

WORKS CITED

Althusser, Louis. "Ideology and the Ideological State Apparatus." *Critical Theory since 1965.* Ed. Hazard Adams and Leroy Searle. Tallahassee: UP of Florida, 1986. 238–50.

Bakhtin, Mikhail. *The Dialogic Imagination: Four Essays by Mikhail Bakhtin.* Trans. Caryl Emerson and Michael Holquist. U of Texas Slavic Ser. 1. Ed. Michael Holquist. Austin: U of Texas P, 1981.

Baudrillard, Jean. *Simulacra and Simulation.* Trans. Sheila Faria Glaser. Ann Arbor: U of Michigan P, 1994.

Bourdieu, Pierre and Jean-Claude Passeron. *Reproduction in Education, Society, and Culture.* London: Sage, 1977.

Burns, Philip. "Supporting Deliberative Democracy: Pedagogical Arts of the Contact Zone of the Electronic Sphere." *Rhetoric Review* 18.1 (1999): 128–47.

Castells, Manuel. "Flows, Networks, and Identities: A Critical Theory of the Information Society." *Critical Education in the New Information Age.* Ed. Donaldo Macedo. New York: Rowan and Littlefield, 1999: 37–64.

Cooper, Marilyn. "Postmodern Possibilities in Electronic Conversations." *Passions, Pedagogies, and 21st Century Technologies.* Ed. Gail E. Hawisher and Cynthia L. Selfe. Logan, UT: Utah State UP, 1999. 140–60.

De Zengotita, Thomas. "The Numbing of the American Mind: Culture as Anesthetic." *Harper's Magazine* 304.1823 (April 2002): 33–40.

Gilpin, Robert. *The Challenge of Global Capitalism:The World Economy in the 21st Century.* Princeton, NJ: Princeton UP, 2002.

Halasek, Kay. *A Pedagogy of Possibility: Bakhtinian Perspectives on Composition Studies.* Carbondale: SIUP, 1999.

Healy, Dave. "Cyberspace and Place: The Internet as Middle Landscape on the Electronic Frontier." *Internet Culture.* Ed. David Porter. New York: Routledge, 1997. 55–68.

Holquist, Michael. *Dialogism: Bakhtin and His World.* New York: Routledge, 1990.

Howard, Tharon. *A Rhetoric of Electronic Communities.* Greenwich: Ablex, 1997.

Johnson, Robert. *User-Centered Technology: A Rhetorical Theory for Computers and Other Mundane Artifacts.* New York: SUNY P, 1998.

Kellner, Douglas. "Theorizing Globalization." *http://www.gseis.ucla.edu/faculty/kellner/papers/theoryglob.htm.*

Knapp, James A. "Essayistic Messages: Internet Newsgroups as an Electronic Public Sphere." *Internet Culture.* Ed. David Porter. New York: Routledge, 1997. 181–97.

Landow, George. *Hypertext 2.0: The Convergence of Contemporary Critical Theory and Technology.* Baltimore: John Hopkins UP, 1997.

Lanham, Richard. *The Electronic Word: Democracy, Technology, and the Arts.* London: U of Chicago P, 1993.

McLuhan, Marshall. *Understanding Media: The Extensions of Man.* New York: McGraw Hill, 1964.

McLuhan, Marshall and Bruce R. Powers. *The Global Village: Transformations in World Life and Media in the 21st Century.* Oxford: Oxford UP, 1989.

Myers, Greg. "Reality, Consensus, and Reform in the Rhetoric of Composition Teaching." *College English* 48 (1986): 719–30.

Neilson, Jakob. *Designing Web Usability: The Practice of Simplicity.* Indianapolis: New Riders Publishing, 2000.

Pratt, Mary Louise. "Arts of the Contact Zone." *Profession 91.* New York: MLA, 1991. 33–40.

Rheingold, Howard. *The Virtual Community: Homesteading on the Electronic Frontier, revised edition.* Cambridge: MIT P, 2000.

Said, Edward. "The Clash of Ignorance." *The Nation* Oct. 22, 2001.

———. *Covering Islam: How the Media and the Experts Determine How We See the Rest of the World.* New York: Vintage Books, 1997.

Selfe, Cynthia L., and Gail E. Hawisher. "Introduction: Testing the Claims." *Global Literacies and the World Wide Web*. Ed. Cynthia L. Selfe and Gail Hawisher. London: Routledge, 2000. 1–18.

———, eds. *Global Literacies and the World Wide Web*. London: Routledge, 2000.

Selfe, Cynthia L., and Richard J. Selfe, Jr. "The Politics of the Interface: Power and Its Exercise in Electronic Contact Zones." *College Composition and Communication* 45 (Dec. 1994): 480–504.

Trimbur, John. "Consensus and Difference in Collaborative Learning." *College English* 51 (1989): 602–16.

Winner, Langdon. "Do Artifacts Have Politics?" *The Whale and the Reactor: A Search for Limits in an Age of High Technology*. Chicago: The University of Chicago Press, 1986. 19–39.

Young, Iris Marion. *Justice and the Politics of Difference*. Princeton: Princeton UP, 1990.

Presence in Absence

Discourses and Teaching
(In, On, and About) Trauma

Peter N. Goggin and Maureen Daly Goggin

> The disaster—experience none can undergo—obliterates (while leaving perfectly intact) our relation to the world as presence or as absence.
>
> —Maurice Blanchot (120)

> A strange lostness
> Was palpably present.
> —Paul Celan (139)[1]

IN WHAT MAY be called a *traumatic turn*, scholars from a variety of disciplines have focused unprecedented attention on trauma and discourses of trauma over the last couple of decades.[2] Through this turn, some scholars have gone so far as to claim that we are living in a time marked by trauma (LaCapra xi), with others claiming we are in a "post-traumatic century" (Felman "Education" 1). As a partial warrant for these observations, scholars draw attention to the explosion of testimonies appearing in academic and popular presses, videos, television shows, and other digital media in the last 20 years or so (Berger). Consider, for instance, the long-running confessional talk shows of the likes of *Sally Jesse Raphael, Montel,* and *Jerry Springer,* and the more recent rise in popularity of court TV and reality TV shows as well the increase of trauma novels such as Toni Morrison's *Beloved* and documentaries such as Claude Lanzmann's 1987 *Shoah*. Consider as well that on July 31, 2002, just ten months after 9/11, Bruce Springsteen released his CD, *The Rising*—a tribute to 9/11.

Shoshana Felman, thus, calls our times "the age of testimony" (53). Concurrent with the steep rise in testimony as discourse practice has been a rising scholarly interest in, and acceptance of, research on testimony over the past 20 years (LaCapra 86).[3] Testimony, that is, has become a salient object for scholarly gaze. Whether or not this is indeed an era of trauma or post-trauma unlike all preceding eras is an open question; however, it clearly appears to be an age of burgeoning testimony and scholarship on testimony.[4]

Given the public and scholarly turn to trauma and discoursing (about) trauma, it is somewhat surprising that until this volume little scholarly ink has been spilt on the subject of trauma and its discourses in pages devoted to the teaching of writing.[5] In this essay, then, we contribute toward ways of conceptualizing trauma and ways of understanding the discourses both generated by and surrounding it. This exploration serves as a crucial ground for considering questions concerning the teaching of writing trauma and of writing (about and during) trauma. We begin by defining trauma and exploring its complex relationship with discourse practices. We then explore a pedagogical model robust enough to accommodate the complicated web of discursive practices that both are generated by and surround various kinds of trauma. This model is not a panacea but a flexible framework to consider writing course designs that by their very nature must be localized to meet both kairotic conditions of time and place, diverse student needs, and particular institutional and departmental missions and resources.

(DE)LIMITING TRAUMA

> Trauma is a disruptive experience that disarticulates the self and creates holes in existence; it has belated effects that are controlled only with difficulty and perhaps never fully mastered.
>
> —Dominick LaCapra (41)

LaCapra's definition of trauma is at once both a surplus and a jejuneness in that it attempts to limit, as all definitions do, those literally and figuratively *unspeakable* events that are existentially experienced (and, thus, discursively constructed) differently by different people and even by one person over and across time. The fault lies not in LaCapra's (de)limiting of *trauma* as a unique phenomenon but in the nature of trauma that both demands and resists discursive construction.[6] For our purposes in this essay, we further limit the term *trauma* by distinguishing among three different kinds: *national, natural,* and *personal.* The distinctions are to some degree artificial, for these three kinds intersect in profound ways. *National traumas,* those that are perpetrated (whether malevolently or inadvertently) particularly in times of political struggle by human agents certainly affect individuals on intensely personal levels.[7] For instance, those who lost loved ones in the Oklahoma City bombing and in the 9/11 terrorist attacks on the twin towers of the World Trade Center and the Pentagon as well as those who survived these horrific events clearly suffered on deeply personal levels. National traumas are also generated by the loss of one person whose personhood transcends, and stands in for more than, the individual. Consider, for instance, the national and personal responses to the political assassinations of President John F. Kennedy and Martin Luther King as well as those to the horrific accidental death of Princess Di. Moreover, national traumas have transnational economic, political, social, and cultural implications that ripple worldwide and are experienced differently by different countries and by the individuals within those countries.[8] Similarly, *natural traumas,* those created for instance by floods, fire, violent storms, and earthquakes, not only affect individuals on the level of personal trauma but also have national and transnational traumatic effects and implications. The former manifested, for example, when a public official declares a traumatized place a disaster area and diverts public funds for restoration of the area. Finally, *personal traumas,* those perpetrated on and experienced by individuals such as rape, incest, home invasions, and the like, have national implications as well. Personal traumas often serve as exigencies for laws and enactment of laws meant to deter such horrendous acts and protect the polis. Consider, for instance, the exigencies that gave rise to organizations such as MADD (Mothers Against Drunk Drivers) or the bills and laws that bear the names of victims such as the Brady Bill and Shannon's law.[9]

   Although distinctions can be drawn in the abstract among national, natural, and personal traumas, these all converge in significant ways on an epistemic level. The process of learning, knowing, coming to grips with, and attempting to comprehend trauma of any kind requires encountering individual discursive constructions of the trauma. As Cathy Caruth observes, "trauma is not locatable in the simple violent or original event in an individual's past, but rather in the way that its very unassimilated nature—the way it was precisely *not* known in the first instance—returns to haunt the survivor later on" (4). In other words, *trauma* can only be tackled/approached/grappled with discursively; it is not until it is spoken/written that trauma is made present. As French philosopher and literary scholar Maurice Blanchot puts it, "Writing (or Telling, as distinct from anything written or told) precedes every phenomenon, every manifestation or show" (11). There is no one referent but only the multiple stories told by the one and many who were there as first-, second-, or even third-degree witnesses (distinctions we explicate later in this essay). Yet the speaking/writing (about) trauma is a stuttering struggle. It is, in Blanchot's words, "beyond the pale of writing or extratextual" (7). Herein lies the paradox. As Shoshana Felman notes, trauma refers to "events in excess of our frames of reference" ("Education" 5). As such, a traumatic event as both exigency for and object/subject of writing poses powerful problems for the rhetor, for it is by its very nature both beyond language a rhetor possesses and yet can only be constituted by the language s/he produces.[10]

RHETORICS OF TRAUMA

Writing lies before us as a challenge, an extreme exigency that bears witness to the irreducible futurity of that which is still to come.
—Leslie Hill (19)

In explicating Blanchot's theoretical treatment of writing the disaster, Leslie Hill draws attention to the complex interdependent relation between discourse and traumatic event. Writing is both a challenge and an extreme exigency—that is, it is both called forth by and constitutes the trauma. But writing both exceeds and is inadequate to the task; it is both unavoidable and impossible. Blanchot puts the paradox this way: "Neither reading nor writing, nor speaking—and yet it is by those paths that we escape what has been said already, and knowledge, and reciprocity, and enter the unknown space, the space of distress where what is given is perhaps not received by anyone" (99). Individuals are both compelled to and repelled by discoursing on the trauma—some respond with outpouring of oral and written discourses while others are silent. As Blanchot proclaims, "One must just write, in uncertainty and in necessity. Not writing is among the effects of writing. . . . [Yet] [t]o want to write: what an absurdity. Writing is the decay of the will, just as it is the loss of power, and the fall of the regular fall of the beat, the disaster again" (11). The social condition of language makes discourse (writing or speaking) not the sovereignty of any one person but that of one with an "other." As Bakhtin reminds us, "*word is a two-sided act*. It is determined equally by *whose* word it is and *for whom* it is meant. As word, it is precisely the *product of the reciprocal relationship between speaker and listener, addresser and addressee*. Each and every word expresses the 'one' in relation to the 'other'" (933).

Although Blanchot seems to want to vilify writing precisely because he envisions it as a "decay of the will," this view can only be sustained if one sees the will or the conscious as *a priori* (if not pure) to discourse—a perspective Bakhtin challenges in useful ways. For Bakhtin, "consciousness takes shape and being in the material of signs created by an organized group in the process of its social intercourse" (930). More importantly, he reminds us that "meaning does not reside in the word or in the soul of the speaker or in the soul of the listener. Meaning is the *effect of interaction between speaker and listener pro-*

duced via the material of a particular sound complex" (Bakhtin 944). Meaning occurs in discursive *praxis*, in the act of discoursing—speaking/writing and listening/reading. This constructivist view complicates Blanchot's somewhat Platonic view. The diverse responses to trauma are not merely generated by an autonomous will or pure self, rather these are authorized responses. That is to say, political, institutional, social, and cultural (*pace* rhetorical) conditions permit some to speak while eclipsing others, permit some views while silencing others, and permit some forums while ignoring others.[11] In short, who gets to speak and be heard, who has access to public forums, when and where this happens, and what can and cannot be said and heard are crucial rhetorical questions that problematize in important ways the understanding of trauma and writing (about) trauma.

WRITING (*ABOUT* AND *DURING*) TRAUMA AND METADISCOURSE

Trauma as both constituted by and generative of discourse becomes enveloped and glimpsed (albeit obliquely) by multiple discursive practices and authorized genres that function very differently being constituted by radically different rhetorical situations. Thus, what Bernard-Donals terms *the rhetoric of disaster*, we argue, may be more properly understood in the plural as the *rhetorics* of disaster. LaCapra offers a useful binary for thinking about this when he distinguishes between *writing about trauma* versus *writing trauma*.

For LaCapra, *writing about trauma* "is an aspect of historiography related to the project of reconstructing the past as objectively as possible without necessarily going to the self-defeating extreme of single-minded objectification that involves the denial of one's implication in the problems one treats" (186). By contrast, *writing trauma* "involves processes of acting out, working over, and to some extent working through in analyzing and 'giving voice' to the past—processes of coming to terms with traumatic 'experiences,'" (186). LaCapra's distinction is important, for it calls attention to the very different webs of rhetorical relations among the rhetors, topical objects, contexts, purposes, audiences and genres. In the former, writers reconstruct events not from personal or first-hand experience but from the discourses of those who have been involved and affected in some direct way with the trauma. In the latter, the writer authors from an existential position, having survived a trauma. As LaCapra notes, however, "*Writing trauma* is a metaphor in that writing indicates some distance from trauma (even when the experience of writing is itself intimately bound up with trauma). . . . Trauma indicates a shattering break or cesura in experience which has belated effects" (186). In this way, the concept of writing trauma is somewhat misleading for it must always necessarily involve (re)writing trauma, an activity taken not during but after the experience.

To LaCapra's bipartite definitions of writing and trauma, we want, for powerful theoretical and pedagogical reasons, to add two more: *metadiscourse on writing* (about) trauma, and *writing during trauma*.[12] *Metadiscourse on writing* (about) trauma involves critical or scholarly practices of studying and writing about either of the two discourses LaCapra identifies. *Writing during trauma* involves any kind of writing undertaken during a traumatic period whether or not it is directly linked to or generated by the trauma.

These four different discourses, as we show below, can be mapped according to the subject positions of the rhetors in relation to the trauma, the exigencies and purposes for the discourses and the genres in which those discourses take shape. In characterizing different subject positions in relation to disastrous or traumatic events, psychoanalyst and psychology scholar Dori Laub usefully delineates three levels of witnessing: "the level of being a witness to oneself within the experience; the level of being a witness to the testimonies of others; and the level of being a witness to the process of witnessing itself" (75). These three roles, or levels as Laub would have it, resonate with the distinctions we draw here among *writing trauma* (undertaken by first-degree witness), *writing about trauma* (undertaken by second-degree witness), and what we term *metadiscourse on writing (about) trauma* (undertaken by third-degree witness). The fourth type, *writing during trauma* can incorporate any of the subject positions, exigencies, and genres of the three discourses above or may be unrelated, at least on the surface. Each of these subject positions gets configured differently according to its unique rhetorical situation, and in turn, gives rise to different kinds of genres and hybridized genres. We provide fuller descriptions of each of the four discourses in the following sections.

Writing Trauma, as LaCapra so well explains, consists of a working through, and acting out, by those who are first-degree witnesses (or perhaps it is more accurate to say wit[less]nesses)—that is, those who experienced the traumatic event first-hand. Most common among the genres of writing trauma is testimony (although art, music, poetry, and other literary forms are also produced in response to trauma). Through testimony, "the witness is making *present* an *absence* that so disrupts his present that they become absolutely inseparable" (emphasis added, Bernard-Donals 78). As Laub explains, the function of testimony is integral to the process of working out and through trauma:

> What ultimately matters in all processes of witnessing, spasmodic and continuous, conscious and unconscious, is not simply the information, the establishment of the facts, but the experience itself of; *living through* testimony, of giving testimony.
>
> The testimony is, therefore, the process by which the narrator (the survivor) reclaims his position as a witness: reconstitutes the internal 'thou,' and thus the possibility of a witness or a listener inside himself. (85)

Thus, testimony, according to Laub and others, can be therapeutic and restorative.[13] The power of it cannot be overstated. Laub found in his clinical work with survivors of the Holocaust that they "not only need[ed] to survive so that they could tell their story; they also needed to tell their story in order to survive" (78). Testimony creates *presence* in *absence*. Put simply, in Blanchot's words, "loss goes with writing" (121). Put in more complex terms, Laub explains that testimony is "a dialogical process of exploration and reconciliation of two worlds—the one brutally destroyed and the one that is—that are different and will always remain so. The testimony is inherently a process of facing loss—of going through the pain of the act of witnessing, and of the ending of the act of witnessing—which entails yet another repetition of experience of separation and loss" (91). Absence and loss become palpable through discoursing, but there are always fissions marbling what is given presence that can be neither bridged nor filled. As Bernard-Donals observes in his discussion of the diary kept by Holocaust victim Lewin, "It is here that events . . . are *omitted* from the language of the writing but are made *present in the absence* of writing. The intention to write is shattered by the event's ability to elude writing" (emphasis added 83). The first-hand accounts come out of and return to a state of wit(less)ness.

Writing about Trauma consists of discourses that draw on, comment on, and interpret first-degree testimony. Those who write *about* trauma are second-degree witnesses. Second-degree witnesses (witnesses of the witnesses or witnesses of the testimonies of first-degree witnesses) include, for instance, those who write histories, literary, rhetorical, and cultural critical analyses on trauma as well as psychological tracts and treatment plans for victims of traumas. Their data consist almost exclusively of first-degree wit(less)ness accounts. The role of those who write about trauma, however, is not so clear-cut from the role of those who construct the discursive objects they select for scrutiny. As Felman observes, second-degree witnesses can serve "as catalysts—or agents of the process of reception, agents whose reflective witnessing and whose testimonial stances aid our own reception and assist us both in the effort toward comprehension and in the unending struggle with the foreignness of signs, in processing not merely (as does the professional interpreter) the literal meaning of the testimonies but also (some perspectives on) their philosophical and historical" ("The Return" 213). Second-degree witnesses thus both authorize and interpret trauma discourse. At times, they also serve as catalysts in prompting first-degree witnesses to tell their story (when, for instance, oral historians conduct interviews or documentary film artists ask for a recounting of the trauma).

In dealing with testimonies, second-degree witnesses confront the fissures and gaps left in these first-degree witness accounts. Patching together testimonial accounts creates yet additional fissures and gaps, leaving holes for others to attempt to stitch or correct. As LaCapra wisely notes, there is a danger when writing about trauma becomes conceived of as a stand-in for the trauma, an explanation of it in its utter totality. As he suggests, "the historical text becomes a substitute for the absent past only when it is construed as a totalized object that pretends to closure and is fetishized as such" (10–11). In other words, the danger lies in believing that any one text or set of texts can possibly capture the past in all its complexities let alone the traumatic past. Such a perspective ignores (and we'd argue with some peril) Bakhtin's point that "*Any utterance,* no matter how weighty and complete in and of itself, *is only a moment in the continuous process of verbal communication.* But that continuous verbal communication is, in turn, itself only a moment in the continuous, all inclusive, generative process of a given social collective" (939). And to put it even more clearly, as Bernard-Donals notes: "we do not establish truth through discourse as much as we produce arguments for a certain view of it, and no argument, no matter how strong, and no matter the integrity of the speaker, will settle a matter once and for all" (90).

Metadiscourse on writing (about) trauma refers primarily to scholarly discourses that explore questions concerning the complex relationships between trauma and writing. Metadiscourse is constructed by third-degree witnesses who both seek to theorize and interrogate the discourses generated by second-degree witnesses. Their data consist primarily of second-dress accounts. LaCapra's *Writing History, Writing Trauma,* Cathy Caruth's *Trauma and Memory,* Blanchot's *The Writing of the Disaster* offer good cases in point— as does this very chapter. These are texts that explore historiographical questions, literary and psychological questions, and philosophical questions concerning the discourses of and about trauma. A common goal in this kind of discourse is to come to understand how accounts come to be constructed, what purposes they serve, and who they serve. These then are the questions that also occupy those in rhetoric and composition, questions, for instance, that guide Michael Bernard-Donals's "The Rhetoric of Disaster and the Imperative of Writing." As such, this discourse should be of particular interest to both teachers and students of writing.

Writing during trauma refers to all those discourses generated during a time of trauma that are not necessarily directly related to the trauma but cannot help but be affected, and in some way respond to, and be shaped by, the trauma. For instance, on the day of 9/11 and in the wake of the furor following it, discourses of all kinds ostensibly unconnected with the national trauma were taking place; the question is: to what degree were these shaded by, directed toward/against, selected/deflected in unanticipated ways by the turmoil of the trauma? Consider, for example, John Schilb's review of John Trimbur's edited collection *Popular Literacy: Studies in Cultural Practices and Poetics* that appeared just months after 9/11. Schilb opens his review with these words:

> The terrorist attack on the World Trade towers and the Pentagon targeted those buildings as American icons. Moreover, subsequent media cov-

erage treated them as such. Yet the disaster generated more local forms of art. When the Towers fell, ordinary New Yorkers responded with a stunning visual array. Through murals, graffiti, and posters of the missing, citizens of an often-fragmented city joined in mourning, while also using their spontaneous public sphere to debate whether and how to retaliate.

I suspect that John Trimbur would see this deployment of images as 'popular literacy' in action (196–97).

Schilb's opening is a good example of the kind of writing generated during trauma. On the most obvious level, his introduction could not have been written without the horrific events of 9/11. His use of these events to draw readers into his book review nevertheless demonstrates the powerful intervention of trauma on discourses that are not directly targeted at the trauma. Moreover, just as Schilb notes that "the disaster generated more local forms of art," it also generated his local opening for a scholarly book review—and lots of other local forms, some of which have receded into the shadows while others have been put under the glaring lights of the critical gaze. The concept of *writing during trauma* has (as do those of the other kinds of discourses related to trauma) significant pedagogical implications as those of us who stepped into our classrooms on 9/11 and the dizzying days following it can attest to.

TEACHING WRITING (DURING/ABOUT/ON) TRAUMA

September 11, 9/11, as it has become known, was an event so startling and profound on so many levels for the millions who witnessed and shared in it via the unblinking, slow motion replay medium of "live" television that it defies (as trauma is wont to do) language. Analogies fall woefully short; definitions seem impossible; explanations are simply inconceivable. This violent, gruesome, ravishment of a nation and the lives of so many individuals generated question upon question. For those who teach writing, the terrorist attacks and the aftermath of grief, retribution, and reconstruction on a national scale have challenged us to re-examine and reconsider scholarly theories on and pedagogical assumptions about the teaching of writing.

Among the more salient questions raised by this disequalibrium are: why and how should a trauma of such magnitude be brought into the teaching of first-year writing in the university? How do our rhetorical and pedagogical theories and approaches serve us when the trauma is so great that we don't even have the language during the event to be able to grapple with it directly in the writing classroom context? What do we do when all of our arguments, conceptions, and research concerning written communication and the teaching of writing are seemingly so instantly trivialized by the magnitude of an event so extreme that it blots out and refigures all other functions, events, and emotions? What is our ethical responsibility to our students when the discursive practices and texts generated by and surrounding trauma can themselves reconstitute the trauma? What role should our assignments play or not play in such times? Eating, sleeping, marriage, death, grocery shopping, teaching, studying, writing an essay all become measured, conceived, constructed, disseminated, and filtered through the context of national trauma. How do writing instructors, especially those who teach a (multi)cultural approach to writing, cope with forceful popular sentiment opposing anything that might be construed as an "anti-American" attitude, with a Federal government whose stated position is that Americans should watch what they say,[14] or with the nationally authorized polemic discourses of good and evil, right and wrong, American and Arab? How do we attend to the infinitely diverse reactions—the grief, anger, ambivalence, hatred, silence—that individual students may demonstrate in class and in their writing?

Question heaps upon question: the potential for using events such as 9/11 for teaching and having students investigate, construct, and produce writing is so vast as to be almost incomprehensible. On the one hand, the trauma along the magnitude of 9/11 is such a particularized horror that perhaps it ought not serve as the linchpin of any one pedagogy; on the other hand, it is now part of the national fabric and so is unavoidable. A significant lesson for scholars and teachers in this incomprehensible trauma is that it brings to the fore the virtually inescapable role of trauma in teaching and writing. It challenges us to think about what it means to teach *during* times of trauma. The challenge is important, for it could be argued that we are already always immersed and surrounded by traumas of all sorts—bombarded daily by personal, natural, national, and international traumas in digital and print media not to mention the individual personal traumas we and our students cope with throughout our lives. Thus, like it or not, we are in some ways always already writing *during* trauma. In this light, considerations of teaching *during* 9/11 raise insights that may be more widely applicable.

It is not unreasonable to assume that virtually every instructor who walked into the writing classroom for the first time after the news of 9/11 remembers having to make decisions about how or if to broach the subject of the attacks. It is likely that many instructors in the eastern United States walked into their early classes that day without knowledge of the events that morning and did not find out until later. It is likely that many found out during their classes from students and colleagues. Other instructors may have heard the news broadcast as they were leaving for work, or before they left, or at the coffee shop, or on the train, or in their offices. Still others may have had time to prepare themselves for their classes later that day or for the following days. Some instructors may have cancelled their classes that day or for the next few days due to their own personal reaction to the trauma, concern for their students' reactions, or by administrative decree. Regardless of the timing between getting the news and facing the class, probably most, if not all, had to consider the political dynamics of their classes: students who had ties and connections to victims of the attacks, students from Middle-Eastern countries, students eligible for military service or already serving in the military, Moslem students, and so forth. The variables on an individual level are so overwhelming that any generalization that attempts to be inclusionary about a shared experience in national trauma will serve only to exclude. Here we want to stress that the answers and routes taken are less important than the questions raised and tackled by teachers, for we believe these serve a broader heuristic function in making pedagogical decisions about teaching writing.

PEDAGOGICAL IMPLICATIONS

The questions generated by 9/11 in particular and by considerations of traumas more generally call attention to a need for distinguishing among the different kinds of discourses related to trauma. As we suggest in the previous section, writing *during* trauma is unavoidable. How we handle such discourse is what is important, a point we consider later in this essay. Of the other three discourses related to trauma, there are potential dangers surrounding assigning/demanding *writing trauma* as well as assigning reading and writing *about* trauma (see note 13). Although *metadiscoursing on writing (about) trauma* is also not without its perils, if conducted with sensitivity as part of a larger set of course objectives, it may be useful.

Consideration of the interdependent relation between trauma and writing, and the discourses that both (re)construct and surround trauma can serve to illuminate the shadowy aspects of safety and community that are often (and naively) presumed in the writing class and provide students greater latitude in the choices they make when writing in connection to trauma. One key issue to recognize is that the classroom is *not* a safe place. This is not to say that a classroom is not relatively secure for most students, but rather to say that the classroom is not hermetically sealed off from the world in which it is situated. Moreover, we need to interrogate the concept of community, even in a national trauma, to show it not as an essential truth but as ideological construction. In extending and challenging Pratt's metaphor of the classroom as "safe house," Read reminds us:

> There are dangers in *assuming* a community—in the class(room)—based on the utopian concepts of equality, fraternity, and liberty (Pratt; Ellsworth). In the context of contemporary multicultural national realities (in the United States specifically), Mary Louise Pratt suggests that the class(room) should more properly be defined as a "contact zone." . . . In the

contact zone of the class(room) then, students and teachers negotiate knowledges, conflicts and debates born out of real social differences and interests, and the classroom is not "safe." (108)

Whether one confronts directly, as Read advocates, the "conflicts and debates born out of real social differences and interests" or attempts to ignore these, the fact of the matter is that the classroom is a site of difference and is situated in national, regional, and local spaces of difference that make it not "safe" in the sense of being immune to all that goes on outside its walls. If this fact was not abundantly clear before, it certainly should be in these post-9/11 times.

The shattering of previously held assumptions concerning the classroom and its participants provides a unique teaching opportunity and asks us to reconsider how our classes are constructed—discursively and otherwise. For instance, despite the tendency of the popular news media and political appointees to present 9/11 as events that cut across social and ideological identities, unifying all Americans in their shock and horror in the wake of national trauma, the notion of a legitimized homogenous community is not only an illusion but also an imposition. The assumption of legitimate community in the writing classroom is no less an imposition, especially if individual students have little choice about whether or not to be there and whether or not to write trauma or write about trauma. That is, the power, and potentially devastating effects, of these kinds of discourses should give us pause to consider the costs of demanding them.

However, to exclude national (or for that matter personal and natural) trauma in the writing classroom would also be an imposition. As Read goes on to state, "one of the challenges in the class(room) . . . is to find ways of making different knowledges public and to produce different knowledges in the process. And one of the ways in which this happens is through the exploration of trauma" (116). The paradox here is that while it is crucial that we do not mandate writing trauma, it is equally crucial that we also do not silence it. That is, as teachers we need to create spaces in which students may discuss or write trauma, in whatever form they choose, if they initiate this level of trauma discourse.[15] But we should not end there. We should also introduce students to, and open spaces for, the four levels of writing and trauma to provide them with rhetorical strategies for engaging in and understanding these discourses.

What is necessary then for exploring multiple rhetorics of trauma in the classroom is a model that allows students to engage in a variety of literate practices concerning trauma, and especially to participate in a metadiscourse of critical reflection on writing and not writing trauma. In short, what is needed is a robust model that can accommodate multiple constructions of knowledges, discourses, and literate practices in the writing classroom.

Toward a Pedagogical Framework for Teaching Writing (in, about, on) Trauma

The events of 9/11 and our reflections on our pedagogical choices then affirmed and crystallized for the two of us Bill Cope and Mary Kalantzis's recent observation that "there cannot be one set of standards or skills that constitutes the ends of literacy learning. . . . Gone are the days when learning a single, standard version of the language was sufficient. . . . No longer do the old pedagogies of a formal standard, written national language hold the utility they once possessed" (6). Cope and Kalantzis writing in pre-9/11 days could rightfully observe that in the *kairos* where discourses of all sorts are being shaped by twin, seemingly opposing, forces of increasing local cultural diversity and global connectedness as well as by rapidly evolving multimedia contexts, students need to learn (perhaps as never before) a wide range of different kinds of literate practices. This realization was brought home to us poignantly and powerfully when within the context of 9/11 and post-9/11, we found ourselves in our classes grappling with the four kinds of discourses related to trauma that we describe above. *Discoursing the trauma* manifested itself as we and our students discussed the events face-to-face and on an electronic board; discoursing *about* trauma manifested itself, for example, as we explored the ways various news media were reporting the events and the ways others (teachers, friends, family members) were and were not discussing 9/11; *metadiscoursing about trauma* occurred, for instance, as we discussed ways to rhetorically and critically analyze the conflicting reports and coverage, and to account for the multiple, diverse reactions to the trauma; discoursing *during* trauma incorporated the other three levels and all other discourses that took place in and around our classroom apart from those focusing on the events.

As Bernard-Donals observes, "the pedagogical implication of a rhetoric[s] of disaster is complicated and potentially troubling" (84). In thinking through the tough pedagogical questions raised by the national trauma of 9/11, the two of us have found new literacy theories (Gee; Street); and activity theory (Russell "Activity," "Rethinking"; Lee and Smagorinksy) particularly useful, and the pedagogical model advocated by Cope and Kalantzis especially robust.[16] Their model is constructed by four tenets: *situated practice, overt instruction, critical framing,* and *transformed practice. Situated practice* assumes that students learn best when immersed in the contexts in which actual literate practices take place and when they engage in real literate tasks; when, in short, they experience meaning-making in real contexts and through a variety of media. *Overt instruction* is based on the concept that students who develop metacognitive skills through studying theory are better able to select and use appropriate literate strategies. *Critical framing* assumes that when students learn rhetorical tools that permit them to interpret social and institutional contexts in terms of diverse purposes and audiences, they discern the most effective ways to communicate in particular rhetorical situations. *Trans-formed practice* holds that students become effective meaning-makers by trans-forming strategies they already control to engage in new rhetorical situations (7). In what follows, we briefly sketch out in very broad strokes how these four tenets guide our own teaching of first-year writing, and how they were man-ifested in our classrooms during and following 9/11.[17]

Before we begin our sketch, we offer a brief description of our first-year writing class. We teach in one of the largest state universities in the country. Our student population tops 49,000, with an entering first-year population of near 7,000. However, our school also serves an equally large influx of transfer students, many of whom are required to take first-year writing. Thus, our classes are often diverse in terms of age range and experience. Our first-year program offers traditional face-to-face classes, hybrid classes, and on-line classes in writing. The two of us teach the hybrid version in which we meet students face-to-face half of the time and in an asynchronous online forum setting for the other half. This dual arrangement of meeting in phys-ical and virtual space allows for an expanded range of settings for various reading and writing practices as well as for different arrangements of stu-dent-to-student and student-to-teacher interactions. Built into the course then are diverse opportunities for students to engage in multimodal literate practices via diverse writing technologies. We further encourage multimodal reading and writing practices by the kinds of projects we assign and by their sequencing. Students pursue a topic area of their own choosing and conduct four projects, each requiring a different mode of inquiry: hermeneutical (semiotic and cultural analysis of a website related to their topic), empirical (an ethnographic study of a public space related to their topic), historical (analyses of historical treatments of their topic), and cultural critical reflec-tion (a synthesis of the various perspectives taken to arrive at an analysis of their topic). These projects (and the relevant genres to which they give rise) build on each other as students engage in layers of interconnected reflective analysis throughout the course, utilizing various communication media and discussion formats to analyze texts they read and write, and the social and cultural contexts that these texts circulate in and are shaped by, and their own assumptions and values they bring to rhetorical situations. The central ques-tion driving our course is: What is writing? Over and over we return to this deceptively complex question. As students engage in multiple modes of inquiry and through multiple media, they begin to build a more complicated picture of what writing means. As they keep returning to the question of what is writing, they are able to raise new questions, insights, observations, and problems to develop a richer understanding of what is clearly a complex question. Instead of asking a question such as "How do I become a better writer?" this approach allows them to ask "What does it mean to be a writer in this situation?" and "What is meant by 'better'"?

Situated Practice

As best as we are able given the artificiality of the writing classroom, we immerse students in real-world reading and writing tasks that emerge out of their multiple studies of an area in which they have some investment (whether personal, academic, or professional). For better or worse, 9/11 provided a multilayered context in which to examine and enact a variety of real world discursive practices. In our case, prior to that day, we had been examining public space as a discursive construct. Students had been reading, discussing, and writing about various arguments and interpretations of the concept of public space as it appears in the readings anthologized in Diana George and John Trimbur's *Reading Culture*. While these assignments and activities were meant to prepare the ground for tackling their first project, an analysis of a virtual public space, they became grist for thinking and discoursing on how the attacks and their aftermath impacted on our conceptions and reconceptions of public space. And they provided critical rhetorical tools for exploring the various kinds of discourses generated by and about the traumatic event and for participating in these discourses. Through situated practice, then, we engaged in voluntary *discoursing trauma,* discoursing *about* trauma, and *metadiscoursing* (about) trauma.

Overt Instruction

We introduce students to the rhetorical and cultural theories that we draw on ourselves for teaching writing as well as competing theoretical views that they have likely encountered in their years of school-based literacy instruction. One of our goals is to emphasize the notion of design—that writing consists of socially negotiated literacy acts and practices, imbued with tacit and overt cultural values and embedded assumptions—including our own course. Throughout the semester we discuss various rhetorical theories and engage students in a variety of rhetorical heuristics that help to explain and demonstrate knowledge construction as design and to help them to begin to construct the kinds of questions relevant for particular rhetorical situations. In the extreme case of 9/11 and post-9/11, we now recognize (though we have to admit we didn't at the time) the need to bring in theories of trauma and discourse—such as those with which we open this essay. If we understand that we are in some ways always already immersed in trauma to one degree or another, such theoretical frames and the questions and discourses they give rise to ought to serve students in fruitful ways beyond the immediacy of one (albeit overwhelming palpable) trauma. In other words, grappling with theorizing and questioning ought to provide students with strategies to help them participate in trauma discourses on various levels.

Critical Framing

We work with the students to help them defamiliarize the familiar as a means of helping them gain critical distance from the reading and writing activities they are engaged in and the social and cultural contexts in which their meaning making occurs. To do this, we teach (via overt instruction) critical tools for analyzing rhetorical situations and the ways these both permit and constrain what may be written. Critical framing was particularly important as we explored with our students what was being said/written and not said/written by others through various media and in various personal and academic contexts. It further gave us tools for considering how notions of public space were being tested, contested, and legislated over this extraordinary time.

Transformed Practice

We begin with the assumption that students are not lacking in literate practices—what Brian Street refers to as a deficit model—but come to the course with all sorts of socially acquired literacies and discourses. They come, that is, with a diverse variety of conceptual and material tools that shape their literate practices and that emerge out of their past literate experiences. In this, we find activity theory particularly useful. Literate practices may be best understood as an activity that takes place alongside and with other activity systems. As David Russell notes, "an activity system is any ongoing, object-directed, historically conditioned, dialogically structured, tool-mediated human interaction" ("Rethinking" 510). Engaging in a literate task means not only responding to a web of other texts in which the text one is reading or writing is situated, but it also means working with material tools (pen/paper, keyboard/screen, physical and digital pages) and rhetorical tools of language. None of these is ever simply created anew with each new task but is drawn on and adapted as new rhetorical situations present themselves. Known strategies and tools, in other words, are engaged for new tasks. The key to helping students understand this is to get them to become more critically reflective about the literate practices they have engaged in previously and to develop a meta-awareness (which requires overt instruction and critical framing) of the ways in which these converge and the ways these diverge from the texts they are reading and writing at any given time. In grappling with the widely contested discourses generated by and circulating around 9/11, students were asked to recognize the kinds of practices—e.g., first-degree witness accounts, second-degree witness accounts—that were coming to the foreground and were in harmony or clashing with one another. In this, they acted as well as third-degree witnesses, metadiscoursing on discoursing. They also came to recognize that they had to confront other discursive situations from which they could draw conceptional, physical, and rhetorical tools to adapt to this unspeakable of speakable events.

Some Concluding Thoughts

We have explicated, in admittedly very sketchy strokes, our approach to teaching writing and have reflected on how this approach played out (at least as we recall it) during the tumultuous times of 9/11. We offer it not as a panacea but as a way to think through issues concerning the teaching of writing in general and, specifically, the teaching of writing—during, in, and about—trauma. In other words, we offer our explication as a heuristic not as an answer because course designs must take local conditions and populations into account. However, a few general observations are worth making. Our approach, adapted from Cope and Kalantzis pedagogical model, requires that we view our students not only as writers (broadly defined), but also as students *of* writing. That is, we help them to discover that written communication is indeed a body of study, not merely (as one of Peter's students put it) "just something you do." From such a perspective, students can examine what it means to explore various kinds of writing in a context of national trauma. Nonwriting, personal expression, editorializing, testimony, and historical and political analysis can all be examined as acts of communication—as literate practices. Further, we can also introduce theory that supports metadiscourse concerning why and how we study writing connected to trauma, thereby bringing the writing course itself and the approaches to teaching writing into the arena of inquiry.

In writing or not writing during the immediate aftermath of national trauma, and in the weeks and months following, students who choose to write about the event can express personal reactions—can *write trauma*, in other words. They can also critically consider the questions that they bring to their own texts in constructing the event, and to their analysis of other published print and digital texts to *write about trauma*. Also, they can begin to discover questions concerning the institution of academic inquiry and the discursive practices these permit and discourage as they engage in *metadiscourse on writing (about) trauma*. Perhaps most importantly, they can begin to examine how and why certain discourses about national trauma are authorized while others are excluded or ignored. They can discover with our help what it is that we as rhetoricians and writing instructors theorize and recognize—that there *are* questions, and that cultural, social, political, personal, and academic responses and reactions to writing about trauma—or anything—are embedded with tacit and overt values, experiences, and theories that shape the public (discursive) construction of knowledge.

Notes

1. Also quoted in Felman "Education" p. 49.

2. For a review of the literature in literary studies that has turned its attention to trauma, see Geoffrey Hartman, "On Traumatic Knowledge and Literary Studies." As

an indication of the rise of scholarly interest across many disciplines, also see Paul Antze, and Michael Lambek, eds., *Tense Past: Cultural Essays in Trauma and Memory;* James Berger, *After the End: Representations of Post-Apocalypse;* Maurice Blanchot *The Writing of the Disaster;* Cathy Caruth, *Trauma: Explorations in Memory;* and *Unclaimed Experience: Trauma, Narrative;* Kai Erickson *A New Species of Trouble: Exploration in Disaster;* Kirby Farrell, *Post-Traumatic Culture: Injury and Interpretation in the Nineties;* Shoshana Felman, and Dori Laub, *Testimony: Crises of Witnessing in Literature, Psycho-analysis, and History;* Judith Lewis Herman, *Trauma and Recovery;* Dominick LaCapra, *Writing History, Writing Trauma;* Ruth Ley, *Trauma: A Genealogy.* Bessel A. van der Kolk, Alexander C. McFarlane, and Lars Weisaeth, eds. *Traumatic Stress: The Effects of Overwhelming Experience on Mind, Body, and Society* to name just a handful.

3. One indicator is the turn toward oral history and oral historiography, and the validation of oral testimony as acceptable evidence. For a discussion of the role of oral testimony in history in our field, see Nelms.

4. It is beyond the scope of this essay to debate the claims that bracket off our times as more or less traumatic than other ages. Yet it is worth close scrutiny elsewhere to explore those claims and to ponder the question that if this is an age of unprece-dented testimony to traumas of all sorts, is it the case that the testimony is being gen-erated by the existential fact that we are living in a more potent time of trauma? Or is the construct, the belief, that this is a more traumatic era creating the conditions that generate more testimony? That is, do we take an empirical rise in testimonies as a symptom of a more heightened and powerful traumas or is it the reverse?

5. With rare exception, those in rhetoric and composition have been curiously silent on the subject of trauma, disaster, and the discursive practices and texts associated with and surrounding such events. For examples of these exceptions, see Bernard-Don-als; Bishop; Giroux; and Read. Our observation of the relative silence on trauma in our field is not meant as a fault-finding move; indeed, we as authors would probably not have turned our eye toward trauma and writing had we not been asked to contribute to this volume and had not the traumatic events of 9/11 served as an exigency. The gap functions as a rhetorical move for inserting our argument into the scholarship but more importantly it also exemplifies the powerful role trauma itself plays in generating/silenc-ing discourses of all kinds—a point we develop more fully later in this essay.

6. This oppositional pull comes in part because the subject positions of those responsible for and those affected (even victimized) by specific traumatic experiences are not stable sets of relations but are contextually constituted and rhetorically con-structed and reconstructed in complex ways.

7. See McFarlane and van der Kolk who ask: "Do nations, in order to function effectively, need a shared history of trauma to forge a sense of national community that creates a sense of belonging and security in its citizens?" (24; also qtd. in Read 105). That is, might national trauma be understood as a social, if not political, glue? There is an interesting tension worthy of exploration elsewhere between the shattering of trauma (national or otherwise) and the notion that it might serve as a glue and sense of security.

8. For an insightful discussion of how trauma is configured, understood, experienced and inscribed differently by different subject positions, see Caruth *Unclaimed*. In her discussion of Alain Resnais and Marguerite Duras's 1959 French film *Hiroshima mon amour*, Caruth draws attention to the opening dialogue through which a French woman speaks her "understanding of Hiroshima from the perspective of a national French history" (29). Caruth explains that "for the French, Hiroshima did not signify the beginning of the suffering of the Japanese, but rather precisely the end of their own suffering. The knowledge of Hiroshima, for the French, understood not as the incomprehensible occurrence of the nuclear bombing of the Japanese but as the knowledge they call 'the end,' effaces the event of a Japanese past and inscribes it as a referent, into the narrative of French history" (29).

9. On June 14, 1999, as 14-year-old Shannon Smith stood in her own backyard talking on the phone, a stray bullet from a gun shot straight in the air by a nearby neighbor fell directly into Shannon, killing her on impact. Shannon became one of the many victims in Phoenix, Arizona, who have been killed or injured by random gunfire. Her parents successfully fought for amending the lenient Arizona law regarding the unlawful discharge of firearms within a city or town to raise it from a class 2 misdemeanor to a class 6 felony that carries greater penalties. The provisions for amending the law, 13–3107, stipulated that it be designated as "Shannon's Law."

10. The crucial problem here has to do with frames of references that permit individuals to make sense of each unique event—even though it is experienced for the first time. As Young, Becker and Pike point out in their first maxim of their tagmemic rhetoric, "*People conceive of the world in terms of repeatable units.* In the continuously changing, dynamic flow of events, there are always recognizable, namable, recurring 'sames'—discrete units of experience. Although every instant in life is different from all previous instants, people act as if things were constant, as if situations or events could occur repeatedly. We may never be able to step into the same river twice, but we act as if we can" (26). Yet, as Maria Root notes, trauma as an event represents "the destruction of basic organizing principles by which we come to know self, others and the environment" (72). In the case of a traumatic event of the magnitude of 9/11, a whole new river was being forged.

11. For example, during the tumultuous weeks following 9/11, those who did not adhere to the approved discourses were publicly chastened or fired from their jobs. Richard Berthold, Bill Maher, and Tom Gutting immediately spring to mind. The resignation of Richard Berthold, a history professor at the University of New Mexico, was called for when he "joked" that anyone who blew up the Pentagon would have his vote. In response to calls for Berthold's resignation, New Mexico State legislator William Fuller suggested that as a state employee at a public institution, Berthold should be held accountable for his statement. Bill Maher, host of ABC's *Politically Incorrect*, was chastised in the media for suggesting that the 9/11 terrorists were not cowards, and that what was cowardly was lobbing cruise missiles from 2,000 miles away. Tom Gutting, a city editor for the *Texas City Sun*, was fired by the publisher for an opinion column in which he criticized President George W. Bush.

12. We find this quadripartite distinction necessary and significant, though it is not one that has been made. Indeed, often in the research literature on writing (about) trauma scholars conflate the writing trauma with writing about trauma, and thus do, to our minds, violence to both.

13. The therapeutic effects of writing and trauma were recently studied in controlled conditions by Schoutrop et al. Their study revealed that the group engaged in writing assignments showed marked differences in terms of coping with the traumas and with depression as compared with the control group. However, we want to be quick to point out that such findings should not be taken lightly outside of these controlled conditions. That is, we do not take such findings as warrants for using testimony in writing classes as a form of therapy. In fact, we see great danger in making the leap from the psychologist forum to the classroom forum. If anything, we see such findings as warrants for why we as rhetoricians and teachers of writing ought to be cautious about dabbling in areas for which we are not trained (cf. Bishop). The potential for creating crisis among students when they all are required to testify (or even delve into testimonials on trauma) is great as Shoshana Felman found when she taught a graduate course titled Literature and Testimony (see "Education"). In the context of a national trauma on the scale of 9/11, requiring students to connect themselves to the event through testimony is to our minds unethical. And tackling any of the levels of discourse associated with trauma without the rhetorical tools of critical distance and metadiscourse is to potentially do more harm than good. This does not mean that we avoid tackling trauma and the writing of trauma but that we are careful not to mandate confessional and testimonial discourse related to trauma of any kind in our classes. We advocate instead of ignoring trauma that we instead teach tools for understanding the discursive complexities of it.

14. On September 21, 2001, at a Whitehouse press briefing, Ari Fleischer was asked about the President's reaction to Bill Maher's quip about terrorists on *Politically Incorrect*. Fleischer responded:

> I'm aware of the press reports about what he said. I have not seen the actual transcript of the show itself. But assuming the press reports are right, it's a terrible thing to say, and it is unfortunate. And that's why—there was an earlier question about has the President said anything to people in his own party—they're reminders to all Americans that they need to watch what they say, watch what they do. This is not a time for remarks like that; there never is.

15. Indeed, many of our students, and we suspect those of other writing teachers, were grateful that we did open a space in class for such discussions. One of Maureen's students spoke passionately about the frustration and pain he felt when on the afternoon of 9/11 his economics' professor did not even acknowledge the event.

16. See the edited collection *Multiliteracies* by Cope and Kalantzis for discussions of how this pedagogical model might be enacted in a variety of contexts, and for considerations of its limits and for cautions about importing it into local contexts.

17. In offering this broad sketch, we want to point out that our recollections and emplotment of those days is fraught with fissions—gaps—and the description makes it seem far more coherent than it no doubt was. We admit to stumbling and stuttering (as we expect many did) through the early days and weeks following 9/11. It is only in the relative calmness of hindsight that we have been able to begin to understand the lessons we learned from those frantic times.

WORKS CITED

Ankersmit, Frank. "Reply to Professor Zagorin." *History and Theory: Contemporary Readings*. Eds. Brian Fay, Philip Pomper, and Richard T. Vann. Malden, MA: Blackwell, 1998. 209–222.

Antze, Paul, and Michael Lambek, eds. *Tense Past: Cultural Essays in Trauma and Memory*. New York: Routledge, 1996.

Bakhtin, Mikhail. From *Marxism and the Philosophy of Language*. Trans. Ladislaw Matejka and I. R. Titunik. *The Rhetorical Tradition: Readings from Classical Times to the Present*. Eds. Patricia Bizzell and Bruce Herzberg. Boston: Bedford, 1990. 928–44.

Berger, James. *After the End: Representations of Post-apocalypse*. Minneapolis: U of Minnesota P, 1999.

Bernard-Donals, Michael. "The Rhetoric of Disaster and the Imperative of Writing." *Rhetoric Society Quarterly* 31 (2001): 73–94.

Bishop, Wendy. "Writing Is/And Therapy?: Raising Questions about Writing Classrooms and Writing Program Administration." *JAC* 13 (1993): 503–16.

Blanchot, Maurice. *The Writing of the Disaster*. Trans. Ann Smock. Lincoln: U of Nebraska P, 1986.

Caruth, Cathy, ed. *Trauma: Explorations in Memory*. Baltimore: Johns Hopkins UP, 1995.

———. *Unclaimed Experience: Trauma, Narrative, History*. Baltimore: Johns Hopkins UP, 1996.

Celan, Paul. "Dumb Autumn Smells." *Poems*. Trans. Michael Hamburger. New York: Persea Books, 1980. 139.

Cope, Bill, and Mary Kalantzis. "Introduction: Multiliteracies: The Beginnings of an Idea." *Multiliteracies: Literacy Learning and the D4esign of Social Futures*. Eds. Bill Cope and Mary Kalantzis. London: Routledge, 2000. 3–8.

Culbertson, Roberta. "Embodied Memory, Transcendence, and Telling: Recounting Trauma, Re-establishing the Self." *New Literary History* 26 (1995): 169–95.

Erickson, Kai T. *A New Species of Trouble: Exploration in Disaster, Trauma, and Community*. New York: W. W. Norton, 1994.

Farrell, Kirby. *Post-Traumatic Culture: Injury and Interpretation in the Nineties*. Baltimore: Johns Hopkins UP, 1998.

Felman, Shoshana. "Education and Crisis, or the Vicissitudes of Teaching." Felman and Laub 1–56.

————. "The Return of the Voice: Claude Lanzmann's *Shoah*." Felman and Laub 204–83.

Felman, Shoshana, and Dori Laub. *Testimony: Crises of Witnessing in Literature, Psychoanalysis, and History*. New York: Routledge, 1992.

Gee, James Paul. *Social Linguistics and Literacies: Ideology in Discourses* 2nd ed. London: Taylor and Francis, 1996.

George, Diana, and John Trimbur. *Reading Culture: Contexts for Critical Reading and Writing* 4th ed. New York: Longman, 2001.

Gill, Carolyn Bailey, ed. *Maurice Blanchot: The Demand of Writing*. London: Routledge, 1996.

Giroux, Susan Searls. "The Post-9/11 University and the Project of Democracy." *JAC* 22 (2002): 57–91.

Hartman, Geoffrey H. "On Traumatic Knowledge and Literary Studies." *New Literary History* 26 (1995): 537–63.

Herman, Judith Lewis. *Trauma and Recovery*. New York: Harper Collins, 1992.

Hill, Leslie. "Introduction." *Maurice Blanchot: The Demand of Writing*. Ed. Carolyn Bailey Gill. London: Routledge, 1996. 1–20.

LaCapra, Dominick. *Writing History, Writing Trauma*. Baltimore: Johns Hopkins UP, 2001.

Laub, Dori. "An Event without a Witness: Truth, Testimony and Survival." Felman and Laub 75–92.

Lee, Carol D., and Peter Smagorinsky, eds. *Vygotskian Perspectives on Literacy Research*. Cambridge, England: Cambridge UP, 2000.

Ley, Ruth. *Trauma: A Genealogy*. Chicago: U of Chicago P, 2000.

Loewenstein, Andrea Freud. "Confronting Stereotypes: *Maus* in Crown Heights." *College English* 60 (1998): 396–420.

McFarlane, Alexander C., and Bessel A. van der Kolk. "Trauma and Its Challenge to Society." van der Kolk, McFarlane, and Weisaeth 24–46.

Nelms, Gerald. "The Case for Oral Evidence in Composition Historiography." *Written Communication* 9 (1992): 356–82.

New London Group. "A Pedagogy of Multiliteracies Designing Social Futures." Cope and Kalantzis 9–38.

Newman, Michael. "The Trace of Trauma: Blindness, Testimony and the Gaze in Blanchot and Derrida." Gill 153–73.

Office of the Press Secretary, the White House. Online Posting. 26 Sep. 2001. Press Briefing. 14 Aug. 2002. *http://www.whitehouse.gov/news/releases/2001/09/20010926–5. html.*

Read, Daphne. "Writing Trauma, History, Story: The Class(room) as Borderland. *JAC* 18 (1998): 105–121.

Root, Maria P. "Reconstructing the Impact of Trauma on Personality." *Personality and Psychopathology: Feminist Reappraisals*. Eds. Laura S. Brown, and Mary Ballou. New York: Guilford P, 1992.

Ropars-Wuilleumier, Marie-Claire. "On Unworking: The Image in Writing According to Blanchot." Gill 138–52.

Russell, David R. "Activity Theory and Its Implications for Writing Instruction." *Reconceiving Writing, Rethinking Writing Instruction.* Ed. Joseph Petraglia. Mawah, NJ: Lawrence Erlbaum, 1995. 51–78.

———. "Rethinking Genre Theory in School and Society: An Activity Theory Analysis." *Written Communication* 14 (1997): 504–54.

Schilb, John. Rev. of John Trimbur, ed. *Popular Literacy: Studies in Cultural Practices and Poetics. Rhetoric Review* 21 (2002): 196–200.

Schoutrop, Mirjam J. A., Alfred Lange, Gerrit Hanewald, Udi Davidovich, and Henriette Salomon. "Structured Writing and Processing Major Stressful Events: A Controlled Trial." *Psychotherapy and Psychosomatics* 71 (3) (2002): 151–57.

Street, Brian. *Social Literacies: Critical Approaches to Literacy in Development, Ethnography and Education.* Harlow, England: Longman, 1995.

van der Kolk, Bessel A., Alexander C. McFarlane, and Lars Weisaeth, eds. *Traumatic Stress: The Effects of Overwhelming Experience on Mind, Body, and Society.* New York: Guildford P, 1996.

Young, Richard E., Alton L. Becker, and Kenneth L. Pike. *Rhetoric: Discovery and Change.* San Diego: Harcourt Brace Jovanovich, 1970.

Here and Now

Remediating National Tragedy and the Purposes for Teaching Writing

Richard Marback

THAT THE WORLD we live in was changed by the tragedy of September 11 is now familiar to everyone. From travel through airports to the reorganization of the federal government and the increased urgency of international relations, our experiences have been altered and our expectations transformed. The processes and purposes of all these activities, and many more besides, have been redefined to address the demands of a different world. What has made our world so different is how we have directed our attention following the events of September 11. On the one hand, we were drawn into a different awareness of ourselves and our world. The shock and horror of that day could not but compel our attention and come to dominate our lives. Images of the destruction and of the rescue efforts were immediately pushed into our daily awareness, pushing out other, more mundane concerns. On the other hand, the events themselves do not dictate the kind of attention we should pay the tragedy and its aftermath. Nor do the events themselves dictate the difference our awareness should make for how we now live our lives together.

The simultaneous dominance and indeterminacy of September 11 in our conceptual horizon should lead compositionists to take a hard evaluative look at the purposes of teaching first-year writing. I make this claim knowing full well the activities of teaching writing have no direct relationship to heightening airport security, reorganizing the federal government, or improving international relations. At the same time, the manner by which current events compel attention and organize activities in the world should give us pause to weigh the value of what we compositionists do. I say this not so much because recent events have compelled everyone to take stock of what they do. Rather, I say this because what we do when we teach writing is direct the attention of students to the audiences, contexts, and purposes of their making of meaning here and now. With regard to audience, we teach students how to pay attention to the people they write for, in order to best direct those people to, in turn, pay attention to a specific topic at a specific time and for a specific purpose. Similarly, with context and purpose, we teach students to pay attention to where they write and why they write, so that they might most effectively direct the attention of an audience to consideration of a topic. That the events and aftermath of September 11 so dominate our lives, so assert themselves on our considerations of who we interact with, where we are, and what we do, demonstrates something about the phenomenology of attention and circumstance that has bearing on the attention we ask our students as writers to pay to audiences, contexts, and purposes.

I say this because the events of September 11 that shattered lives in New York City, at the Pentagon, and in rural Pennsylvania were felt far away from those specific places, and they continue to resonate, long after that day ended. What the vast majority of Americans experienced on that Tuesday in September was not the destruction then and there. They experienced images of wreck and rubble, reports of death and destruction, and representations of despair and heroism, again, and again, and again.

The ability of the mass media to mobilize global communications technologies and provide immediate, broad access to events almost anywhere challenges our sense of what we can and what we should make ourselves pay attention to as literate citizens here and now. However, this does not mean we can know anything anywhere at any time. Federal officials in the executive branch and the justice department continue to exert their authority to withhold information; reporters still shape newscasts out of their uneven access to people and places; and information in general cannot but be tailored to fit within the rhetorical structures of television broadcasts, print journalism, and digital media. The formation of our attention through the technological and organizational mediation of what we can know has consequences both for our awareness of ourselves as having a voice and for our understanding that our expressions somehow matter. The organizing of our attention to the events and aftermath of September 11 has altered our world, challenging us to evaluate who we become through lives lived in a world of mediated representations, compelling us to imagine what we can make of ourselves through our rhetorical activities, and leading us to locate occasions for purposeful writing within the dynamics of mediated representation and individual rhetorical activity here and now.

I develop my view that the events and aftermath of September 11 have profoundly shaped our attention by arguing my claim for compositionists to reflect on the mediation of current world events in directing our attention to the purposes of teaching writing. I do this in three sections. In the first section, I narrate the experience of having my attention, and the attention of my basic writing students, dominated by the events of September 11. My narrative documents the experience of world events as compelling, but removed from the context of here and now. The experience of world events as both compelling and distant at the same time removes us from the prospects of rhetorical participation. Such an experience dissociates audience, context, and purpose, and so disorganizes our attention to the rhetorical situation, undermining our capacity for meaningful response. The second section explains the dissociation of our attention to events from our rhetorical capacity to respond to those events by appealing to the mediation of our attention through current information and literacy technologies. As will become clear, my argument here is that literacy technologies in use today demand of us a new response. In the final section, I conclude with a proposal for reinvigorating the public purposes of writing instruction as a necessary response to the disorganizing force of event mediation on our rhetorical capacities as citizens here and now.

A Personal Experience of
Composition Instruction Here and Now

I experienced the immediacy of September 11 on the teaching of writing because I was teaching the second of two sections of basic writing when students walked into class bringing news of a plane having crashed into a building. Their accounts conflicted. One said the Sears Tower in Chicago had caught fire. Another said a plane had crashed in New York. Whatever happened did not seem reason enough to prevent us from continuing with class as usual. After class, as I stepped out of the building, I was confronted by several people, all stunned by what they knew. Something profoundly tragic had happened, yet the world around me appeared unchanged. I returned to my office and turned to the Internet for a more accurate report of events. As I read initial reports and waited for more information, the events of September 11 drew me in. Not that I wanted to isolate myself or avoid it. I wanted to know what happened. I wanted to know what would happen. As the day went on, and as the days passed, I listened to the radio, read the newspaper, and scanned the Internet searching for information. The events simply absorbed my attention.

Media coverage of the events absorbed the attention of my students as well. With events unfolding in New York and Afghanistan and so absorbing our attention, I did not think I could just ignore it all in the classes I was teaching. I felt compelled to bring discussion of the terrorist attacks and the unfolding events into my writing classes for a number of reasons. Even though

I recognized we had an obligation to continue what we were already doing, we could not act as though the attacks had not happened, or that the prospects of war did not loom large. Like everyone else, students in my courses were both interested in and horrified by what they witnessed and by what was happening. They wanted an opportunity to make sense of what they were hearing and seeing without having that concern take over their lives. So I felt compelled to incorporate current events into my writing courses that semester. World events pressed our attention and changed the context and strained the purposes for teaching and learning writing that semester. As much as I had to acknowledge the changed context for writing instruction, I also felt compelled to not let the writing courses I was teaching devolve into forums for rant. Whatever else we might do in response to that day, I did not think we should surrender over to it the purposes we had for learning and teaching writing. Retaining the direction we had prior to September 11 seemed at least as important, if not more so, given the intensity of focus given over to waiting for war.

My solution to the dilemma of continuing work that should still matter, while acknowledging events pressing in on our attention, almost to the exclusion of all else, was to use media coverage of September 11 as an object lesson in the rhetoric of public ideas. This resolution of the dilemma did not compromise the curriculum of my courses. From the beginning of that semester, I had stressed that people make and are subject to public arguments all the time, that good writing matters because writing does work in the world, and that learning to write is learning to do public work in the world. Before the semester began, I had designed my syllabus around assignments teaching students some of the kinds of public arguments there are and how to make those arguments. After September 11 and through the remainder of that semester, public arguments about Afghanistan and homeland security dominated the media and absorbed our attention. While the volume of dialogue and information and opinion provided students in my courses ample opportunities for analysis, it also exposed for me a serious constraint on the capacity of students as citizens to construct public responses.

So the decision to bring media representations of the aftermath of September 11 into my classes was more than simply acknowledgment of shifts in context and purpose brought about by world affairs. It was at least as much an attempt to make sense of the attention focused on world events, to make sense of those events in terms of the attention-organizing capacities of representations. But as I incorporated engagement with the events into the classroom, it seemed the interest and horror expressed by students were responses more to a media event than to any direct experience of a national tragedy. Sure, this is a trivial observation. Obviously, the unfolding events were available to the majority of people only through mass media representations. What is less trivial and not always obvious is the influence of event presentation in the media on our perceptions of our own expressive agency. A new dimension of the influence of mass media on agency and voice was made apparent to me in student responses to several assignments. In one assignment in particular, I asked students in each of my basic writing courses to analyze the appeals made in a media representation of their choice. It could be a magazine or newspaper photograph or article or even an editorial. They could also choose from any number of Internet or audio representations. The source mattered less than what I directed them to do with it, for the purpose was to redirect the attention these representations seemed to demand of us, to redirect it by thinking hard about how the representations capture and hold our attention. I gave them typical questions to guide their thinking: Who is the audience? What assumptions are made in the narrative about that audience? How does the narrative develop from those assumptions? What does the author accomplish with the narrative? What does the author leave out of the narrative? How do you imagine the narrative would need to change if the projected audience were different?

Two responses stood out to me as indicative of something important about the manner by which mass media representations grab our attention and frame our capacities for spectatorship and agency. The Detroit area where I teach is home to the largest Arab American community in the United States. It quickly drew the attention of federal investigators and became the focus for angry, frustrated, and outraged citizens. For Arab Americans in the area, events were all too real. It was real that they became victims of hate crimes, real that they were targeted for questioning and suspicion, real that some of them were detained or deported, real that they felt obligated to pledge their allegiance, even though many are American citizens. Local newspapers, radio, and television ran stories chronicling anti-Arab American hate crimes and portraying Arab Americans as loyal citizens. Non-Arab students in my courses could understand the fear and frustration of Arab Americans living in the area. They could see how the media representations of events assumed a non-Arab audience in need of reassurance, and they could understand how that reassurance appealed to a dominant set of personal values. Given all that, when it came to the question of how successful the representations were at providing reassurance, students were less able to see beyond the personal stories of the portrayed Arab Americans. As a group, they did not see that the representations were persuasive. The stories certainly engaged everyone: They all talked eagerly and energetically about additional instances of hate crime they had heard about from friends and family. But when I tried to get them to move past their fascination with sharing anecdotes to consider how those narratives served to justify or not the events unfolding around us, everyone fell silent.

I would have considered student preference for sharing anecdotes as typical of first-year students, a preference for the tangible over the abstract understandable given their age and experience. But I resist explaining away the preference for anecdote here because there was something else, something about another response to a different media representation that led me to not make such a dismissive generalization. Shortly after September 11, newspaper stories compared the terrorist attacks to the bombing of Pearl Harbor 60 years earlier. In a version of the comparison brought to class by a student, the reporter interviewed men who had been teenagers in 1941, who explained how the event then inspired in them feelings of patriotism, and how they were then inspired to enlist in the armed forces. I was familiar with stories of how Pearl Harbor inspired a generation because I had heard those stories from family members as I was growing up. With this kind of awareness, I made a particular kind of sense of the comparison between then and now. There seemed much for us to discuss. So I was initially taken aback when none of the students in the class made sense of the comparison. Not wanting to let it go, I pushed on the comparison in discussion, asking how they thought the events were being compared in the article, how they thought the events could be compared based on their own knowledge, and what they saw as the persuasive potential of the comparison. I asked, "What national passions does the story of Pearl Harbor arouse? What purposes does the appeal to that story and to those passions serve today?"

After some discussion, it became clear that we were simply at odds over our readings of the article. Students in the class just did not think Pearl Harbor had anything to do with the World Trade Center. No one understood the appeal to the past or that such an appeal could possibly have any force. It was not that they were ignorant of what happened at Pearl Harbor 60 years earlier. They were all well aware of it. They were aware of it from its central place in histories of the United States, histories they had learned in school. They were also keenly aware of the availability of those events in popular culture, the most recent example at that time being the widely publicized film, *Pearl Harbor*. During our discussion, many students expressed their awareness of those events through education and entertainment. They had seen photographs and film from Pearl Harbor, and they were immersed in images from New York City. Even with recognition of their awareness of both events, I could not manage to get any students in the class to attend to the appeal made by comparing the attacks on Pearl Harbor to the attack on the World Trade Center. No one could make sense of the narratives as constructing and/or appealing to nationalist sentiments.

Perhaps, in expecting such a reading I was expecting too much. As became clear to me, students did, through our discussion, make a meaning out of the comparison. In 1941, those young men who enlisted did so because they were personally moved to do so. It may have been patriotism, but no one could say that for sure. Although, they could say that those men must have felt it deeply and directly. In 2001, we were again being personally motivated by events of horrific proportion. If both events compared in any way, it was in that each was an attack neither on a nation nor on a way of life; each was an attack *on us*. Both attacks at Pearl Harbor and on the World Trade Center were attacks that concern us because they expose our personal vulnerability as people, not as *a* people.

I could understand student attention to media representations as expressing inexperience with reading and writing, nothing more nor less than the level of sophistication they brought as entering college students to the tasks at hand. Leaving it at that, I could have simply resolved to teach them to be more critical. But I think more is going on. The way students gave attention to events following September 11 cannot be explained only in terms of what students do and do not do by themselves. Like any of us, what students can and cannot do with texts is shaped by the availability of texts for their use. The kinds of images, representations, and texts they have available, how they are made available, the form their availability takes, as well as the context of their availability provide people opportunities for developing and exercising rhetorical abilities, and for recognizing their capacity for meaningful exercise of those abilities. To understand the responses of my students in these terms, I turned to reflect on how the dynamics of representations call forth our attention.

THE MEDIATION OF HERE AND NOW

We were called to pay attention to world events in the fall of 2001 not simply out of an inherent interest in what happened. We were called to pay attention to world events by the structure of appeals made to us in the mass media. The need to acknowledge that our world, and so our present, are somehow mediated by current communications technologies has been widely recognized and has been commented upon by contemporary theorists ranging from Noam Chomsky to Jurgen Habermas to Jean Francois Lyotard. While all agree on the fact of information mediation, these theorists disagree about the nature and consequences of information mediation. Without reviewing the nuances of the debates about information mediation, I do focus on one instance of it that is central to any current proposal for promoting civic agency in a composition course.

The debate over theories of mediation and prospects for agency most famously drew attention during the presidency of the first George Bush, when Jean Baudrillard proclaimed the Gulf War would not take place, and then, after hostilities ceased, that it did not take place. His initial claim that the war would not take place was grounded in an argument that the threats and counter-threats of political leaders, taken together with the media display of military technology and capability, had effectively erased the line separating the event of war from the representation of war. Whatever else war is, according to Baudrillard, it has become in our media-saturated world, a representation. It is a representation from military leaders, a representation for political leaders, and a representation to the public. After the Gulf War, Baudrillard remained steadfast in his claim, arguing that the multiple representations of the war, taken together with the massive imbalance of forces, effectively nullified understanding of events on the ground as "war" in any traditional sense. Dismayed by Baudrillard's claims, Christopher Norris responded, not just to Baudrillard, but also to Baudrillard's way of thinking. Norris argued at length that the claim denying consequential reality to events on the ground demonstrates the emptiness and irrelevance of postmodern theories.

I discuss this here because more is at work in this debate than a ludicrous remark. Clearly, the Gulf War did happen. Just as clearly, it was not simply a military campaign in the deserts of Kuwait and Iraq. It was also a global media spectacle, a media spectacle that served multiple narrative purposes in the United States, not the least of which was to burnish the image of a post-Vietnam military. The events of that war, like the events of September 11, were mediated, and whatever those events are, they are that and not anything else because of their mediation. Baudrillard overstated it, but he was right to observe that the sum total experience of the Gulf War was greater than the military action that took place on the ground in Kuwait and Iraq. Then, as now in the "war on terror," events unfold largely in and through mediated representations.

Differences in understanding the nature and consequences of mediating events such as the Gulf War and the "war on terror" form the substance of Norris's response to Baudrillard. These differences are worth addressing here as a way for me to consider the personalizing of the attention my students paid to mediated representations of national tragedy. The differences are simply stated. Norris rejects virtually everything Baudrillard has to say regarding the Gulf War. Norris explains in considerable detail what it is that compels him to so vehemently deny Baudrillard. He begins, however, by acknowledging that the Gulf War "is indeed in some sense a 'postmodern' war, an exercise in mass-manipulative rhetoric and 'hyperreal' suasive techniques, which does undoubtedly confirm some of Baudrillard's more canny diagnostic observations" (25). Particularly relevant here is Norris's agreement with Baudrillard regarding "the prevailing sense of 'hyperreality,' the mood of collective indifference to issues of factual or documentary truth that enabled such a mass of false information to circulate largely unchallenged from day to day" (26).

While he may grant the rhetorical hyperreality of the Gulf War, Norris rejects critical indifference to the war's mediation, and so he must take seriously the claim that the war did not happen. As he explains, "it brings home with particular force the depth of ideological *complicity* that exists between such forms of extreme anti-realist or irrationalist doctrine and the crisis of moral and political nerve among those whose voices should have been raised against the actions committed in their name" (27). Another way to put Norris's point is to say that postmodern theories negate the very possibility for our critical rhetorical agency. The weight of Norris's point rests on his view that principled critical opposition is possible, taking the form of demystification and telling the truth to power, which can have real consequences on political actors and social policy. Baudrillard presupposes the impossibility of such opposition and discounts the ability of any critical opposition to unmask propaganda and thereby leverage political leaders to act with greater accountability. For Norris, Baudrillard and postmodern theory are complicitous with an ineffectual critical stance that makes everything into rhetoric through incessant mediation in which every representation becomes infused with a power against which there can be no effective critique. If power is everywhere, then we can do nothing to change it. The best we can do is lament the ubiquity of both power and our powerlessness.

But for Norris, everything is not power. He acknowledges power's seeping quality, all the while holding out the possibility for normative principles. As much as people may be fashioned as subjects by mediations of texts and images, Norris asserts they are also agents capable of choice and discretion. He gives clear expression to this view explaining his preference for Chomsky over Foucault:

> Unlike Foucault, [Chomsky] attaches real significance to the values, principles and elective self-image by which most citizens in a liberal democracy prefer to think themselves (and their government) guided. That is to say, he rejects the Foucauldian option of viewing them as so many ruses or alibis in the service of an omnipresent will-to-power, one which scarcely leaves room for any meaningful distinction between democratic systems—however badly compromised in practice—and other (e.g., totalitarian) regimes. For Chomsky, such differences not only exist but require just the kind of critical vigilance that prevents power-interests from advancing their hegemony to the point where a sceptic like Foucault might be justified in professing his Hobbesian theses. (120–21)

I have quoted Norris at length because his argument in this passage captures what seems to me crucial in theories of composition: the need for, and the possibility of, a critical capacity among citizens in a democracy. At its core, the disagreement between Baudrillard and Norris is a disagreement over the dynamics of critique and representation, over how to read the structures of multimedia, and over the extent to which meaningful response is possible within those dynamics and structures,

The disagreement between Baudrillard and Norris should sound familiar to compositionists as it echoes the questions of agency and subjectivity, individual integrity and collective authority we consider among ourselves all the time. The debate between Baudrillard and Norris about responses to the first Gulf War repeats options that still trouble our capacities as compositionists to promote literacies of democratic participation. The mediation of current events in Iraq does seem to confound critical response. At least students in my writing classes during the fall of 2001 were confounded in their capacities to respond by a media that brings world events directly into their lives in a manner that invites sympathetic stasis rather than encouraging critical engagement. As Norris proclaims, finding a public purpose for writing in the wake of September 11 involves identifying the capacity of the self to create texts having critical purchase on mass-mediated representations. The self is more than the product and reflection of multiple discourses. This is not just a faith necessary for teachers of writing. It is a commitment essential for citizens in a democracy. At the same time, Norris does not have it completely right. His description of the self and its access to critical discourse and independent expression seems unrealistic. We have enough experience with the day-to-day authority of independent voices to be skeptical. Not that we do not want to encourage rhetorics of critical engagement. It is just that teaching students to write for public purposes demands we acquire a better grasp on the rhetorical capacities of the self as these are structured by contemporary media experiences.

Jay David Bolter and Richard Grusin describe the consequences following upon the mediation of events for the experiences and perceptions of media users. Their description seems to me to offer the best option for navigating between nihilistic surrender to power everywhere and heroic stand against power anywhere. Avoiding the choice between nihilism and heroism matters for finding a response adequate to the attention demanded by the events of September 11. Bolter and Grusin argue that medias from radio to television to the Internet all strive for immediacy; the medias are designed to provide people a more direct and so a more authentic experience than previous medias. Proliferation of technologies claiming ever more direct, ever more authentic and immediate experience is a hypermediation. Bolter and Grusin call hypermediated immediacy the logic of remediation. They characterize the logic of remediation as a dual impulse, "Our culture wants both to multiply its media and to erase all traces of mediation: ideally, it wants to erase its media in the very act of multiplying them" (5).

The cultural logic of remediation has consequences for the structure of experiences and so of the self. Our experiences of any event are experiences of representations in picture, sound, or word, at the same time that they are experiences of technologies we manipulate and interact with to represent objects. Bolter and Grusin draw out the implications of mediation technologies for our experiences. We experience things through our manipulations of a wide variety of devices, everything from cell phones, to camcorders, to computers.

By experiencing through interaction with technologies, we change how we are in the world. We adapt our practices and perceptions to devices in exchange for various kinds of access. Much as Baudrillard had argued, our experiences of an event such as the Gulf War are experiences crafted and contained by the mediation of technology.

Where Bolter and Grusin part company with Baudrillard is in their observation that his claims regarding simulacral reality rest on the very same distinction between the real and the representation that Norris so vigorously restates. As Bolter and Grusin put it, "Baudrillard expects us still to believe that the Renaissance logic of transparency is the norm from which our culture has diverged. For our culture, however, the logic of hypermediacy is at least as compelling. Just as reality and mediation have become inseparable off-screen, so hypermediacy has become the formal mark of liveness on television" (194). The important point for my purposes is that the logic of remediation is a different logic than that shared by both Baudrillard and Norris. The technological intensity of reality and encroaching reality of technology make the distinction between reality and representation less relevant. Hypermediacy makes the choice between seeing power everywhere and critical opposition to power anywhere less workable as well. Instead, opportunities for critical agency rest in reconceptualizing agency and subjectivity in a hypermediated world.

The self in a hypermediated world is fashioned through the dual logics of remediation: immediacy and hypermediacy. As Bolter and Grusin put it, "under the logic of transparent immediacy . . . we see ourselves as a point of view immersed in an apparently seamless visual environment." Under the logic of hypermediacy, the self "is a network of affiliations, which are constantly shifting. It is the self of newsgroups and e-mail, which may sometimes threaten to overwhelm the user by their sheer numbers but do not exactly immerse her" (232). Opportunities for agency exist within this logic that are unavailable in the cultural logics of Baudrillard and Norris. The first opportunity for agency lies in the choice of point of view. People can make choices about how they constitute their identities and how they present themselves by making choices among and within technologies of representation. The second choice is one of connection. People can make choices, again within and across technologies, regarding their interrelations and affiliations. Choices for point of view and connectedness are never static. People make these choices and remake them, over and over, to suit an ever-changing sense of the self with others through the here and now of remediation. Unlike the binary logic of reality and representation, which constrains choices for critical engagement, the logic of remediation creates options for agency in the constant interaction of selves with new media.

Drawing from the logic of remediation, I started considering how student responses to recent events are responses to the hypermediacy and immediacy of media representation. I considered, as well, how teachers of writing might intervene in the dynamics between technologies of representation and student response. The logic of remediation helps make sense of the personal and voyeuristic responses to current media representations of national tragedy. As hypermediated selves, as identities individuated in and through technologies of representation, people experience a national identity not as a collective commitment, but as a personal experience. The immediacy of experience is accentuated by participation in engines of representation, by people fashioning themselves and their desires through the process of accessing and managing access to representations. The hypermediacy of experience directs our attention to the horrors of terrorism as an attack *on us* as persons. Any larger sense of collective commitment to national ideals or national interests is translated into personal terms, a translation that thwarts critical engagement with larger issues of national interest and terrorism.

PURPOSES FOR TEACHING WRITING HERE AND NOW

Our awareness of any national tragedy cannot but be mediated. The very concept of nation itself is, as Benedict Anderson so aptly phrased it, an imagined community. We should not let the insight that our national community is imagined dissuade us from recognizing that it is nonetheless real. The community we sometimes share is the experience of observing terror. It is a real remediation. It is experienced as real through its representation, it is made real in the consequences that follow from its representations. It is real.

Still, we need to avoid the cynicism of Baudrillard and admit that remediation by itself does not explain the kind of attention paid to September 11. Also, remediation does not provide a full account of the kind of attention we need to pay to the teaching of writing in the face of responses to September 11. What remediation does give us is a point of departure from which to direct our attention to the purposes for writing instruction post-September 11. The concept of remediation reminds us we live, now more than ever, in the world with and through technologies of communication, information, and representation. Our actions and our interactions are hypermediated by these technologies. Our immediate awareness of ourselves and our attention to the world are produced through our interactions with technologies. We become who we are in the world at the human/machine interface. We are here, now, as we are, because that is how uses of technologies enact our attention to ourselves, to others, to our world, and to the interactions among these.

Applying the logic of remediation to the teaching of writing should encourage us to avoid pedagogies that parallel the counterproductive disagreement between Baudrillard and Norris. Taken to its logical conclusion, remediation enables us to think across the divide separating the ludic from the critical. On the one hand, teaching practices grounded in remediation avoid pedagogies of ludic postmodernism that conceive of everything as text while reducing all power to the play of signification. The Gulf War, like the destruction of the World Trade Center, did happen, even though both events were thickly mediated, immediately gaining wide audiences and acquiring complex significance. The logic of remediation simply does not deny the materiality of actions. Quite the opposite. Remediation pushes signification in the direction of the material by locating meaning in the technologies of hypermediation and immediacy. On the other hand, teaching practices grounded in remediation also avoid pedagogies of hypercritical modernism, such as might be inspired by Norris, which retain the material ground outside of texts while reducing texts themselves to the task of always signifying abuses of power. Hypercritical modernism fails to get to the insight that war and terrorism as actions people take are inextricable from war and terrorism as events people witness. Remediation lends force to the project of critique by linking the hypermediacy of actions to the immediacy of events. Here, what we say cannot but intersect with what we do.

Remediation also reinvigorates the significance of literacy education for students. Pedagogies that teach the play of signification empty acts of writing of any consequence. Teaching students to be critical of power everywhere renders them disengaged at worst and disenchanted at best. A pedagogy of remediation avoids extremes of inconsequentiality and disenchantment by locating the play of texts within a network of technology-mediated interactions that does not simply reduce everything to text. Different consequences and alternative engagement can be promoted by asking students to reorient the call made to their attention by their interactions with technology. Attending to the immediacy and hypermediacy of commanding events, teachers of writing can move students to reconceive and remake the networks of their identities and relationships within representational technologies.

When I asked my students during the fall of 2001 to analyze media representations for constructs of audience and purpose, I was limiting their potential engagements with events that technologies of representation had forced upon our attention. I was participating in the no longer useful logic of represented/representation and so falling victim to the trap of unproductive debate between ludic and critical. The questions I asked got the unproductive responses they did because I had misunderstood what was happening. I had misunderstood the dynamic of rhetoric, self, and technology in the construction of reality. Realizing this, I started thinking hard about what contemporary technologies of communication contribute to events, how those technologies participate in constructing national tragedy, how student uses of those same technologies create an experience of national tragedy, and what teachers of writing might do to intervene in the dynamics of student use of literacy technologies.

I saw limits to the current formulation of critical pedagogies. Critical pedagogies have so far concerned themselves with engines of representation and their construction of collective identities and individual desires. Contemporary digital technologies and events such as the mass destruction on September 11 challenge the one-dimensional nature of critical pedagogies. Not only do structures of representation fashion identities and desires, but individuals also participate in those constructions through their interactions with technologies. The flexibility of literacy technologies allows individuals to create not only their own desires and identities but also, to a degree, their engines of representation. This is not to suggest that people have the freedom and opportunity to make themselves over any way they see fit. Options are still limited. It is to say people create themselves and their world together through their manipulations of technologies. Critical pedagogies must account for this process and rethink its goals as possibilities for intervening in technologies of becoming self-aware. The multiliteracies pedagogy of the New London Group, and the various uses of it, seem promising in this regard.

Returning to the responses of students to my assignments in the fall of 2001, I would say now that they were not so much expressing inexperience with critical thought as they were expressing their greater experience with current literacy technologies. What they said could not but be structured by an engagement with technologies that crafted their attention. The nature of the engagement allowed for, perhaps even encouraged, a more personal, depoliticized response. On the one hand, the ready availability of information as events unfolded brought the death and destruction to bear directly on all our activities. In this, the horror was immediate and visceral. On the other hand, the presentation of available information, its presentation as well as its sheer quantity, confounded the civic responsiveness of students. It captured their attention at a personal level that heightened emotional interest while diminishing political engagement. When it came time to write, they could not see that what they had to write made a difference, if we understand making a difference as a transformative intervention, which is the way most people typically understand it. Nor could students see that what they heard or read had anything but a personal impact. Their capacity to respond was diminished in the here and now, by the here and now, as the media made that here and now available to us all, and so, as we were made available to ourselves through that mediation.

Drawing upon the logic of remediation, the personal does become a site for students to produce writing that does make a difference. Writing, using the technologies of literacy and representation, is their point of entry into networks of meaning. It is where they change those networks and change themselves through their participation, through acts of reading and writing. These are small changes, changes of point of view and interaction. These changes likely do not force greater accountability on elected officials, as Norris wants.

But these changes are more than the simulacral play described by Baudrillard. To get at these changes with my students, I would have had to redirect their interrogation of media representations. Instead of asking them to analyze and describe appeals to audience and purpose, I should have asked them to remediate those representations, to express their relationship to the media representations through design of media productions such as web pages. These productions would have served the purpose of contributing to a purposeful and thick network where the students find agency and meaning.

Almost every day throughout the closing months of 2001, I listened, read, and watched for news of events that unfolded hundreds, even thousands, of miles from me. Reports from Afghanistan, updates from Washington, stories from New York continued to dominate the media and my attention. The destruction of September 11 had destroyed lives and property. The destruction made vivid through the media and in our attention generated and justified a massive restructuring of the national government. The subsequent reordering of agencies and bureaucracies served the purposes of foreign policy and trickled down to the reorganization of a number of daily activities becoming, on an individual level, a shift in our general attention to the world. It is a shift that challenges our capacities for communication here and now. I may have initially thought my teaching of writing paled in comparison to the significance of world events unfolding around me. I was wrong.

WORKS CITED

Anderson, Benedict. *Imagined Communities*. New York: Verso, 1991.

Bolter, Jay David and Richard Grusin. *Remediation: Understanding New Media*. Cambridge, MA: MIT Press, 2000.

New London Group. "A Pedagogy of Multiliteracies: Designing Social Futures." *Harvard Educational Review* 66 (1996): 60–92.

Norris, Christopher. *Uncritical Theory: Postmodernism, Intellectuals, and the Gulf War*. Amherst: U of Massachusetts P, 1992.

Teaching in the
Wake of National Tragedy

Patricia Murphy, Ryan Muckerheide,
and Duane Roen

INTRODUCTION

SOON AFTER THE tragic events of September 11, 2001, the University of
Minnesota published a 9/11 story on the institution's website. A faculty member in the Department of Geography, Eric Sheppard, described how his students in a 100–level course needed to talk in class on 9/11 about the shock of
the events ("Teaching in the Midst of Tragedy"). Psychologically they could-
n't do anything else that day. However, two days later they didn't want to talk
about it at all. Sheppard then accounts that after a month had passed the students were ready to be more reflective and analytical.

Reading about Eric Sheppard's geography students at the University of
Minnesota reminds us that Abraham Maslow's hierarchy of needs describes
our students' learning as occurring within a complex array of factors: (1) *Phys-
iological Needs:* food, water, oxygen, shelter, clothing; (2) *Safety Needs:* feeling
secure, which can be challenging during natural disasters or periods of social
unrest; (3) *Love, Affection, and Belongingness Needs;* (4) *Esteem Needs;* and
(5) *Self-Actualization Needs.* Our work as teachers of writing can traditionally
be viewed as addressing Maslow's highest levels, but during times of national
tragedy in particular our students are struggling to satisfy other needs.

In this essay we analyze how students' needs changed after 9/11. Our experiences come from three distinct perspectives: an English 101 teacher reacting
to her students on the day of the attacks during fall 2001, an English 102

teacher who revised his spring 2002 syllabus to address the events, and a campus administrator responsible for preparing teachers to better understand how to attend to students' perceptions after 9/11. By offering these perspectives, we hope that we show respect for those who suffered most from the tragic events of September 11, 2001. Further, we hope that these perspectives offer practical support for those who teach students to write, read, and think critically.

Just like Eric Sheppard, we quickly understood that the events of 9/11 made it necessary for us to shift attention from students' esteem needs and self-actualization needs—the standard focus of much university teaching—to safety needs (Maslow). We realized that trying to force students to stay focused on the normal course material and activities would not result in much learning. However, once we had invested a modest amount of time addressing safety, students offered clear cues that they were ready to return to the study of rhetoric and writing.

PERSPECTIVE ONE: PATRICIA MURPHY, TEACHING FIRST-YEAR COMPOSITION 101

In the fall of 2001, I was teaching two first-year composition courses using a recently published book, *Scenarios for Writing* (Glau and Jacobsen, 2001), that fosters a realistic sense of civic responsibility for students. The book describes situations in which there is some public debate, and the students are asked to write a persuasive letter to the board governing the controversy, whether it is a library, a college, or a high school. The premise of the book is that students are more likely to consider concerns of audience and purpose if something is at stake, so the text sets up realistic situations in which students are called upon to share their opinions with the public in a persuasive manner. I read the first drafts of the first paper with great pride, because students not only articulated their own opinions, but they also made those opinions clearly persuasive to a well-defined audience.

The final draft of the first paper was due on September 11. On that day at 6:00 A.M. I was driving to South Mountain for my twice-weekly mountain bike ride, and I was surprised to hear the announcer on National Public Radio comment that a Cessna-sized plane had just hit one of the World Trade Center Towers. I suspected that it was somehow related to a recent prank where a man tried to parachute off the top of the Statue of Liberty. I dismissed it, imagining that the damage was minor. I arrived at the parking lot, mounted my bike, and took off on the trail. The hour-long ride was tough in the morning heat, and when I returned to the parking lot, I was tired and covered with sweat. A man had his radio cranked up, and as I passed his car I heard the solemn voice of Tom Brokaw as he confirmed reports that a passenger jet had just crashed into the Pentagon. I hit my brakes and listened to the description of the scene while other riders slowly gathered around to hear details.

I will never forget that moment. I slowly came to the realization that American citizens had been attacked on American soil. I listened for a few more moments and thought, "We are at war." America had been at war during my lifetime, but this was different. This was a violent act of massive proportions taking place in my own back yard. My uncle lives two miles from the Pentagon. My best friend passes it every day on her way to work. While I listened, the second plane hit the second tower. I drove home and turned on the television just in time to watch the Twin Towers fall.

My office hours that semester were on Tuesday, and as I sat listening to the news broadcast on the portable radio behind my desk, Brian, an honor's student from the previous semester, popped his head into my office and said "What's up!" He sat across from me as he had on many occasions and seemed anxious that I did not return his cheerful greeting.

"Well, just listening to the reports here." I replied, certain that his demeanor would adapt.

"What reports?" He queried, pulling his hand through the shock of red hair atop his head.

I weighed my response carefully, understanding that he very well might not know yet, as impossible as that seemed. I even tried to imagine what it was like not to know—to feel that nothing had changed. "You have not heard? There was an attack on The Pentagon and the World Trade Center Towers in New York. The towers, well, they are gone."

I watched his face carefully, realizing he may have family, friends there. His brows furrowed with recognition. "The students in the Union—I thought they were watching sports or something." We listened to the radio together for a few minutes, and he told me that he had just visited New York City that summer, that he had stood at the foot of the towers himself.

As I walked from my office to the Computing Commons that day, I wondered what I would find in the classrooms I entered. More importantly, I wondered about my responsibility to these young adults. I was obviously in a state of shock, with no time to prepare myself much less my course plan for what I imagined would be a group of confused, vulnerable, and shaken first-year students. What could I possibly say to them that might be of some comfort? What types of emotional needs might they have? Would they even be there?

In my first class I was surprised that most of the students were present, some even offering to turn in their papers, which I had no intention of collecting. The first words I could manage were, "How do you feel?" The students were eager to talk. The first reply came from a polite and attentive mechanical engineering major who always responded thoughtfully to class discussions, "I want to take my gun, and I want to kill whoever did this."

This was not the reaction I expected—especially not from this particular student. What could I possibly say in response? In my ten years of teaching, I have learned that the best way for me to lead a class discussion is to listen closely to each student and validate their voices even if I disagree with their ideas. I find that not only will the students feel more free to openly express their opinions, but they also then have the chance to hear a wide range of thoughts that would not have been heard had mine been the prevailing voice. By nature of my position, my voice carries authority in the classroom, and students will usually censor themselves based on my opinions if I voice them first. Therefore, I facilitate discussions by encouraging all student voices and by limiting my input. Inevitably, to my great satisfaction, there are students who verbalize my very thoughts, which are much less politicized when coming from a peer than when coming from a professor. I view class discussion as a way for students to clarify their own opinions and to understand how those ideas relate to others around them. So I responded with, "That is certainly a strong emotion. Are others of you angry also?" I hoped to better gauge the prevailing sentiment.

The next comment came from a lively and bright pre-business major from Nebraska: "I wouldn't say I am angry, but I am scared. I have heard rumors that major universities could be the next targets. A gun is not going to stop that kind of aggression. We may be in grave danger, and there is nothing we can do about it. It is not going to help to get angry."

An aerospace engineering major entered the conversation next. He was one of my most articulate students in class discussion, though he struggled with written work: "The fact is that hate and anger caused these attacks in the first place. Someone obviously wants to hurt us, and they must have some reason. This was by no means a random act. You know, not everyone around the world thinks the United States is a shining beacon of opportunity. There are other countries where they burn our flag and curse our leaders. To hate them back will not help. We would do better to try to understand them."

I was relieved when the first speaker refined his previous comment this way: "No, I just mean that I really want to defend my country and what it stands for. This action makes me want to join the armed forces so that I can have a part in protecting our nation. It makes me feel a sense of patriotism and pride in my country. I feel like I need to do something." What he was actually trying to articulate was a common sentiment echoed by citizens across the country in the days, weeks, and months following the attacks. People felt helpless and wanted something to do.

The conversation continued with students asking questions about details of the attacks, and other students adding information they had gathered from various news channels. We talked about why it had happened and what its effects might be. After the discussion ebbed, I decided it was time to bring up the business of the course, so I said that we would move slowly. Before they left, I thanked the students for coming, and asked them to stay strong.

My next class was much different. Only six students arrived that Tuesday, and two of them were talking on their cell phones trying to reach family and friends back east. I received several e-mail messages from other class members who were not attending school that day because they knew people who worked in the Twin Towers or at the Pentagon. This class was hit hard in a very personal way, so it seemed that a discussion such as the one in my previous class would be completely inappropriate. I spoke with the students who did come to class, asking them to spread the word not to worry about the assignments, and that we would meet the following Tuesday.

Was my reaction on that day fair? I left both classrooms feeling a sense of desperation and hopelessness. As someone in a leadership role, as someone whose job it is to help students understand their world so that they might express themselves more clearly, I felt a responsibility to offer the students some insight, some answers, and moreover, some comfort. I left campus wondering whether I had helped or hurt my students. I wondered whether I had made any impression at all. I hoped desperately that my presence in the classroom amounted to "doing something" to make the situation better, at least for this small group of people.

When I met again with my classes a full week after the attacks, the discussions took on a very different tone. We knew much more about what had happened and why. We had more time to understand how our lives would be changed. We had determined who was safe, and who was missing. One after one, my students told stories of how they were affected—an aunt at the Pentagon got out safely but lost several colleagues; a cousin in the FDNY arrived on scene just as Tower One started to fall; a father was booked on one of the fated American Airlines flights but changed travel plans last-minute. The students drew comfort from each other's stories, and we spent the class period recalling how we found out, who we knew, how we reacted.

As the semester wore on, we continued with the syllabus—the students writing papers about violence in high schools, living wills, and Internet censorship. I did not feel the need to change the curriculum, but I was very careful to respond to changes in student needs. One student commented at the end of the semester, "Everybody was still affected emotionally and it showed on everybody's faces, the students and the teachers." But I continued each class period with the same gentle philosophy I had at the beginning of the semester. When a student had something to say, I was going to listen.

PERSPECTIVE TWO: RYAN MUCKERHEIDE, TEACHING FIRST-YEAR COMPOSITION 102

In the Fall 2001 semester, I was teaching a Monday–Wednesday–Friday schedule, so I did not see my students on 9/11. On September 12, I sat down in front of them, backwards on a typical student desk, and told them that for the next few days, the planned assignments were off. I asked if they wanted to talk about what had happened and if they had any questions. One student wanted to know if we were safe; rumors abounded that ASU or the Palo Verde nuclear power station west of Phoenix might be targets of future terrorist attacks. This question seemed to stir more fear and inject more uncertainty into the classroom. I told the class that the Pentagon and the World Trade Center were targeted because of their symbolic value and that there was frankly nothing in Phoenix with that kind of value. Another student asked, "Do they know who did it?" I said that Osama bin Laden was a suspect, and, I thought, a likely one. As I looked around the room, I noticed a large number of blank stares. I asked if they knew who bin Laden was. Only a handful had ever heard of him, and they only knew that he was "a terrorist or something." Most remembered the 1993 World Trade Center bombing, and a few had heard of the Taliban, but no one had heard of the Khobar Towers, and only a couple recalled the bombings of the embassies in Kenya and Tanzania.

Before the class period was over, I had become concerned that my students were not adequately informed about matters that were about to be of paramount importance. How could they understand the developing situation—a situation they would have to live through and cope with—if they did not have an understanding of the underlying causes? My students, like Patricia Murphy's and many others around the country, did not feel safe—a condition aggravated by a lack of knowledge and understanding of the threat. A few weeks later, when the Writing Programs issued a call for textbook proposals, I decided to develop a themed research-based 102 class, hoping to help students understand the causes of terrorism, new developments, and the impact of these events in a post-9/11 world.

The choice of textbooks was relatively easy because I was already familiar with several good possibilities. I had used John Ramage, John Bean, and June Johnson's *Writing Arguments: Brief Edition* in previous classes with great success, and I had planned on using the complete edition in future classes. However, when I decided to teach "Terrorism 102," the extensive readings contained in that edition would have been irrelevant. I chose instead the *Concise Edition*, which includes all the essential material on argument styles but omits all of the readings.

In addition, I needed materials for discussion and readings that would give the students some much-needed background on al-Qaeda. My choice, Peter Bergen's *Holy War, Inc: Inside the Secret World of Osama bin Laden,* is well-suited to this class for several reasons. Bergen, whom many will recognize from his role as CNN's terrorism analyst, traveled to Afghanistan on several occasions and, along with Peter Arnett, interviewed bin Laden for CNN in 1997. The manuscript of the book had just been delivered to the publisher in August 2001, so Bergen was asked to incorporate the events of September 11 before publication. Particularly useful are the chapters on the history, background, and ideology of al-Qaeda. *Holy War, Inc.* is a very accessible and engaging text that many of my students actually enjoyed reading. This text has since been updated with additional information on post-Taliban Afghanistan.

I have used course Web pages as repositories for syllabi, handouts, and relevant links to online resources in several other classes. This course, based in part on news sources and held in a computer-mediated classroom, positively demanded such a Web page. The site provided, in addition to the components listed above, a place to post updates, links to online articles, and PowerPoint presentations. I also used an online discussion board where students could post homework assignments and interact outside of class.[1]

When I began to plan the schedule of assignments, I realized that the issue of time management would be crucial, as I would have to spend a great deal of time at the beginning of the term teaching the background material. The first third of the semester was spent intensively discussing the mechanics of argument, how to evaluate sources, and how to do research. Interspersed with this were readings from *Holy War, Inc.* and news articles on the history of bin Laden and Islamic extremism. During the rest of the term, students were asked to combine various writing and research activities with the subject matter. For instance, students were asked to bring in articles related to terrorism, discuss them in groups, and analyze the arguments. They were asked to look for biases, logical fallacies, insufficient evidence, false claims, and possible agendas. Students found this exercise to be very beneficial.

One concern I had regarding the papers was that students were expected to learn and write several different argument styles throughout the course. In the past, I had taught one style at a time, so that I could more carefully focus on the finer points of the style. I did not think that this strategy would work well this time. The basic problem was that every student would come in with different interests, and might not have sufficient background knowledge to know what possibilities existed for, say, a definitional argument. I decided to teach several argument styles in the beginning of the term and allow students to choose, for each paper, their own argument style and topic. This allowed them to pursue their own interests and choose the argument style that would best fit their topic. The only restriction: A student could use each argument style only once. This arrangement worked well and had another benefit: When a student was having a difficult time choosing a topic, he or she could start by choosing an argument style, then asking what topics would best fit the style. Further, if a student wanted to write on, for instance, women under the Taliban, but did not know precisely what angle to take, the choice of style would often help him or her decide.

Whenever possible, I tried to take advantage of the capabilities of the computer-mediated classroom (CMC). I used many online sources to help make my points and provide news and various perspectives on the issues at hand. Students were occasionally asked to do group work and either post their results on the online discussion board or e-mail them to me. I used several PowerPoint presentations and showed several videos. The CMC allowed the class to take a global reach via the Internet and to explore rapidly-developing situations.

Based on my experiences with "Terrorism 102," I offer the following suggestions, many of which are general in nature and attempt to address the teaching of this class in any setting (traditional classroom, CMC, online, hybrid, etc.). They reflect my own experience and teaching style and may not work for everyone.

1. Because the world situation can change rapidly with new developments, and those events must be discussed for the class to keep its relevance, I found that a tightly structured syllabus was more of a liability than an asset. The syllabus I currently use is structured by topical unit and week. For instance, one might set aside four weeks to discuss the Israeli/Palestinian conflict. Each week lists several background readings, which will likely not change much from semester to semester. A week in advance, I find news articles that discuss the most current developments and add those to the assignments. Class discussions and group work are based on a situation as it stands during that week. During the last class of each week, I discuss briefly the goals and assignments for the following week. Students who wish to read ahead may begin with the background readings already assigned. The papers alone have fixed due dates. This provides some basic structure for the class, yet allows for flexibility.

2. Prepare "packets" of teaching material for each topic. For instance, one might have a packet on the background of Osama bin Laden and al-Qaeda, one on the history of the Israeli–Palestinian conflict, one on Iran, etc. The benefit is that all of the background materials would be ready, and only a little updating would be necessary in order to teach a specific topic. This would be very useful if one wished to change topics at the last minute to accommodate some new development.

3. Teach the argument styles students will be expected to know at the beginning of the term, and let them choose their own style and topic for each paper. This works very well because it allows students to pursue their own interests and still meet the requirements of the assignment, a combination that will invariable produce better papers. It does, however, involve a little more mental footwork on the part of the instructor. While this could be seen as a disadvantage, I see it as an opportunity to individually encourage and motivate students, a practice that can only be beneficial to them in the long term. Further, since we could not possibly cover every aspect of the war on terrorism in class, and since students often have a difficult time choosing topics, this approach enables students to explore topics on which we spent relatively little time in class: women's issues, airport security,

cyberterrorism, etc. One student who was having difficulty choosing a topic came to my office one day to seek advice. I began by asking what her major was, hoping that we could find a topic that fit her interests. Her response: "Exercise science." She ended up writing a paper on the Taliban's crackdown on sporting events and physical entertainment.

4. Teach them how to do basic research early, and give them some online sources for information, such as the CIA World Factbook[2] and LexisNexis Academic Universe.[3] Students frequently used the resources I put online on the course Web page, and several commented on their usefulness.

5. Discuss how to evaluate websites early in the term. One potentially useful exercise would be to have students do an evaluation exercise on an obviously biased site. Using articles from American newspapers might be especially helpful, as students often do not think about the bias inherent in the American perspective. Do in-class exercises with news articles. Have students evaluate them or do a "believing/doubting" exercise. Show them how any source can be biased toward a certain point of view and how the credibility of articles can be determined by looking at their sources, the publications in which they appear, what information they give or omit, etc.

6. Conduct a question-and-answer session at the beginning of class. Allow them to ask questions, and give them questions to debate. This can generate lively discussions, and it has the added benefit of getting the students engaged and thinking at the beginning of the class period.

Most importantly, research the topics, both general and specific, as much as you can. I have had several students come to my office asking for clarification on both background information (I had to explain bin Laden's anti-Americanism to one student by beginning with the Soviet invasion of Afghanistan and the Persian Gulf War) and specifics (one student, while writing on women under the Taliban, needed clarification on the role of women in pre-Taliban Afghanistan and in the new interim government). In this type of class, the instructor cannot be merely a "facilitator"; he or she must also be prepared to disseminate basic information, or at the very least, be able to help the student find good information on both general and specific topics. The instructor should have a list of varied reference material available, whether on paper or online.

PERSPECTIVE THREE: DUANE ROEN,
SUPPORTING TEACHERS CAMPUS-WIDE

As Director of the Center for Learning and Teaching Excellence at Arizona State University *(http://clte.asu.edu)*, I worked with administrators from other campus service units to provide support for faculty, staff, and students dealing with the aftershock of 9/11. Our team included staff from Counseling and Consultation, the Campus Environment Team, Residential Life, the Registrar, Employee Assistance, Human Resources, Student Health and Wellness, Campus Safety, the Intergroup Relations Center, and other campus offices. My particular focus was to provide faculty with resources to engage students in the "teachable moments" in the weeks following 9/11.

As I worked with faculty and their students, several factors reminded me to be sensitive to the need to balance our academic responsibilities with our responsibilities to students' well-being. The most immediate reminder is that one of my sisters-in-law, Sheila Earley, had worked in the World Trade Center. On September 11, 2001, she stayed home from work because she was battling a cold that day. The second reminder came in the form of a spontaneous flashback to Maslow's hierarchy of needs, which explains that our safety needs have priority over our other human needs.

Patricia's and Ryan's students, like Eric Sheppard's at the University of Minnesota, seem very similar to many other students with whom I spoke shortly after the events of 9/11. Some of them were saddened, shocked, and angered that some faculty did not even acknowledge the events of September 11, 2001. Some of them said that they needed the trusted older adults in their daily lives to help them process the events of 9/11. Beyond that, though, students talked about how the events of 9/11 made it very difficult for them to learn as effectively as they normally do. Some, for example, needed extra time to complete projects because family tragedy consumed their time and emotional strength. Some reported that they didn't feel safe leaving their apartments at night, which meant that they were unable to come to campus to use the library or computing facilities after dark.

There are common tools that faculty can use to assess students' learning or readiness to learn. For example, some faculty asked students in class whether they needed to process the events of 9/11 as a group or individually during office hours. For some students, though, it can be risky to express such needs in public. During class, teachers were encouraged to allow time to address the most obvious needs of safety and emotional stability, though as time passed, they moved on to addressing the need to process and analyze the events of 9/11. When encountering such horrible events, students—and faculty too—struggle to comprehend as much as possible about the situations that have occurred, but we serve student needs most effectively when we ask them to use that knowledge as a basis for higher-level thinking. This section details three activities that were designed to be used during class time after the initial shock of the tragedy had worn off.

The first activity involved asking a variety of questions to help facilitate critical thought about the events. When we ask students to analyze events such as those of 9/11, we help them to develop strategies for considering a wide range of perspectives and to ask difficult questions:

- Why did the attacks of 9/11 occur?
- What could the United States have done during the past two decades to lessen the likelihood of the events of 9/11?
- What are the most effective methods of preventing events such as those of 9/11—political, diplomatic, economic, military, educational?
- What comparisons can you make between the contexts for the events of 9/11 and the contexts for other events?

These questions help students explore the full range of Bloom's taxonomy of cognitive skills—knowledge, comprehension, application, analysis, synthesis, and evaluation. At different points in time after the events of 9/11, students seemed to demonstrate a readiness to engage in various kinds of cognitive activity. As faculty, we can seize upon such moments to engage students fully in learning that will serve them not only in the academic realm of life, but also the professional, personal, and civic realms. When we ask students to apply rhetorical principles, they learn how speaking and writing can lead to constructive solutions to even the most difficult conflicts. When we ask them to synthesize various rhetorical approaches and to evaluate the effectiveness of those syntheses, we help students understand that successful solutions are complex and that they require collaborative rather than competitive approaches. These questions were used to help facilitate discussion in a nonthreatening manner so that students could process and apply new information about what happened on 9/11.

In the wake of the events of 9/11, these questions can also help students engage with ideas in the ways that Lee Shulman suggests in his recently devised, profoundly insightful "Table of Learning," which includes the following six categories: (1) Engagement and Motivation, (2) Knowledge and Understanding, (3) Performance and Action, (4) Reflection and Critique, (5) Judgment and Design, and (6) Commitment and Identity. Shulman explains how the progression can work:

> Learning begins with student engagement, which in turn leads to knowledge and understanding. Once someone understands, he or she becomes capable of performance or action. Critical reflection on one's practice and understanding leads to higher-order thinking in the form of a capacity to exercise judgment in the face of uncertainty and to create designs in the presence of constraints and unpredictability. Ultimately, the exercise of judgment makes possible the development of commitment. In commitment, we become capable of professing our understandings and our values, our faith and our love, our skepticism and our doubts, internalizing those attributes and making them integral to our identities. These commitments, in turn, make new engagements possible—and even necessary.

The events of 9/11 motivated Patricia's and Ryan's students, as well as the students of many colleagues, to engage in the sequence of learning that

Shulman describes. Their initial emotional engagement led to the need to be more intellectually reflective and action-oriented. In some ways the students engaged with the real-world text of 9/11 in the ways that resemble Louise Rosenblatt's reader-response approaches to texts—begin with whatever responses emerge and then temper them with intellectual "transactions" with the text.

The second activity designed to help students better understand the world in the wake of 9/11 addressed cultural attitudes after the tragedy. During the months following the attacks, nationalism was high, and xenophobia led to further tragedies such as the "revenge" murder of an Indian immigrant in a suburb of Phoenix. This action raised a question about the balance of free speech: how can we use national events to discuss the mix of rights and responsibilities protected by the First and Fourteenth Amendments to the U.S. Constitution? The following passages are excerpted from the U.S. Constitution:

> *Article I.* **Congress shall make no law** respecting an establishment of religion, or prohibiting the free exercise thereof; **or abridging the freedom of speech,** or of the press; or the right of the people peaceably to assemble, and to petition the Government for a redress of grievances [emphasis added].

> *Article XIV. Section 1.* "All persons born or naturalized in the United States, and subject to the jurisdiction thereof, are citizens of the United States and of the State wherein they reside. No State shall make or enforce any law which shall abridge the privileges or immunities of citizens of the United States; nor shall any State deprive any person of life, liberty, or property, without due process of law; **nor deny to any person within its jurisdiction the equal protection of the laws.**"

Discussion Questions

1. As teachers and students, what can/should we each do in class to balance one another's rights and responsibilities—especially in times of national crisis?
2. How can/should each of us act in classes—in words and deeds—to acknowledge both the First and Fourteenth Amendments of the United States Constitution?

The purpose of this activity is to encourage students to consider the full range of rights and responsibilities that each of us has in a college or university classroom. For free speech to function as a free exchange of ideas, all participants in the conversation—not just those with greater political power—need to feel safe. In times of national crisis, it is sometimes too difficult to foster such a free exchange.

The third exercise encourages students to contextualize actions that occurred after 9/11. National tragedies can offer moments for pondering issues as large as U.S. international policy. For instance, Stanley Fish offered the following perspective:

> How many times have we heard these new mantras: "We have seen the face of evil"; "these are irrational madmen"; "we are at war against international terrorism." Each is at once inaccurate and unhelpful. We have not seen the face of evil; we have seen the face of an enemy who comes at us with a full roster of grievances, goals and strategies. If we reduce that enemy to "evil," we conjure up a shape-shifting demon, a wild-card moral anarchist beyond our comprehension and therefore beyond the reach of any counterstrategies.
>
> The same reduction occurs when we imagine the enemy as "irrational." Irrational actors are by definition without rhyme or reason, and there's no point in reasoning about them on the way to fighting them. The better course is to think of these men as bearers of a rationality we reject because its goal is our destruction. If we take the trouble to understand that rationality, we might have a better chance of figuring out what its adherents will do next and preventing it.
>
> And "international terrorism" does not adequately describe what we are up against. Terrorism is the name of a style of warfare in service of a cause. It is the cause, and the passions informing it, that confront us. Focusing on something called international terrorism—detached from any specific purposeful agenda—only confuses matters.

Fish encourages students to question the overly simplified explanations that can follow events such as those that occurred on September 11, 2001. Instead of accepting the easy response, "They are evil," students are encouraged to consider other motivations, other causes. As a result, students are positioned to develop more thoughtful solutions.

CONCLUSION

If we claim to offer a rhetorical education that is relevant to students' academic, professional, personal, and civic lives, we must engage them in discussions that challenge their understanding of local, national, and international events. During times of national tragedy, this can only be accomplished after students have been able to address one of their most basic needs—the need to feel secure. Once this has been accomplished, we can then help students to develop a set of critical lenses for analyzing a full range of discourses—moderate, conservative, liberal, nationalistic, xenophobic, inclusive—to consider the assumptions and motives of those who engage in those discursive practices.

By being aware of the full range of students' needs, we do much to strengthen ethos because, as Richard Light observes in his study of students' satisfaction with college, "Those students who make connections between what goes on inside and outside the classroom report a more satisfying college experience" (14). National tragedies offer strong reminders that we who teach writing have a collective responsibility to make topics meaningful. Not only are we now teaching different students because of what happened that September morning, but in fact we are different teachers.

At end of the fall semester 2001, one ASU student commented, "I think everything changed on September 11 for everyone, everywhere, in every aspect of life." While this could also be true of many events that have occurred in our nation's history, we would still be wise as teachers of writing to use this tragedy as a lesson. We must remember that students are goal-oriented, driven, passionate, and interested. We must prioritize the desire to help students understand more clearly how they fit into the world. We must ask students to be engaged in current controversies and to constantly deconstruct who we are as a nation and what privileges we enjoy.

NOTES

1. Due to restrictions on server space, I cannot be certain how long the original site will remain active. Currently active pages may be accessed from my root directory at *http://www.public.asu.edu/~muckerrm/index.htm*.

2. *http://www.cia.gov/cia/publications/factbook/*.

3. *http://web.lexis-nexis.com/universe*.

WORKS CITED

Bergen, Peter L. *Holy War, Inc: Inside the Secret World of Osama bin Laden*. New York: Free Press, 2001.

Bloom, Benjamin S., ed. *Taxonomy of Educational Objectives: The Classification of Educational Goals. Handbook 1: Cognitive Domain*. New York: David McKay, 1956.

Fish, Stanley. "Condemnation Without Absolutes." *New York Times* (online version) 15 October 2001.

Glau, Gregory R., and Craig B. Jacobsen, *Scenarios for Writing: Issues, Analysis, and Response*. New York: McGraw-Hill, 2001.

Light, Richard J. *Making the Most of College: Students Speak Their Minds*. Cambridge, MA: Harvard University Press, 2001.

Maslow, Abraham H. *Personality and Motivation*. 3rd Ed. New York: Harper & Row, 1987.

Ramage, John D., John C. Bean, and June Johnson, eds., *Writing Arguments*. Concise ed., 2nd ed., New York: Longman, 1989.

Rosenblatt, Louise. *The Reader, the Text, the Poem: Transactional Theory of the Literary Work.* Carbondale and Edwardsville: Southern Illinois UP, 1978.

Shulman, Lee S. "Making a Difference: A Table of Learning." *<http://www. carnegiefoundation.org/elibrary/docs/making_differences.htm>.*

"Teaching in the Midst of Tragedy." Kiosk. October 2001. Minneapolis: University of Minnesota. *<http://www1.umn.edu/urelate/kiosk/1001kiosk/midstoftragedy.html>.*

United States Constitution. *<http://www.law.emory.edu/FEDERAL/usconst.html>.*

Teaching Writing in Hawaii after Pearl Harbor and 9/11

How to "Make Meaning" and "Heal" Despite National Propaganda

Daphne Desser

IN THE AFTERMATH of September 11, professors at the University of Michigan from composition-related fields such as education and psychology were asked by the administration to provide guidance to their fellow faculty members on how to address the national tragedy in their classrooms. In a published version of the advice they gave to their colleagues, Kardia and colleagues open with the following questions: "How do we discuss the unfathomable? How do we learn in the face of violence and threat, making meaning out of events that seem meaningless by their very nature?" (19). They then offer the following postulation as a foundation for their recommendations:

> . . . education is based on the development of skills and structures that promote discussion of complex and contradictory events and viewpoints and also engage people in critical thinking, creativity, and problem solving. By developing higher-order critical thinking, people can interpret, analyze, sort, find patterns, and support arguments in the midst of data that might appear arbitrary, random or absurd. Thus, through education, people develop the capacity to confront seemingly incomprehensible experiences and create new possibilities in response (19).

As a composition and rhetoric specialist, I find this outline of the foundations of the educational enterprise to be superficially rhetorical; that is, I interpret the primary pedagogical goal according to the above passage to be that students acquire the ability to confront chaos, contradiction, and confusion by imposing an interpretive and argumentative lens upon the raw material of life, history, observation, and event. But because the above characterization of the educational enterprise makes no note of the larger socioeconomic and political contexts that locate, define, and limit educational institutions, I find this opening premise and the subsequent suggestions for classroom practice limited by their apolitical thrust. I have two specific concerns about such a depoliticized approach to teaching in times of national trauma: (1) it seems to suggest that the goal of interpretation, analysis, and argumentation is to make the "seemingly incomprehensible" safe for consumption by transforming it into material that is manageable, orderly, civilized, and palatable, ignoring trauma's inevitable inability to be fully defined, processed, or understood; and (2) the authors seem to have in mind a narrow kind of meaning making that easily lends itself to accommodations to dominant cultural productions.

By dominant cultural productions I mean the pervasive ideologies constructed by governing socioeconomic forces—examples relevant to the events of 9/11 are jingoism and unthinking patriotism represented by, for example, Jack in the Box's "Let's keep America rolling" advertising campaign and Dan Rather's famous speculation that the reason for the terrorists' attack is that they are "jealous" and "hate our freedoms." Such directives and justifications exemplify a too-easy "will to closure," one to which Kardia's recommendations feel dangerously close. To find meaning behind the events of 9/11 amidst overwhelming media and governmental influence necessitates first a critical investigation of the master narratives created by the socioeconomic powers, which define, control, and limit our national discourse. These constructions are destructive and antithetical to the kind of intellectual awareness necessary for authentic meaning making and/or healing to occur. My suggestion is to transform the writing classroom into a space where the master narratives produced by national propaganda and promotion are deconstructed. To put the same in Althusserian terms, I argue for pedagogical approaches that minimize the extent to which the writing classroom, as part of the larger educational institution, serves often unconsciously and unwillingly the purposes of the ideological state apparatus that surrounds and penetrates it.

To counteract the pervasive influence of such master narratives, writing teachers can teach students how to let the mystery and "unfathomable" nature of trauma remain in their writing and thinking; I suggest a deconstructive type of meaning making that is incomplete, partial, and deferred and that comes out of and contributes to a critique of dominant cultural production. Similarly, I suggest that writing teachers avoid the pressure to emotionally and/or spiritually heal their students by giving in to the temptation of the will to closure;

we can, instead, rely on disciplinary knowledge to provide insight and structure that can offer students intellectual tools of critical analysis and investigation to create a different type of healing—one that is more politically aware. I further suggest that an emphasis on the rhetorical dimensions of civic discourse and practical political action can be healing in a more productive way since (1) these are our areas of professional expertise, not emotional or spiritual counseling; and (2) these intellectual investigations may very well result in a kind of intellectually aware and complex healing, one that also comes out of and contributes to a critique of dominant cultural production.

As a professor at the University of Hawaii, I will develop these arguments further in a context that is familiar to me. I will argue for teaching students how to let the mystery of trauma remain in their writing as a way to critique master narratives by referring to witness accounts and oral interviews located in Hawaii and the mainland after the bombing of Pearl Harbor. And I will argue for a redefinition of healing that emphasizes our disciplinary knowledge of rhetorical analysis and production. I find that some scholarship which argues for "the writing teacher as healer" unwittingly promotes the superficial "will to closure" mentioned above, the artificiality of which becomes more evident when viewed against a local context of practical political action, namely the protest activities of a University of Hawaii faculty organization called "Professors Opposed to War" that arose as an immediate response to the events of 9/11.

Before I develop these arguments in more detail, I think it may be helpful to note that I do not see the pedagogical goals that I describe above as contradictory but rather complementary to research that values the spiritual, emotional, and interpersonal aspects of both the process of writing and the teaching of writing. As a human being, a teacher, and a fellow writer I want to reach my students in humane and productive ways. Like many teachers, I have found this role vexed and complicated by the sometimes contradictory personae of "fellow human being," "fellow writer," and "teacher" that we all to some extent embody and must continually renegotiate. My purpose in this essay is not to devalue or critique a scholarly emphasis on the humanizing aspects of our profession but rather to offer a model that blends political activism and an emphasis on disciplinary knowledge with a nurturing pedagogy that recognizes the emotional and spiritual aspects of writing. This is a tall order, and I do not pretend to have it all figured out. Rather, I offer these goals as ideals for us to discuss, imagine, and, perhaps, strive for.

Making Meaning More Meaningful

If we view the classroom as a site that is often an unwilling and unconscious participant in the role of education as ideological state apparatus as described by Clifford, Berlin, Spellmeyer, and others, then the push toward artificial closure ought to be resisted by both students and teachers since the "meaning" created under such circumstances is likely to be colored by prevailing political and economic structures that promote interpretations of national events that are conducive to their ongoing dominance. Because the power of such prevailing world views is not easily resisted, I believe that as writing teachers we need to be wary of the pressure to push our students toward an artificial and too-easy resolution in their writing about traumatic events.

Such tropes—tragedy teaches us courage, moral strength, and compassion, for example, or that acts of evil can be redeemed by acts of kindness—can easily be appropriated to ensure students' ongoing loyalty to existing political and economic structures. For students to acquire moral and spiritual lessons in ways that would allow them to move toward meaning making despite the influence of predominant world views (which, in times of national crisis often take the form of national propaganda and promotion), these lessons need to be hard-earned; they will not come easily nor quickly and may remain laced with elements of bitterness, despair, fear, and confusion for many years after the traumatic event has occurred. Such reflections and reconsiderations may cause students to question, evaluate, assess, and reassess previously held political and religious beliefs in ways that feel destabilizing and scary to students rather than reassuring and comforting.

To demonstrate the complexity of interpreting trauma and to show the often unresolved, partial, and deferred meanings that accompany such interpretations, writing teachers can turn to oral or written witness narratives of ordinary citizens during times of national trauma. These accounts function to allow intellectual work in the classroom that works against an artificial will to closure. These narratives often demonstrate how difficult it can be for people to construct meaning out of extraordinarily traumatic events and thus how challenging it would be for faculty and students to make meaning out of "meaningless events." In Hawaii, the local newspapers provided useful classroom material for such discussion in their coverage of residents' recollections of Pearl Harbor on its 60th anniversary in light of the events of September 11. Their witness accounts provided useful examples of how incomplete our understanding of the human experience of trauma is.

Betty Oda Dietz, for example, describes her experience watching the movie "Pearl Harbor" in a special edition of the *Honolulu Advertiser*. Dietz, who left Hawaii for the mainland as a young woman, believes that the trauma of watching her sister die from enemy attacks on December 7, 1941, led her to flee Hawaii without clearly understanding why she did so and made her less confident and emotionally stable throughout her adult life. She describes how she has recently begun to face how the events of Pearl Harbor affected her sense of self and security throughout her adult life with the help of group counseling: "I hurt so bad for so many years," she said. "I didn't know that the war had such a trauma on my life. When I saw that movie, I cried. That's how fresh the pain was inside of me." Although not all of us were so immediately affected by 9/11, it is hard to imagine that any student could reasonably resolve the impact of 9/11 during its aftermath or even many years afterward when many Pearl Harbor survivors describe how they are still processing the event 60 years later. How trauma affects us, in the immediate and long term, is complex and ultimately mysterious. Some may initially respond with vigor and resistance and only later when they are in more safe and secure environments allow themselves to feel anger and fear. Others may go into shock immediately and become paralyzed or emotionally numb. We may, over the years, come to interpret the same events in various ways. When writing teachers ask students to reflect upon national traumas, the students and the teacher must come to grips with the radical nature of individual suffering and struggle to reflect this complexity in their writing and writing prompts.

One way for students to gain a sense of the far-reaching and unpredictable impact of national tragedies on individual lives is to critically analyze accounts of survivors of previous national tragedies. Writing students can then be asked to interpret the ways in which stylistic choices in language and narrative structure reveal the extent to which the authors remain perplexed by the extremity of the suffering they witnessed. Nancy S. N. Miller's account of Pearl Harbor is an example of a narrative that does not end with a resolution but rather with enduring questioning and sadness. Rather than model the process of meaning making in response to a national tragedy, Miller seems interested in making the horrific nature of the events real to the reader. She plays the role of witness and asks the reader to join her in experiencing her pain and confusion. She does not attempt to comfort the reader nor does she offer sentimental statements, encouragements, or advice. Rather, her account is a stark retelling that defies the simplified platitudes that characterized the prevailing jingoism of her time:

> The sky was blue with very few clouds that Sunday morning. I was 9 years old and lived with my parents and brother in the second story of an old four-unit wooden structure in Ma'o Lane, Kalihi. My popo (grandmother) owned the structure and lived on the first floor with two of her sons.
>
> It was a peaceful morning, I watched our kimono-clad neighbor who lived diagonally from us in his two-story home greet his talking Myna bird by saying, 'Ohayo.' The bird would echo the 'ohayo.' It was a ritual every morning between the two. After a while, I watched people walking down to the church at the end of the lane, the church bells were ringing. I wondered whether I should go back to church as I waved to a friend walking down the lane with her family.
>
> My dad and uncles and the other riders were all back home that afternoon. Being Asian, they were denied entrance to the bases and sent away. A few days later, my dad read in the newspaper that our kimono-clad neighbor committed suicide because he was so ashamed of what happened on Dec. 7.

When students encounter this narrative, they will not rush to interpret it in simplified ways but rather will be asked to consider the complicated position of divided national loyalties and the long-range effects of military action on citizens and the unanticipated cost national political decisions have on individual lives. Such accounts break through the dominant narratives that surround our common retelling of Pearl Harbor—the predominant representation of the attack as a surprise, despite good evidence that Roosevelt knew that the Japanese were planning an attack on the Pacific (Scott 9–10) and the resultant pervasive prejudice against the Japanese as "naturally sneaky."

Indeed, this false construction remains popular today with many educational materials sponsored by the U.S. government perpetuating the myth of the Japanese catching America unaware. The National Park Service's materials provide students and teachers with a largely balanced source of information that includes excerpts of accounts of Pearl Harbor in Japanese history textbooks published in the 1960s for students to compare with U.S. history books of the time. Yet even this source of mostly varied and complex information refers unquestioningly to "the surprise attack" (Vierra, 26). The long-term and widespread effect of the construction of the attack on Pearl Harbor as unanticipated and, by implication, unwarranted, is evident in oral interviews with 34 WWII-generation residents of Muncie, Indiana (Brant et al.). These interviewees often express an overriding dislike for "the Japs" brought on largely by the production of the false narrative by the government that the attack on Pearl Harbor was unexpected. The extent to which the average American living far from Pearl Harbor and its cultural complexity faithfully absorbed the government's intended interpretation of the events is reflected well in such comments by Kathalene Rainey as "the Japanese were sorta sneakin' is what we figured" (11) and this longer reflection by Cleo Savage:

> There were a few Japanese people scattered around, you know, working in this area, and everything. And I know a lot of people thought they should be sent home, or to camps, or somewhere. They just felt that they shouldn't be around here. [These people] felt that those people were the ones who did what they did to Pearl Harbor, so they should be run out [of the United States]. Nobody considered the Japanese people that lived here as Americans at all. I was really very hostile toward the Japanese. Every time I looked at one of them, I just wanted to say, 'Go home where you belong.' (19)

Reading such direct perspectives from citizen accounts from Muncie, and comparing them to the witness accounts of Japanese Americans who lived in Hawaii and served in WWII, can allow students to embark on the process of critical examination of master narratives, individual accounts of lived experience, and historical representations to begin to make meaning of these complex events. However, the meanings they derive may not coincide with their earlier assumptions about the political role of their government and/or they may not see meaning in these events that is redemptive or hopeful. The witness account of Ramsay S. Hishinuma, 76, of 'Aiea, Hawaii is a valuable account to present alongside the Muncie interviews as it will produce another set of probing questions for students to consider:

> Since the attack, things changed drastically for our family, beginning with the internment of my father, who was a soldier in the Japanese army during the 1904 war with Russia. He immigrated to Hawai'i in 1907, seven years prior to World War I.
>
> Early in 1943, I tried to volunteer for the all-Nisei unit, later known as the famed 442nd Regimental Combat Team, but was denied the chance to serve because I was underage at 17. In 1945, soon after I was reclassified from 4C to 1A, I was drafted into the U.S. Army and served my country as a member of the occupation forces in Japan.
>
> During the early days of the occupation, I had a very unusual experience of meeting my cousin, who was a former kamikaze pilot who was demobilized when the war ended. For obvious reasons, he didn't seem happy to see me in a U.S. Army uniform. . . .

Taken together, these citizen accounts provide the general reading public with a history that is at once collective and individual, complex, incomplete, and shot through with the unfathomable and the mysterious—all of which may help, in some small way, to counter, or at least complicate, the overdetermined jingoism coming from dominant cultural productions. These citizen accounts show the unresolved, partial, and deferred aspects of meaning making in response to trauma and can serve as models and research material for writing teachers and students in writing their own accounts of national trauma, accounts that may in turn resist simplified notions of what national trauma is and embody more critical intellectual responses to it. Such writing, as I hope to show in the next section, is not antithetical to healing; it can in fact be a productive means of processing trauma in socially responsible and self-empowering ways—a form of healing in and of itself that moves beyond "making sense" and "feeling better."

THE HEALING ASPECTS OF
RHETORICAL INQUIRY AND ACTION

The writing teacher as healer of students' trauma is a motif that runs through much of composition and rhetoric's current literature; not coincidentally perhaps, there is a recent increase in interest in the emotional aspects to the act of writing and to the teaching of writing. Although I sympathize with teachers' concerns for their students and recognize that we all negotiate complex roles of personal and professional in our positions as writing teachers, I believe that we teach our students more effectively when we balance our desire to solve the world's problems or even one particular student's problems with our professional responsibility to share our disciplinary knowledge. This approach encourages us to maintain a certain amount of emotional distance from our students and to model for them how writing about national trauma can result in civic participation and political action. Just as a premature and apolitical rush toward meaning will actually impair the process of authentic meaning making as I have described it above, so will an overemphasis on healing students' emotions, especially when this process is separated from an intellectual critique of dominant cultural productions and results in a healing that is superficial and limited.

This is not to suggest that we ignore emotions in our teaching or our scholarship. Our disciplinary knowledge about the civic dimensions of rhetorical practice, after all, includes consideration of the emotions, since rhetoric traditionally recognized them as a legitimate target for persuasive appeals; involving students in analyses and productive uses of emotion in their reading and writing can help students begin to process—perhaps even heal from—the effects of national trauma. I wish to be clear in my position here: I am arguing for emotion as engaged through our existing professional expertise in rhetorical inquiry and civic response, rather than for an expansion of our roles to include those of confidante or counselor. I hope thereby to question what I see as a common false dichotomy between the writing teacher as conveyor of disciplinary knowledge and the writing teacher as healer by arguing for the healing effects of a process of rhetorical inquiry that complements or results in civic participation.

To further develop my discussion of the limitations of an approach toward healing that deemphasizes civic discourse and/or the cultural critique of dominant ideologies, I will analyze in more depth a recent book that argues for the caring involvement of writing teachers in their students' lives. In their book *Letters for the Living: Teaching Writing in a Violent Age*, which consists primarily of their e-mail exchanges about their pedagogical and personal responses to traumatic events in their students lives, Blitz and Hurlbert argue for a writing pedagogy that unapologetically places the teacher smack in the middle of their students' personal lives. The authors describe their approach to writing pedagogy as follows: "We have chosen to make our pedagogies an extension of our commitment to the value of correspondence between caring people. Our students know we care about them, and their writings are always, in part, one-half of a correspondence, the other half of which is our responsibility and our privilege" (51). I sympathize with Blitz and Hurlbert's desire to infuse the writing classroom with compassion and to see their roles as composition teachers and something beyond gatekeeper, grammar teacher, or dispensers of tools for critical thinking. However, even after reading through their book a few times, I still find this passage unclear. I don't know what Blitz and Hurlbert mean when they state that their students know that they "care" about them. What does such caring involve and how can they state with such confidence what their students "know"?

Such lack of clarity in language disturbs me because it points to one of my primary concerns: where do the boundaries lie for those who argue for the writer teacher as healer? How should we distinguish, for example, between the caring we do for our immediate family and closest friends and the caring that is supposed to take place between our students and ourselves? What does it mean to care as a writing teacher; does it mean that we will fix our student's car, babysit his/her child, loan him/her money? Or does it mean we will read his/her papers with compassion before we set a mark on its pages? Are all students in Blitz and Hurlbert's classrooms equally cared for, or do some receive more emotional attention than others, and on what grounds are these distinctions made? Need? Merit? Compatibility with the teacher's temperament and/or intellectual interests? These are some of the areas that proponents of this pedagogical approach often leave unexamined.

If we extrapolate this type of writing pedagogy, incomplete in its expression as it is, to a scenario where students are experiencing trauma on a national rather than individual scale, similar questions arise. What might it mean to care for the students in this circumstance? How are the students meant to respond to such caring? Blitz and Hurlbert suggest that there is a two-way relationship in their writing classrooms, which implies that their students not only are the recipients of care, but that they give care as well. Some students may resist this; others might find it confusing and uncomfortable; some may be emotionally ill-equipped to take such a relationship on; others may thrive on it. To assume that one emotional approach is appropriate for all students ignores the complexity of our students' temperaments, ethnic and racial backgrounds, age, class, and gender—all of which will have some bearing on how students respond to teachers who present themselves as caring about them and their personal lives beyond the classroom. This diversity of possible responses becomes even more complicated when we imagine the range of students' responses to a complex event such as 9/11. Much more needs to be communicated to the students than Blitz and Hurlbert's desire for students to know that the teacher cares about them.

In addition to texts that explicitly encourage writing teachers to get involved in their students' personal trials and painful experiences, there is also a growing argument for consideration of the emotional aspects of the writing process and their implications for writing pedagogy in recent composition scholarship (Perl; Richmond; Mcleod; Brand; and Bishop). The contention that we need to attend more to emotions associated with the writing process, student–teacher relationships, and classroom dynamics is often accompanied by arguments that the writing teacher's role should be expanded to acknowledge, among others, "nonlinguistic knowing," "emotional intelligence," or "emotions as 'social constructs.'" According to these arguments, composition scholars are reluctant to be open about their emotional attachments to their students. Richmond, for example, argues that scholarship that recognizes the emotional dimensions of writing and the process of teaching writing is stigmatized because of composition's current interest in writing as a socially constructed process with critical consciousness and political action as its primary pedagogical goals.

According to Richmond, scholars concerned with the emotional dynamics of teaching writing tend to disguise their interest by discussing related but more acceptable topics such as the pedagogical merits of assigning personal writing and the value of self-reflection (67, 74). Richmond herself is wary of being misidentified with the wrong camp; although she argues for "repositioning emotions in composition studies," she does not want to be misunderstood as advocating the writing teacher as healer; she states: "Regrettably, emotions are often viewed as tied to healing or rehabilitation, a connection that supposes a therapeutic relationship between writer and teacher—a relationship that causes skepticism among composition specialists (73)." Richmond has a tendency to paint composition studies scholarship in broad strokes throughout her article; the latter phrase is an illustrative example since there is actually an identifiable contingent that upholds the writing teacher as healer as a viable goal (see also recent work by Warnock, Jung.)

More problematically, while Richmond makes a point of distinguishing herself from this group, she does not explain what the writing teacher is then supposed to do—if not heal—with an increased awareness of the emotional aspects of writing and teaching writing. Without much specific information to go on, I imagine Richmond's pedagogical goals to be not so different from Blitz and Hurlbert and to be something like caring for the sake of human connection; for example, she states: "I was taught, during my training as a secondary teacher and in my course on pedagogy in composition, that a student's emotional well-being is not as important to my teaching (or his/her learning) as his or her intellectual development. I believe, however, that this attitude toward students suggests an educational philosophy that emphasizes humanistic education without wanting to view its participants as (fully) human" (79). If I were to take the above authors' advice and use emotional motivation as an analytical lens and employ it to their own writing, I would argue that Richmond and Blitz and Hurlbert appear to be angry at the prevailing approach, which seems to them to dehumanize both teachers and students. Because of this anger they are quite invested in making the argument—that teachers of writing attend more to the emotional aspects of their students' experiences—to such an extent that they leave out a discussion of the most interesting questions of how to enact a caring pedagogy that does not ignore students' emotional lives. I don't find Richmond and Blitz and Hurlbert's pedagogical goals, such as I understand them, to be misguided. I find them not fully articulated, and I find their implied representation of our field's scholarly attitudes toward the emotional aspects of healing not entirely accurate.

To more clearly position my response to Richmond and Blitz and Hurlbert, I offer this emotional analysis of my own perspective: I am less angry about this issue because I believe the training I received as a graduate student did attempt to recognize the significance of all aspects of writing—political, spiritual, and emotional. In fact, for further grounding on how to address the false dichotomy between writing teacher as healer and writing teacher as political agent in a productive way, I turned to Tilly Warnock's "Language and Learning as 'Equipment for Living': Revision as a Life Skill." I looked to this article not only because this piece is part of the most recently published anthology on writing and healing but also because Dr. Warnock was a mentor of mine when I was a graduate student at The University of Arizona. So it is not just her printed words that I read. The profoundly compassionate approach to teaching that she modeled made me read her words in a particular light, not more accurately perhaps but more deeply, influenced as I was by memories of her caring wisdom.

I often turn to the conversations I had with Tilly in my search for an appropriate persona with which to address the complex terrains of personal and professional communication and mentoring. Thus, it did not come as a surprise to hear in her voice some basic assumptions I had carried with me into the writing of this essay. She opens by remarking that Heilbrun's oft-cited *Writing A Woman's Life* presents "seamless, polished, final-copy, reader-based lives, while [she], and most people [she] know[s], live rough-draft lives" and then comments: "the trajectory of our lives is not clearly discernible. . . . Similarly we write along, only sometime reaching a final-copy stage . . ." (34). It is this respect for truth balanced with a realization of the messiness of our lived experience that underlies my first argument: a call for modeling a way for students to write pieces about national trauma that deny conclusion, that are not finished, to present themselves as injured or flawed rather than healed. It's an approach to writing and to the teaching of writing that I see as compassionately flexible, that allows both teacher and students room to grow intellectually, morally, spiritually, and politically.

In contrast to pedagogical methods that argue for the reconstruction of writing teacher as healer of the emotions and spirit, I wish to briefly turn to the example of the protest activities of the Professors Opposed to War at the University of Hawaii (POW). This grassroots organization, initially representing faculty and later expanded to include students, staff, and members of the community beyond the University, has as its purpose to offer a sustained alternative to prevailing media representations of 9/11 and subsequent government policy and propaganda. POW uses various avenues—film, lectures, the Internet, distribution of print media—to reach different audiences and to create and to maintain public spaces in which critique and debate may take place. An illustrative recent pedagogical activity was a collaborative writing assignment across disciplines and class levels that asked students to contribute to literary and artistic productions that critically evaluated the proposed war on Iraq and the ongoing war on terror. POW's pedagogical philosophy, although not explicitly stated, is to engage students in rhetorical practices (speech giving, website productions, multimedia display, listserv discussion) as well as rhetorical analysis (essay writing, research assignments, cultural critique) in not only classroom but also community fora—public arenas and civic gatherings in which the students collaborate with faculty, staff, and members of local and national communities.

Writing teachers, with their particular disciplinary knowledge of the political dimensions of language production, the history of persuasive action as civic participation, and the process of cultural critique ought to be at the forefront of such organizations. To contribute as faculty members will demonstrate their expertise to colleagues and will model for their students the practical, political, and ethical dimensions of their academic field of study. To engage students in the major national events of their time in ways that move beyond the classroom and into their local communities has long been a goal of service-learning and literacy advocates (Herzberg; Cushman; Ervin); we have in front of us a rare opportunity to make such lofty goals concrete. To push ourselves and our students beyond the comfort zones of national propaganda toward cultural critique will result in a process of meaning making and healing that we can be proud of.

To close, I will suggest that I owe the spirit of my second argument to Tilly's intellectual flexibility and emotional tolerance as well. I think she would have appreciated my emphasis on openendedness in writing and teaching writing about national trauma. And whether she would have agreed with it or not, I think she would have allowed me the room to push this argument further to arrive at my second point: that political critique and action can also contribute to the healing aspects of the process of writing. It is this type of intellectual, spiritual, moral, and political room—to discover, disagree, contend, and to contradict—that we must continually strive to provide: for our students, our colleagues, and our selves. It is down this path that healing, as close as we may come to it, lies.

WORKS CITED

Althussser, Louis. "Ideology and Ideological State Apparatuses." *Lenin and Philosophy and Other Essays*. New York: Monthly Review Press, 1971. 127–188.

Berlin, James. *Rhetorics, Poetics, and Cultures: Refiguring College English Studies*. Urbana, Illinois: NCTE, 1996.

Bishop, Wendy. "Writing is/And Therapy?: Raising Questions about Writing Classrooms and Writing Program Administration." *Journal of Advanced Composition* 13.2 (1993): 503–16.

Brand, Alice G. "Healing and the Brain." *Writing and Healing: Toward and Informed Practice.* Eds. Charles Anderson and Marian M. MacCurdy. Urbana: NCTE, 2000. 201–221.

Brant, Heather et alia. "Muncie Remembers that Day of Infamy." Muncie: Muncie Community Schools, 1993.

Blitz, Michael and C. Mark Hurlbert. *Letters for the Living: Teaching Writing in a Violent Age.* Urbana: NCTE, 1998.

Clifford, John. The Subject in Discourse." *Contending With Words.* Eds. Patricia Harkin and John Schlib. Modern Language Association, 1991. 38–51.

Cushman, Ellen. "The Public Intellectual, Activist Research, and Service-Learning." *College English* 61.1 (1999): 68–76.

Ervin, Elizabeth. "Academics and the Negotiation of Local Knowledge." *College English.* 61.4 (1999): 448–470.

Herzberg, Bruce. "Community Service and Critical Teaching." *CCC* 45 (October 1994): 307–19.

Jung, Julie. "Revision Hope: Writing Disruption in Composition Studies." *JAC* 17 (1997): 437–52.

Kardia, Diana, Crisca Bierwart, Constance E. Cook, A.T. Miller and Matthew Kaplan. "Discussing the Unfathomable: Classroom-based Responses to Tragedy." *Change* 34 (2002):18–22.

Mcleod, Susan. *Notes on the Heart: Affective Issues in the Writing Classroom.* Carbondale: Southern Illinois UP, 1997.

Pearl Harbor Plus Sixty Years. Ed. Marsha McFadden. 2001. The Honolulu Advertiser. 30 Jan. 2003. <*http://www.honoluluadvertiser.com/specials/pearlharbor60/*>.

Perl, Sondra. "A Writer's Way of Knowing: Guidelines for Composing." *Presence of Mind: Writing and the Domain Beyond the Cognitive.* Eds. Alice Glarden Brand and Richard L. Graves. Portsmouth, NH: Heinemann Boynton/Cook, 1994.

Richmond, Kia Jane. "Repositioning Emotions in Composition Studies." *Composition Studies.* 30 (2002): 67–82.

Scott, David K. *The Rhetorical Compact: Toward a New Genre of Rhetorical Criticism.* Central States Communication Association Annual Convention. April 9–13. St. Louis, MO. 1997. ERIC Document Reproduction Service No. ED411567.

Spellmeyer, Kurt. Common Ground: D Englewood Cliffs: Prentice Hall, 1993.

Remembering Pearl Harbor: The USS Arizona Memorial. Ed. John Vierra, Jr. 4 Sept. 2001. National Park Service. 30 Jan. 2003. <*http://www.cr.nps.gov/nr/twhp/curriculumkit/lessons/arizona/5about.htm*>.

University Peace Initiative (UPI.). Ed. Ruth Hsu. 24 Sept. 2001. UPI, University of Hawaii. 30 Jan. 2003. <*http://www.hawaii.edu/upi*>.

Warnock, Tilly. "Language and Learning as 'Equipment for Living': Revision as a Life Skill." *Writing and Healing: Toward and Informed Practice.* Ed. Charles Anderson and Marian M. MacCurdy. Urbana: NCTE, 2000. 34–57.

Consumerism and the Coopting of National Trauma

Theresa Enos, Joseph Jones, Lonni Pearce, and Kenneth R. Vorndran

ONE OF THE EFFECTS of national tragedies is their tendency to foreground our view of ourselves as a nation. In any of the great traumatizing events in U.S. history that the writers of this essay have lived through or know about (World War II, the Korean War, the Cuban Crisis, the assassination of President Kennedy, the Vietnam War, the Challenger explosion, the Gulf War, the 2000 Presidential election, and the terrible events of September 11, 2001), the psychological, interpersonal, economic, and spiritual consequences for our national identity were profound, and we adjusted our national identity in an attempt to weather the storm. In the political arena, in the media, in the workplace, and in schools, our conversations reflected our struggle to define appropriate ways to respond to crises that in one way or other affected us all.

As four teachers of writing—whose experience spans several years to several decades, in settings including high school, the community college, and the university—we shared some common interests in the ways that national trauma presents opportunities in the writing classroom for both self-reflection and cultural critique. Our purpose in this essay is to discuss citizenship and consumerism, to explore how—during the course of the twentieth century—our rhetoric regarding the relationship of these two concepts has been transformed (especially in response to national trauma), and to reflect on the reactions of our students to a call that intimately links citizenship with consumption.

World War II: The Call to Conserve

Prolonged or large-scale conflicts—perhaps the most consistent source of trauma in the twentieth century—have provided intense and focused moments in which we have openly contended with our national identity and with what it means to be American citizens. Through WWI and WWII, we Americans came to view ourselves as fighting for right and good. And attempting to maintain this identity—whether we successfully did so or not—became important in Korea, Vietnam, and both wars with Iraq. Because of our national identity, we have desired for our participation in international conflicts to be viewed as having an ethical dimension, and the political friction over Vietnam and Iraq has to a great extent centered on the ethical tensions inherent in those conflicts. Likewise, our definition of what it means to be a citizen has been transformed over the past century. Our misrepresentation and mistreatment of Japanese Americans during WWII, for example, became a rallying cry for the appropriate representation and treatment of Arab Americans after 9/11. Another shift in our notions of citizenship has taken place in tandem with the rise of consumer culture during the twentieth century. Citizenship and consumerism have become intricately bound to one another; our duty as citizens has become linked to the call to consume. Where once—during times of national trauma—citizens were called upon, in some form or another, to conserve, we are now called upon to spend.

For one of us, the ideal of how citizenship is reflected through the symbolic construct of national identity comes from fragmented memories of World War II with its rationing of food and gas, where school kids supported the ideal of citizenship by participating in paper collection drives. Theresa still has in an old scrapbook her "Paper Trouper" certificate. Also in that scrapbook is a piece of lined paper from a Red Chief tablet, her letter to the world, on the day she arrived home from school to see the screaming newspaper headlines that President Roosevelt had suddenly died. On her front porch, she huddled over her notebook and wrote:

> President Rosevelt died Thursday afternoon. I loved him very much and I cried when I knew about it and said a prayer for us (America). I will respect Mother and Bettye and Margy and grandmother very much, and very much this day I write. It is April 13th 1945, soon after my birthday.
>
>   Amen
> I love Rosevelt. I love God. His last words were "I have a terrific headache."

Roosevelt, who in 1942 worked with Congress to establish the Office of Price Administration (the government bureaucracy that would oversee the rationing of goods such as sugar, gasoline, and rubber), called on U.S. citizens to sacrifice for the war effort by conserving and recycling everything from tires to lipstick tubes. A quotation from a small Utah newspaper typifies the tenor of much of the nation's rhetoric during the initial stages of the war:

> We here in the [Uintah] Basin will probably see no great change; we should not be in danger of air raids or other form of attack, we have no air fields, army posts or munitions factories to take on an increased tempo. But we will be affected just the same . . . we will have to give up many of the things we would like to have, we must begin to produce and conserve far out of proportion to our own requirements. (Barton)

Depicted both through textual and visual rhetoric was the idea that all good citizens should gladly forego the fulfillment of their own material needs for the good of their nation (see figure 1).

What interested us (as writing teachers who study and teach rhetoric) about the thrust of the nation's rhetoric during WWII—especially in light of our most recent national trauma—was that it suggested individuals should participate in the war economy by rationing and conserving, that conspicuous, thoughtless, or selfish consumption were at odds with the patriotic cause of the country. Good citizenship entailed enduring economic hardship in order to help the nation. In the wake of more recent traumas such as Desert Storm and the events of September 11, 2001, it is evident that a dramatic shift has taken place in what we as citizens are called on to do in response to threats to our national security.

DESERT STORM: THE CALL TO QUESTION

Because the scope and duration of WWI and WWII placed heavy demands on the economy's resources, making the connection between citizenship and conservation may have been a necessary rhetorical strategy during these national traumas. The absence of these same stresses during the first Gulf War and the tenuous economic post-9/11 climate may account in part for the differing rhetorics of the time periods, but a fundamental cultural shift occurred in the interim between WWII and Desert Storm, a cultural shift that redefined our concept of ourselves to the extent that a rhetorical appeal juxtaposing citizenship and consumption seemed logical, if not acceptable and/or appropriate.

Ken, who was teaching high school juniors and seniors at the time, remembers dissension seeming relatively acceptable to his students. The suspicion that the primary U.S. interest in the conflict was maintaining a supply of oil appeared to be fairly widespread, but as this sentiment rippled outward and transformed into arguments about environmentalism and capitalism, rancor escalated and

FIGURE 1. Wartime poster produced by the Douglas Aircraft Company (Ross).

dissent became less tolerable. The questions being asked—Had our own core behaviors and values created a situation in which we felt compelled to go to war? Could an alteration of these behaviors and values place us in a position, in the future, when our interests in the Middle East might be more objective? Could an adjustment offer us both better treatment of the environment and a stronger geopolitical position? Would the power of corporations (which seemed to be increasingly prevalent in our politics) set the U.S. political agenda about war?—degenerated into touchy, clichéd, and intractable arguments.

One of the hard-won lessons of Vietnam—that citizens needed to question the pro-war rhetoric of government—was acceptable only up to a point, and that point was where consumerism was called into question. The suggestion that we were in Kuwait fighting for oil was tolerable to most. The implication that we might want companies to produce smaller, more fuel-efficient vehicles was the battle line. In rhetoric, pro-American and pro-capitalism became enmeshed, and the individual's right to consume whatever and however he or she desired became sacrosanct.

In Ken's classroom, his main goal during Desert Storm was to ensure that his students had space to participate in civil discourse. Consequently—and especially in the days immediately following the assault on Iraq—he allowed his students much time to discuss their feelings and to debate the issues. In the rhetorical position of facilitator, Ken was able to moderate the discussion, and his concerns were threefold: He wanted to extend the invitation for his students to enter into and to engage in a substantive debate; he wanted to support students who were willing to dissent and those who were in favor of U.S. policies and actions; and he wanted to maintain a sense of sanctuary in his classroom, knowing the risks that students are required to take in writing classrooms necessitate a feeling of safety and shelter.

What he noticed in the wake of the first assaults—this was the first time an act of war directly affected many of his students—was that most of his students seemed to be grappling with vulnerability. But as his students' sense of vulnerability subsided and the focal point of the conversation changed, it interested him to see how rapidly the discussion became a debate about economics and environmentalism and how vehement the opposing sides were. He was pleased to see his students were astute enough to sense the real debate was not really about Iraq or Kuwait but about America and its values. But Ken was disconcerted to see how entrenched the value of consumerism was in his students. For most, the right to buy was divorced from or simply trumped any sense of responsibility for potential geopolitical consequences. Others, who did see a link between America's consumer ethic and various world crises and inequities, seemed frustrated by the nonchalance with which the repercussions of U.S. consumerism were set aside. The call to consume and the concept of citizenship had not yet become overtly intertwined in our national rhetoric, but it was clear that for many the concept of the rights of citizenship and the right to consume were already overlapping.

September 11 and the War on Terrorism: The Call to Consume

A decade, some 2,500 miles, and a giant leap from high school to community college later, a student e-mailed Ken. He thought his sister was in the

World Trade Center Towers when they were hit. The family hadn't heard anything conclusive, but he wouldn't be in class. Could Ken e-mail him with any assignments?

Over the course of the semester, Bruce's story unfolded. Through his in-class writings, his journals, and his essays, Bruce told his writing group, his workshop, and the class about his sister: She was only a kid, 11 or 12, when he was in the motorcycle wreck that withered his left arm. She was a strong student, who was taking a year off between college and grad school to do a stint with the Peace Corps. She had visited Bruce and his wife in the weeks before she went to New York to ship out. Bruce had given her a letter that he had made into a paper airplane. The letter had his phone number on it. He told her to launch it from the Trade Centers when she visited. It'd be interesting to see if anyone called.

Bruce got the call a few days after September 11. Among the debris, someone had found his letter. The person just wanted Bruce to know the letter had been recovered. He hung up without giving Bruce his name.

While the death and violence that took place on that September 11 may have been in many ways too profound and tragic to be constructively discussed, the subsequent actions of the media, the government, and the business community compelled us as citizens and teachers of writing to examine those actions with our students. They compelled us to analyze the various rhetorical practices that pointed to some of the contradictory ways the call to rally as U.S. citizens was expressed through responses to the attacks on the World Trade Center and the Pentagon and the crash of United Airlines Flight 93 in Pennsylvania.

Some of the more notable demonstrations of citizenship were people's physical responses to the tragedies, responses that resulted in monumental outpourings of generosity, reminiscent of the sacrifices called for in World War II, such as long lines of people waiting to give blood, and medical and emergency workers who drove across the country to assist in the rescue efforts. For those not in the immediate vicinity of the disaster sites, other rhetorical acts such as displaying flags and banners provided the means of showing sympathy for victims and their families, support for rescue workers, and patriotism as U.S. citizens.

There were, of course, the predictable calls for unity and conformity. We were, after all, a country under attack, and the rhetoric of national unity is common to countries at war. But the rhetoric that developed in the wake of 9/11 was in some ways quite new. For example, the initial—and now even relatively sustained—reluctance to dissent against U.S. policy in the war on terror was relatively new to current generations who had grown up in the aftermath of Vietnam. And two additonal pieces of rhetoric were startlingly prominent: The first was our caution against blaming people of the same ethnicity or religious background as the terrorists—though it could easily be argued that our policy has not always matched our rhetoric—and the second was that Americans were being called upon to consume rather than to conserve.

When we reflect on these events—WWII, Desert Storm, and 9/11—in their historical context, we see differing images of what it means to be a U.S. citizen. In most of the twentieth century, we not only were asked to sacrifice, but we also gladly did so. What was to be required of us after September 11 seemed quite different. Citizenship seemed to have been coopted by consumerism. We were not asked, as in earlier times, to conserve; rather, we were asked to acquire. Shopping, dining out, and making other such efforts to support our economy were framed as our patriotic duties.

As teachers who are committed to equipping students to rhetorically analyze the texts in their world, we found it important to pay attention to what students observed about various social, political, and commercial texts that appeared in the media after the attacks. In several cases students commented on the ways that the act of consumption and the practice of citizenship seemed to converge in speeches given by politicians who advised citizens to spend money to help bolster an economy disrupted by the attacks and in marketing campaigns that used images of flags and other national symbols to "inspire" consumers to purchase products or services. One particular campaign, "Dine Out for America," raised over $18 million for the American Red Cross Disaster Relief Fund by urging people to eat out on October 11, 2001, at participating restaurants. Over 7,000 restaurants pledged to send some portion of their revenues from that day to the Red Cross Fund (see figure 2).

THE CALL TO CONSUME: A BRIEF HISTORY

While the merger of consumerism and citizenship is not a new phenomenon in U.S. society, rhetorical strategies employed in campaigns such as "Dine Out for America" provide a powerful opportunity for discussing with students various ways that "citizenship" is defined in our society and how these definitions point to certain assumptions we make about our national identity. In this case, in order to understand how deeply embedded the association is between consumption and citizenship in the U.S. character, Lonni has reviewed some of the key historical developments that trace the ascendance of consumer culture in the United States.

Many scholars have written about the increasing influence that consumer culture has on the economic, social, and political life of people in modern capitalist societies. Almost 30 years ago, Raymond Williams, for example, argued that "the dominant mode of human perception and interaction is very generally mediated by consumption" (70–71). Particularly in the second half of the twentieth century, the power of consumption became closely linked to values that people in the United States claim as central to the "American way of life": political freedom, social progress, and economic productivity.

**A PARTNERSHIP OF THE RESTAURANTS OF AMERICA,
THEIR EMPLOYEES AND GUESTS**

FIGURE 2. Dine Out for America logo, "Dine Out for America."

Although earlier events such as the expansion of the middle class and the development of mass printing and transportation systems sowed the seeds of consumer culture, the rapid spread of mass consumption is generally associated with the period after World War II, a development that in some ways was a response to wartime sacrifices and rationing. Consumption became a kind of signifier for freedom, as Richard Fox notes in his discussion of a 1944 advertisement for Hoover vacuum cleaners: "three years after Roosevelt's 'Four Freedoms'—freedom of religion and speech, freedom from want and fear—the Hoover ad urged that 'the Fifth Freedom is Freedom of Choice'" (ix). Because this valorization of consumption contradicted the continuing influence of the United State's Puritan heritage, a quotation from William Whyte's 1957 book, Organization Man, demonstrates the emerging problem for marketers in the 1950s:

> [W]e are now confronted with the problem of permitting the average American to feel moral [. . .] even when he is spending, even when he is not saving, even when he is taking two vacations a year and buying a second or third car. One of the basic problems of prosperity, then, is to demonstrate that the hedonistic approach to life is a moral, not an immoral one. (qtd. in Ehrenreich 36)

As the Cold War developed, one of the ways this shift to "moral consumption" was accomplished was through the idea that the ability to consume demonstrated the superiority of the U.S. way of life over that of the Soviet Union. Fox points to this trend when referring to the public conversation between Khrushchev and Nixon that took place when Nixon, as Vice-President, visited Moscow:

> Richard Nixon's "Kitchen Debate" with Nikita Khrushchev in 1959 was a pure expression of the times: the American way of life equated with the American "standard of living." The American system worked, Nixon told the Russians, because "44 million families in America own 56 million television sets, 143 million radio sets, and [. . .] 31 million of those families own their own homes." (x)

In the decades since the 1950s, the cementing of this link between the "American way of life" and consumption has meant that "In the second half of the twentieth century, we have gradually learnt to talk and think of each other and ourselves less as workers, citizens, parents or teachers and more as consumers" (qtd. in Lewis and Bridger 1). Culturally, consumption now serves as a primary tool for establishing identity—both individually and collectively, as more traditional means of identity-construction, such as religion or political party, diminish in influence.

This redesigned and reengineered identity has had complicated and wide-reaching implications culturally and politically. Marketing has become the engine that drives our economy, an economy in which—by some estimates—up to two-thirds of the purchases are of nonessential goods and services. We must identify ourselves primarily as consumers to sustain this economy and to accept the levels of advertising necessary to keep it functioning. Logowear, slick television commercials and magazine ads, sports teams supported by and bound to specific companies, Coke or Pepsi campuses (from elementary school through college), spin doctors for politicians, press agents for endless streams of Monica Lewinskies, billboards, spam, pop-up advertisements, and coupon mailers are all extensions of consumerism. And they are all continually redefining the extent of our consumer identity as well. Marketing has become ubiquitous, perhaps inescapable, and we are—in the eyes of increasingly sophisticated advertisers and public relations specialists who create and manage our economic and political markets—essentially (and quite necessarily) sets of demographics.

The connections between political and economic power have always existed, but as we have come to define ourselves and to allow ourselves to be defined as consumers, the nature of political discourse has changed. The American public is openly and continually addressed in its role of consumer.

The degree to which we have accepted this role and have become complicit in its continuation is revealed by the centrality of such discourse to our public lives, by the candor with which our role as consumers is articulated within political and governmental contexts, and by the nonchalance with which we, the public, regard such references. The promotion and expansion of our identity as consumers is also revealed through the discourse of consumerism that has slipped into most public institutions (including schools where students are more and more frequently referred to as customers or consumers of education).

Fueled by the cynicism that resulted from the Vietnam War, Watergate, and a growing perception of the government as a wasteful, unwieldy bureaucracy, the American public has become increasingly skeptical of the efficacy of the traditional means of democracy over the last three decades. Many citizens have withdrawn from the public freedoms of citizenship (the freedom to vote, to participate in government, to express opinions on public issues, and so forth) into the private freedoms of consumption (the freedom to design an identity and lifestyle based on one's choice of available products/services). Between the trend toward individual consumerism and a sociopolitical discourse that frames people predominantly as consumers, it is not surprising that when a national trauma like September 11 occurs, we see responses that explicitly point to the representation of consumption as citizenship.

CLASSROOM PRACTICES IN THE WAKE OF NATIONAL TRAUMA: THE CALL TO RESPOND

Five days after the attacks, Joseph walked into class with an assignment for his Advanced Placement Senior English students. Blandly titled "Rhetorical Analysis Independent Project," the assignment was described as follows: "Your task for this project is to find an aspect of the events of, or events emanating from, September 11 and to consider that aspect in a rhetorical manner. To consider something in a rhetorical manner, then, requires that you analyze as thoroughly as you can answers to the following kinds of questions: What is being said? By whom is it being said? To whom is it being said? How is it being said? What are the reasons for it being said in the ways it is? What are the implications for—and implications of—it being said in that way?" Rather than assigning a paper, however, Joseph required students to prepare a ten-minute presentation to the class: "Presentations may utilize technology and visual aids though that's not a requirement. What is required is an engaging—and engaged—analysis of the aspect of events that you select. Help us understand what you've come to understand. This is important work."

Joseph's students began their presentations in early November. Some students traced a series of columns by a particular political commentator (e.g., George Will, Ann Colter) to see how his or her thinking evolved, or didn't, during the weeks after the terrorist attacks. Others looked at particular publications to see how their coverage handled the news events. One student's presentation analyzed the advertising in *Forbes* and *Business Week* and demonstrated how companies were trying to link commerce and patriotism. Other students dissected the more crudely designed local newspaper ads for the ways businesses, from car dealers to the sellers of vacuum cleaners, invoked patriotic imagery as a means of moving merchandise.

While students snickered and rolled their eyes and dismissed the ads as crass and heavy-handed, they seemed neither offended nor outraged by such business practices. Students may have heard that things were forever changed, but what they saw was business as usual. One student, Jonathan, observed: "Buy. Buy. Buy. That's what we need to do, they say. We're not communists, so we define ourselves by our purchasing and selling goods and services." Another student, Won, noted: "It is amazing how everyone caught this virus of commercial patriotism so quickly. It was all over the news, all over the ads in the papers, all over the billboards, and there were American flags plastered on every car window. 'United We Stand,' they read. United we stand for what? Against what?"

At the center of Joseph's work with high school students is developing students' sense of themselves as users and consumers of texts. His students are savvy about certain aspects of the marketplace. They usually know when marketers are appealing to them and trying to manipulate them. If they don't show the outrage we often think they should, it is because they recognize how pervasive marketing is. They know of no boundaries the marketplace respects. But their awareness of the ubiquity of advertising doesn't—perhaps surprisingly—make them cynical either. Their youth permits them the hope that they might, at last, somehow stand outside the pitch.

As the government made repeated calls on Americans to spend as usual, and as advertisers gingerly or blatantly blended patriotic themes into their post-9/11 appeals, Carter, a particularly insightful student, observed:

> It's not unpatriotic to notice that staying at Ramada Inn won't change or help the victims of September 11, and I often wonder when the bulk of the general public will realize this and practice more intelligent consumer ideals.

Carter's observation is instructive not only for its awareness of consumer manipulation and his attempt to stand outside it but also for its invocation for what some might consider an oxymoron: "consumer ideals."

As Carter illustrates, Joseph's students don't tend to entertain the notion that they can somehow escape consumerism. But they do imagine that they might somehow define themselves against the consumer ethos. The more perceptive students react against the myth of the democracy of the marketplace. They do not suffer from the delusion that freedom might be found in a limitless supply of consumer goods or television channels. Such a posture is richly complicated, however, for they wrestle with a key question: In what manner might they register their dissent? In "Why Johnny Can't Dissent," Thomas Franks demonstrates that advertisers have effectively coopted non-conformity and made it among their most persuasive branding devices, and Joseph's students haven't quite gotten that far in their recognition of how deeply marketing penetrates all aspects of our culture:

> Consumerism is no longer about "conformity" but about "difference." Advertising teaches us not in the ways of puritanical self-denial (a bizarre notion on the face of it), but in orgiastic, never-ending self-fulfillment. It counsels not rigid adherence to the tastes of the herd but vigilant and constantly updated individualism. We consume not to fit in, but to prove, on the surface at least, that we are rock 'n' roll rebels, each one of us as rule-breaking and hierarchy-defying as our heroes of the 60s, who now pitch cars, shoes, and beer. (34)

The countercultural ideals to which students could aspire 30 years ago—as a gesture against "the Establishment"—have been adopted by corporate America as a means of selling products as well as reifying a consumerist ideal that applauds those who strive to stand outside or beyond the cultural marketplace. The hip, the cool, and the underground have proven especially effective marketing devices. Those students who recognize this find it particularly difficult, then, to resist or rebel against the demands of consumerism made upon them at every turn. Frank notes: "Corporate America is not an oppressor but a sponsor of fun, provider of lifestyle accoutrements, facilitator of carnival, our slang-speaking partner in the quest for that ever-more apocalyptic orgasm" (34). It therefore strikes students as neither particularly outrageous nor ironic that consumerism has been used to coopt American tragedy. That businesses would try to link themselves—subtly, artistically, obviously, blatantly or even obscenely, depending on their target markets—to things patriotic is not surprising. Nor is it particularly surprising—given the cultural and political focus on consumerism—that our government would call on its citizens to demonstrate their patriotism by spending. But to have dissent coopted by the consumer ethic to the extent that it (dissent) seems passe or clichéd, that it seems something to be done via purchases rather than political action is the ultimate coup. What we see both in Frank's observations about the coopting of dissent and in calls to patriotic spending is the redefinition of our identity as individuals and as citizens in terms of consumption rather than political action.

In the rhetoric of "patriotic consumption" typified by campaigns like "Dine Out for America," the private act of consumption has in some sense been transformed into the public demonstration of citizenship through rhetoric that urges citizens to demonstrate their patriotism by spending money. And, as Franks' observations tell us, dissent too has been coopted by consumerism and so, whether our duty as citizens is calling us to demonstrate support for our nation or to express our dissent against certain government actions, the rhetoric of consumer culture calls us to express our citizenship through our purchasing choices rather than through civic action. When students raise questions about the motives and effects of such rhetoric, we need to take the opportunity to help them articulate what makes them uncomfortable about this kind of rhetoric. We also need to work collaboratively with them to define the significance of various practices of consumption and citizenship in relation to how students see themselves and their country. Most importantly, for ourselves and for our students, we need to collaboratively imagine the possibilities for reclaiming practices of citizenship that are not enacted through consumption.

In times of national trauma, our values and beliefs are often revealed more starkly than at other times and, therefore, it is in those times that we as teachers must engage with our students in a careful scrutiny of what these moments can teach us about the complicated layers of meaning that inhabit our many views of ourselves as individuals and as a nation.

WORKS CITED

Barton, John D. "The War Effort at Home." *Utah History To Go*. Utah State Historical Society. 3 Dec. 2002. <*http://historytogo.utah.gov/warhome.html*>.

"Dine Out for America." Dine Out for America. 2 Feb. 2002. <*http://www.dineoutforamerica.com/*>.

Ehrenreich, Barbara. *Fear of Falling: The Inner Life of the Middle Class*. New York: Pantheon, 1989.

Fox, Richard Wightman, and T. J. Jackson Lears. *The Culture of Consumption: Critical Essays in American History, 1880–1980*. 1st ed. New York: Pantheon, 1983.

Franks, Thomas. "Why Johnny Can't Dissent." *Commodify Your Dissent: Salvos from the Baffler*. Ed. Thomas Frank and Matt Weiland. New York: Norton, 1997. 31–45.

Lewis, David, and Darren Bridger. *The Soul of the New Consumer: Authenticity—What We Buy and Why in the New Economy*. London: Nicholas Brealey, 2000.

Ross, J. D. "WWII Propaganda Posters." 5 Dec 2002. <*http://www.openstore.com/posters/*>.

Williams, Raymond. *Television; Technology and Cultural Form*. London: Fontana, 1974.

Discovering the Erased Feminism of the Civil Rights Movement

Beyond the Media, Male Leaders, and the 1960s Assassinations

Keith D. Miller and Kathleen Weinkauf

REPORTERS DEFINE NATIONAL traumas in ways that create and reinforce certain perceptions of leadership while eliminating others. During the 1960s, journalists generally explained the assassinations of prominent male leaders—specifically, Medgar Evers, President John F. Kennedy, Malcolm X, Martin Luther King, Jr., and Senator Robert Kennedy—as a series of shockwaves that propelled national horror and revulsion. For many people, the widespread identification of these figures as martyrs for racial equality has blocked any attempt to reassess events and discourse of the civil rights movement that occurred before the martyrdoms were completed. Yet such a reassessment is necessary if we are to understand race relations, gender relations, and social change.

Along with others in the academy, writing faculty often (usually implicitly) teach that historical opposition to racism and sexism involves two separate struggles. When teachers approach the civil rights movement of the 1950s and 1960s, they generally explain the nonviolent campaign simply as large-scale agitation for racial equality. This interpretation is evident, for example, in the teaching of Martin Luther King, Jr.'s "I Have a Dream" and "Letter from Birmingham Jail"—works that often appear in freshman and sophomore textbooks. While presenting "I Have a Dream" and "Letter," faculty customarily erase gender from the civil rights movement and treat anti-racism as a posture unrelated to feminist issues. But doing so perpetuates the illusion that one can understand race and racism without grappling with gender and sexism, even though the issues intertwine throughout the African American freedom struggle of the 1950s and 1960s.

We argue that, in order to teach the rhetoric of the civil rights movement effectively, faculty must recognize its female pioneers, the sexism that these women faced and often overcame, and the wholesale erasure of their efforts by the news media—an erasure that the press cemented in the popular imagination following the assassinations. In this essay we will review female leadership and explore the role of the news media in obscuring feminist issues during the struggle. We will also propose new ways to teach civil rights discourse, including "I Have a Dream."

Consider a few of the many female trailblazers. In 1938, long before the civil rights movement supposedly began, a young woman named Pauli Murray tried to break racial barriers by applying for admission to the University of North Carolina. Two years later she was jailed for failing to move to the back of a bus. In 1944 she and three other activists led 50 demonstrators to sit-in and thereby integrate an all-white cafeteria in Washington, D.C. (Olson). Five years earlier, after the Daughters of the American Revolution (DAR) prevented a spectacular performance by Marian Anderson at Constitution Hall, Anderson protested the DAR's racism by singing from the steps of the Lincoln Memorial before an enormous throng. As Scott Sandage persuasively argues, Anderson's concert transformed the memory of Abraham Lincoln from national unifier to symbol of racial equality; her performance also christened the Lincoln Memorial as a site for African American protest. A year before Rosa Parks's famous arrest in 1955, JoAnn Robinson, Mary Fair Burks, and their Women's Political Council decried bus segregation in a letter to the Mayor of Montgomery, Alabama. Robinson and the Women's Political Council—not Martin Luther King, Jr.—initially orchestrated the Montgomery Bus Boycott of 1955–1956 (Robinson; Garrow, *Bearing*). Daisy Bates exercised crucial, behind-the-scenes leadership in the 1957 crisis of school integration in Little Rock, Arkansas. In 1960, confronting the Mayor of Nashville before a large crowd, Diane Nash successfully pressured him to endorse lunch-counter integration (Lewis). The next year, after Freedom Riders were bloodied and hospitalized by white racist mobs in Alabama, Nash—at great risk of her own life—insisted on reviving the integrated bus rides—a protest that mortified President John F. Kennedy and Attorney General Robert Kennedy (Lewis). In 1963, by directing demonstrations in Cambridge, Maryland, Gloria Richardson prodded the Kennedy Administration to protect racial agitators from retaliation by white racists—a move the brothers Kennedy had not made in earlier, similar situations (Olson). Fannie Lou Hamer, a long-time Mississippi sharecropper, survived police torture and became an extremely energetic and outspoken activist with a public profile large enough to intimi-date President Lyndon Johnson (Lee, Marsh, Payne, Reed). Amelia Boynton played a crucial role in spawning the 1965 voting rights protests in Selma, Alabama, and was beaten and tear-gassed by police (Garrow, *Protest;* Olson). Even before Paolo Freire began his career in Brazil, other women, most notably Septima Clark, spearheaded Freire-like politicized literacy efforts as an important component of movement organizing in numerous states (Clark). Unarguably, Ella Baker was one of the most important figures of the entire civil rights movement. Working quietly, she recruited people to join the NAACP in the 1940s. Impressed with her courageous voyages to the Deep South and her relentless devotion to the cause, the NAACP promoted her to national director of its branches in 1943, a position she held until her resig-nation in 1946. In 1957 Baker, Stanley Levison, and Bayard Rustin founded the Southern Christian Leadership Conference (SCLC), which King headed. Baker remained a central figure in SCLC in 1958 and 1959, attempting, with few resources, to organize King's band of Baptist ministers—all of whom, fol-lowing the pattern of their national church, were men. In 1960, disgusted with the paternalism, sexism, and inefficiency of King and his clergy, Baker resigned her SCLC post (Ransby, Grant).[1]

Baker decided that the ultimate hope for the movement lay with student activists. At a crucial 1960 meeting in Greensboro, North Carolina, she helped create the Student Nonviolent Coordinating Committee (SNCC), a grassroots organization of eager, young dissenters. King firmly suggested that the youths join SCLC and follow his leadership, but Baker urged them to secure autonomy from the "fathering" body. SNCC members agreed with Baker and refused to become a lower part of the SCLC hierarchy (Grant; Carson; Branch; Garrow, *Bearing*).

While Baker mentored many significant women in SNCC, she nurtured their abilities instead of dictating their actions. "My theory," she insisted, "is strong people don't need strong leaders" (qtd. in Cantrow and O'Mally 55). Although SNCC disdained hierarchy so much that, at times, it seemed lead-erless, Baker and SNCC participants believed they would be more effective by remaining highly decentralized. One SNCC activist, Casey Hayden, describes Baker's practice of political organizing:

> Ella was, politically, above all pragmatic. . . . Her notion of the need to raise up new leaders, and to rotate leaders, for example, was pragmatic, based on years of experience in seeing folks, when they became leaders, join the lead-ers' club and leave their constituents behind. (345)

Gently guided by Baker and the self-effacing Robert Moses, SNCC for four years functioned unlike any other group in the South. During the early 1960s SNCC—not King's SCLC—served as the largest and the most important body of nonviolent civil rights agitators in the South. In Georgia, Alabama, and throughout Mississippi, SNCC sparked countless nonviolent workshops, sit-ins, marches, church rallies, and voter registration drives—many of which incorporated exciting speeches and jubilant songfests. White authorities often responded with violence, beating and jailing the enthusiastic, often joyful protestors. The linchpin of SNCC logistics was Ruby Doris Robinson, who coordinated much of the crusade from Atlanta (Fleming).

In his award-winning book about organizing in Mississippi—an enormously significant battleground for racial equality—Charles Payne devotes an entire chapter to explaining the painstaking efforts of SNCC to cultivate local leaders, most of whom were women and some of whom needed little or no cultivation (265–83). Payne observes that virtually everyone, including male SNCC organizers, readily noted that women fueled most of the movement in Mississippi. Women sometimes resorted to shaming their own ministers—who were male—into enlisting in the crusade. In Payne's words, "To SNCC members, the contemporary tendency to assume that movement leadership [in Mississippi] was basically ministerial is laughable" (196).

Some women were so dedicated to the movement that they either had no feminist concerns or subordinated those concerns for fear that wrestling with gender would detract from the crusade for racial integration. Because they were female and because they exerted crucial leadership by effectively resisting male domination (both within and outside the movement), we call such women proto-feminists. Baker and others, however, resisted patriarchal hierarchy in general and in the movement. Not only were these women outright feminists, but they also played significant roles in pioneering the entire Second Wave of American feminism (Evans).

Although Baker, Hamer, Ruby Doris Robinson, and many other women exerted important leadership in SNCC, the organization was not immune to sexism. In 1964, at a retreat in Waveland, Mississippi, Casey Hayden and Mary King (with the help of Emmie Schrader and Elaine DeLott) drafted a position paper to air their grievances. Writing anonymously, these women declared:

> The average white person finds it difficult to understand why the Negro resents being called "boy," or being thought of as "musical" or "athletic," because the average white person doesn't realize that he assumes he is superior. And naturally he doesn't understand the problem of paternalism. So too the average SNCC worker finds it difficult to discuss the woman problem because of the assumption of male superiority. Assumptions of male superiority are as wide-spread and deep-rooted and every much as crippling to the woman as assumptions of white supremacy are to the Negro. (qtd. in Cagin and Dray 424)

These women urged SNCC to change "so that all of us gradually come to understand that this is no more a man's world than it is a white world" (qtd. in Carson 148). Other women in SNCC supported this position while most men in SNCC dismissed the women's protest.

The sexism of Martin Luther King, Jr., A. Philip Randolph, Bayard Rustin, and other male civil rights figures was evident in 1963 at the March on Washington, a day-long event that King capped with "I Have a Dream." Speakers at the March included Roy Wilkins of NAACP, John Lewis of SNCC, Walter Reuther of United Auto Workers, Eugene Blake of the National Council of Churches, Whitney Young of the National Urban League, and Jewish leader Joachim Prinz—several of whom could hardly be considered civil rights agitators at all. Until Lynne Olson's magnificent book *Freedom's Daughters* appeared in 2001, almost no one, including historians of the period, knew that Anna Arnold Hedgeman—the only woman on the 19-member planning council for the March on Washington—seriously attempted to secure a speaking role for a woman—any woman—at the March. Although Hedgeman complained (first politely, then loudly) about the exclusion of female speakers from an occasion that promised to be (and was) a media spectacular, her protest fell on deaf ears. No woman spoke at the March (Olson 284–85).

Preceding it by two days was an address by A. Philip Randolph, the official head of the March, at the National Press Club. Though the club had recently admitted black men, it still denied women the right to join and actually confined the female reporters covering Randolph's speech to its balcony (Olson 287). Pauli Murray was so incensed at this display that she quickly penned a letter to Randolph where her feelings would not be misinterpreted or silenced:

> I have been increasingly perturbed over the blatant disparity between the major role which Negro women have played and are playing at the crucial grass-roots levels of our struggle and the minor role of leadership to which they have been assigned in the national policy-making decisions. (qtd. in Olson 288)

A month earlier Murray objected to separating the twin goals of racial and gender equality: "What does it profit me personally to fight fifty years of my life for the civil rights of Negroes only to have to turn around and fight another fifty years so that I and my sex may benefit from the earlier struggle?" (qtd. in Olson 286).

Reflecting a white, male bias similar to that of the National Press Club, the predominately white, male news media largely ignored the long African American protest tradition after the Civil War, including early 1950s nonviolent agitation in Louisiana that was met with racist violence (Fairclough).

Such wholesale neglect made possible the decision of the press to christen the Montgomery Bus Boycott of 1955–1956 as the birth of a new crusade for racial justice. Entirely neglecting JoAnn Robinson and the Women's Political Council, the media catapulted King into national prominence. For the remainder of the civil rights era, newspaper and television editors covered the movement by dispatching almost exclusively male reporters to the South, reporters who erased Baker-style group decision-making and attributed leadership to individual men, especially King (Olson).

Even when King followed SNCC into places where its workers had been organizing for months—most notably Selma, Alabama, in 1965—the press frequently failed to notice that he was trailing SNCC and immediately proclaimed him the head of the Selma campaign for voting rights. Many in SNCC resented the effect of King's scintillating oratory in mesmerizing and monopolizing the news media, which in turn created the widespread, but entirely erroneous impression that all civil rights protestors worked under his direction. Rather than venerate King, some SNCC workers regarded him as an interloper and mocked him as "De Lawd." For her part, Baker observed, "Martin didn't make the movement. The movement made Martin" (qtd. in Garrow, *Bearing* 625).

Granted, during the early 1960s, reporters were wrestling with the complex racial dynamics of an unprecedented, large-scale, nonviolent uprising in the South that almost no one had anticipated. Unfortunately, however, by constructing the movement as a male-led fight for racial justice, the media erased both crucial female figures and the complications of gender within what the press often depicted as a campaign guided by a singular Great Man of History. While women of the civil rights movement were confronting the billy clubs of segregationist police, the possibility of being raped by police or Klansmen, and sexism within and outside the movement, journalists were rendering them invisible.

Any chance the agitating women had of gaining great national attention disappeared following a series of assassinations. Dramatized by the relatively new medium of television, several tragic murders stunned the nation: Medgar Evers, head of the NAACP in Mississippi, killed in 1963; black nationalist Malcolm X gunned down in 1965; and King slain in 1968. Even though the civil rights records of John F. Kennedy and Robert Kennedy were decidedly mixed, their victimage by assassins' bullets, in 1963 and 1968, respectively, also enshrined them as champions of racial equality. An inestimably immense press coverage defined these killings as cataclysmic national traumas, earthquakes fissuring the landscape. Sympathetic to the cause of racial equality, journalists sculpted marble images of the martyred leadership of Evers, King, and the Kennedys, images that were rhetorically unassailable.[2] When the press monumentalized the Kennedys and King, it relegated even other pivotal male leaders of the movement—including Bayard Rustin, A. Philip Randolph,

Robert Moses, Aaron Henry, John Lewis, Fred Shuttlesworth, and James Farmer—to the status of bit players in a highly theatrical, televised drama.[3] The media fixed its images of Evers, Malcolm X, King, and the Kennedys into a frozen tableaux.

A well-known image in this tableaux is 250,000 marchers listening to King unfurl "I Have a Dream" from the steps of the Lincoln Memorial, where Marian Anderson had sung 24 years earlier. National and international television and radio beamed King's speech to millions of listeners, who ranged from starving sharecroppers in Mississippi to Harvard-educated John F. Kennedy in the White House. Like many who had delivered African American jeremiads before him—including Frederick Douglass, Francis Grimke, Ida B. Wells, and Archibald Carey, Jr.—King embraced Lincoln, marshalled astute Biblical quotations, and cited the Declaration of Independence. Like Wells and Carey, he closed by repeating the lyrics of "America" and, like Carey, by expanding those lyrics in his "Let Freedom Ring" conclusion (Vander Lei and Miller).[4] King also echoed rhythms and reimagined grand, yet simple metaphors common to many African American spirituals and gospel lyrics (Miller, "Beacon"). But, as was his custom, he never directly mentioned gender.

In order to teach "I Have a Dream" effectively, teachers should examine its entire context, not simply the verbiage. Faculty need to ask: Why has so little ever been mentioned about the women present at the March on Washington? Why were no women allowed to speak? Why did reporters not notice their absence? Why were the journalists men? Why did women complain or not complain to the news media? Who made the decision that no women would speak? And who, if anyone, should ever have that right?

Teachers should prompt students to examine "I Have a Dream" (and/or "Letter from Birmingham Jail") alongside other important texts that highlight significant gender issues during the heady days of the early 1960s.[5] These include the 1964 Waveland Position Paper by Casey Hayden and Mary King (Carson, Mary King); Anne Moody's now classic autobiography, *Coming of Age in Mississippi;* Hamer's stunning testimony to the Credentials Committee at the 1964 Democratic Convention (Carson, Lewis); and *Deep in Our Hearts,* a recent collection of nine, fairly short autobiographies by Casey Hayden, Emmie Schrader Adams, Connie Curry, and other women who contributed notably to SNCC.

We especially urge teachers to pair "I Have a Dream" with "Sex and Caste: A Kind of Memo from Casey Hayden and Mary King to a Number of Other Women in the Peace and Freedom Movements," which appeared in a 1966 edition of *Liberation,* a magazine for dissidents. This provocative essay calls for egalitarianism within progressive organizations, some of which, unlike Martin Luther King, Jr.'s SCLC, proclaimed themselves member-centered and democratic—principles fostered by Baker. Addressing a subject that few men would admit was problematic, Casey Hayden and Mary King seek to illuminate the sexism that they thought was "straitjacketing" both genders. Highlighting gender discrimination in the Southern freedom struggle, "Sex and Caste" argues (1) that racism rests, in part, on self-serving claims about the erroneously alleged biological basis for the erroneously alleged intellectual differences between one race and another and (2) that sexism rests, in part, on self-serving claims about the erroneously alleged biological basis for the erroneously alleged intellectual differences between men and women. Hayden and Mary King thus strongly imply that racism and sexism intertwine and reinforce each other—a contention quite foreign to King. The authors hope that individuals most appalled by racial inequality would consider gender inequality equally unacceptable.

In contrast to "I Have a Dream," the audience for "Sex and Caste" consisted of other volunteers in the freedom struggle—not the general public. The authors never fantasized that they would be televised. Nurtured by Ella Baker, Casey Hayden and Mary King did not want their essay to move millions or to be authoritative or final. "Sex and Caste" does not allude to any historical figures, reference the Bible, or resort to highly elevated language. One might ask: why bring into the classroom an essay that lacks eloquent phrasing and literary wordsmithing? Why introduce something that is not a sublime monument, but rather a part of a conversation in process, an attempt to provoke "dialogue" within the movement?

Consider the beginning of "I Have a Dream." Standing a few feet in front of Daniel Chester French's gigantic marble sculpture of a brooding Abraham Lincoln, King started his second sentence with the phrase "Five score years ago," an echo of the first line of the Gettysburg Address. He then hailed the Emancipation Proclamation as a "momentous decree that came as a great beacon light of hope" following "a long night of captivity." He warned that, despite Lincoln's magnificent edict, oppression continued: "But one hundred years later the Negro still is not free." This powerful evocation of Lincoln—and portrait of emancipation of a yet-to-be-completed project—frames the entire speech.

Now consider the subtitle of "Sex and Caste." Instead of commencing with a grand, sermonic pronouncement about American history, Casey Hayden and Mary King announce that they are writing not an essay, but what they modestly title a "memo"—rather, not even a "memo" but merely "a kind of memo." Their first paragraph is unimposing:

> We've talked a lot, to each other and to some of you, about our own and other women's problems in trying to live in our personal lives and in our work as independent and creative people. In these conversations we've found what seem to be recurrent ideas or themes. Maybe we can look at these things many of us perceive, often as a result of insights learned from the movement. (1)

Their aim is simply to bring to a larger group the concerns raised in private conversations, not by one or two, but by a number of organizers. Further, they credit not their own genius, but the movement itself—to which all their readers obviously devoted themselves—with fostering insights about race and gender. They finish their first paragraph by saying, "Maybe we can look at these things. . . ." The use of "maybe" qualifies every single statement in the rest of their "kind of memo," masking their assertive ideas in humility and possibly making those ideas more palatable to male readers.

While Casey Hayden and Mary King conclude by suggesting a far-reaching goal—the eradication of racism and sexism in favor of a "new alternative" for race and gender—the patient, gentle tone of their first paragraph is evident throughout their whole essay. Consider the modesty that characterizes their final sentence: ". . . we'd like to see the discussion begin. . . ." The authors' unobtrusive manner contrasts quite starkly with that of "I Have a Dream," which most definitely does not include the word "maybe" or any other self-effacing hedges.

Having heard "I Have a Dream" many times, students often favor it over "Sex and Caste." At least at first. Then, inevitably, someone mentions gender equity. Because students are often uncomfortable with criticizing an American icon, the discussion begins with much trepidation. Eventually they begin to dissect the rhetoric of both the speech and the article, explaining why they like Martin Luther King, Jr.'s rich metaphors, anaphoras, and quotations—and his passion for racial equality—but can also appreciate the inviting informality of Casey Hayden and Mary King. We suggest prodding students to analyze which argument and which approach they find more persuasive and why. Ask: In addressing a massive national audience, does a writer, an orator, or a whole social movement gain a signal advantage by largely focusing on a single evil, such as segregation? Can a nation repeal racism without addressing sexism, as W.E.B. DuBois, Martin Luther King, Jr., and Malcolm X assumed? Or are racism and sexism so tightly interwoven that progressives must target both, as Maria Stewart, Sojourner Truth, Frances E.W. Harper, Pauli Murray, Casey Hayden, and Mary King did? Does discourse need to be high sounding and authoritative to be effective, or should it be openly dialogic instead? Should speakers and writers definitively proclaim "truths" or ask audiences to join them in a search? Should teachers ask each student to produce writing that argues vigorously for a very specific solution to a problem? Or should students kindly invite readers to explore complex dilemmas and possible solutions? When should a writer's tone be insistent and conclusive? When should a writer construct a persona that is well-informed, but unassuming?

In their unobtrusive manner, Casey Hayden and Mary King also protest women's inability to locate a forum for the discussion of sexism: "Nobody is writing, or organizing or talking publicly about women, in any way that reflects the problems that various women in the movement come across and which we've tried to touch above."

Nearly 40 years after this essay was anonymously submitted, our classrooms can become such a forum. As educators we have not only the opportunity to discuss "Sex and Caste" along with "I Have a Dream," but we also have the obligation to tackle issues that "Sex and Caste" introduces. We can foster dialogue by providing classrooms in which students are comfortable discussing the relationship between racism and sexism. This notion goes hand-in-hand with Baker's philosophy about how to run a political organization, a philosophy that can help teachers develop more democratic classroom practices. Sitting alongside students can help teachers foster an atmosphere in which students guide each other as they wrestle with assertive and unimposing forms of argumentation.

When we teach "I Have a Dream" without mentioning gender, we further reinforce and extend the media erasure of feminist issues within the civil rights community of the early and middle 1960s. Presenting "Sex and Caste" alongside "I Have a Dream," on the other hand, means beckoning students to complicate and interrogate "I Have a Dream" and to find a usable past in 1960s politics beyond the press-defined memories of national trauma occasioned by the assassinations of highly visible, nonfeminist male leaders. Casey Hayden and Mary King longed for a site where race and gender could be openly discussed; as educators we have not only the opportunity but also the obligation to create such a forum.

In an attempt to recover and reassert the many, long-neglected heroes of the African American freedom struggle, educators need to look beyond shopworn interpretations of "I Have a Dream" and beyond familiar images of national trauma associated with male martyrs. Once students become acquainted with women like Pauli Murray, Fannie Lou Hamer, Ella Baker, Casey Hayden, and Mary King, they will develop a greater understanding of the complex relationship between race and gender. Teaching the movements toward racial equality and women's equality as inextricably related will help students comprehend and value these intertwining phenomena.

NOTES

1. Dorothy Cotton, who was for some time the highest-ranking woman in SCLC, also observed the male chauvinism of King and other SCLC leaders. See Cotton.

2. For a selection of the best journalism of the movement for racial justice, see Carson et al.

3. For Rustin, see Levine. For Randolph, see Pfeffer. For Farmer, see his autobiography. For Shuttlesworth, see Manis and McWhorter. For Moses, see Payne.

4. At her renowned concert of 1939, Marian Anderson sang "America" ("My country 'tis of thee'"). She also performed at the March on Washington. See Miller and Lewis.

5. For perspectives on "Letter," see Bass; McWhorter; Manis; and Miller, *Voice*. Bass argues that King caricatured the clergy to whom he addressed "Letter," agglomerating them into a single straw figure.

WORKS CITED

Adams, Emmie Schrader. "From Africa to Mississippi." *Deep in Our Hearts*. 289–332.

Bass, S. Jonathan. *Blessed Are the Peacemakers: Martin Luther King, Jr., Eight White Religious Leaders, and the "Letter from Birmingham Jail."* Baton Rouge: Louisiana UP, 2001.

Bates, Daisy. *The Long Shadow of Little Rock*. Fayetteville: U of Arkansas P, 1987.

Branch, Taylor. *Parting the Waters: America in the King Years, 1954–1963*. New York: Simon and Schuster, 1988.

———. *Pillar of Fire: America in the King Years, 1963–1965*. New York: Simon and Schuster, 1998.

Cagin, Seth and Philip Dray. *We Are Not Afraid: The Story of Goodman, Schwerner, and Chaney in Mississippi*. 1988. New York: Bantam, 1988.

Carson, Clayborne. *In Struggle: SNCC and the Black Awakening of the 1960s*. Cambridge: Harvard UP, 1981.

Carson, Clayborne, et al., consulting eds. *Reporting Civil Rights*. New York: Library of America, 2003.

Clark, Septima. *Ready from Within*. Ed. Cynthia Stokes Brown. Navarro, CA: Wild Trees, 1986.

Cotton, Dorothy. "Dorothy Cotton." *My Soul Is Rested: Movement Days in the Deep South Remembered*. Ed. Howell Raines. New York: Penguin, 1977. 432–434.

Deep in Our Hearts: Nine White Women in the Freedom Movement. Athens: U of Georgia P, 2000.

Evans, Sara. *Personal Politics: The Roots of Women's Liberation in the Civil Rights Movement and the New Left*. New York: Vintage, 1980.

Fairclough, Adam. "The Civil Rights Movement in Louisiana, 1939–54." The Making of Martin Luther King, Jr., and the Civil Rights Movement. Ed. Brian Ward and Tony Badger. New York: MacMillan, 1996. 15–28.

———. *Race and Democracy: The Civil Rights Struggle in Louisiana*. Athens: U of Georgia P, 1995.

Farmer, James. *Lay Bare the Heart: An Autobiography of the Civil Rights Movement*. New York: Arbor, 1985.

Fleming, Cynthia. *Soon We Will Not Cry: The Liberation of Ruby Doris Smith Robinson*. Lanham, MD: Rowan and Littlefield, 1998.

Garrow, David. *Bearing the Cross: Martin Luther King, Jr., and the Southern Christian Leadership Conference*. New York: Morrow, 1986.

———. *Protest at Selma: Martin Luther King, Jr., and the Voting Rights Act of 1965*. New Haven: Yale UP, 1978.

Grant, Joanne. *Ella Baker: Freedom Bound*. New York: Wiley, 1998.

Hayden, Casey. "Fields of Blue." *Deep in Our Hearts*. 333–375.

Hayden, Casey, et al. "Sex and Caste: A Kind of Memo from Casey Hayden and Mary King to a Number of Other Women in the Peace and Freedom Movements." *Liberation* 1965. Rpt. in *www.cwluherstory.com/CWLUArchive/memo.html*.

King, Mary. *Freedom Song: A Personal Story of the 1960s Civil Rights Movement*. New York: Morrow, 1987.

King, Martin Luther, Jr. "I Have a Dream." *Testament of Hope: The Essential Writings of Martin Luther King, Jr.* Ed. James Washington. New York: Harper, 1986. 217–220.

———. "Letter from Birmingham Jail." *Why We Can't Wait*. New York: Harper, 1964.

Lee, Chana Kai. *For Freedom's Sake: The Life of Fannie Lou Hamer*. Urbana: U of Illinois P, 1999.

Levine, Daniel. *Bayard Rustin and the Civil Rights Movement*. New Brunswick, NJ: Rutgers UP, 2000.

Lewis, John. *Walking with the Wind*. New York: Harcourt, 1998.

Manis, Andrew. *A Fire You Can't Put Out: The Civil Rights Life of Birmingham's Fred Shuttlesworth*. Tuscaloosa: U of Alabama P, 1999.

Marsh, Charles. *God's Long Summer: Studies in Faith and Civil Rights*. Princeton, NJ: Princeton UP, 1997.

McAdam, Doug. *Freedom Summer*. New York: Oxford, 1988.

McWhorter, Diane. *Carry Me Home: Birmingham, Alabama: The Climactic Battle of the Civil Rights Revolution*. New York: Simon and Schuster, 2001.

Miller, Keith D. "Beacon Light and Penumbra: African American Gospel Lyrics and Martin Luther King, Jr.'s 'I Have a Dream.'" *The Role of Ideas in the Civil Rights South*. Ed. Ted Ownby. Oxford: U of Mississippi P, 2002. 55–68.

Miller, Keith D. *Voice of Deliverance: The Language of Martin Luther King, Jr., and Its Sources*. Second edition. Athens: U of Georgia P, 1998.

Miller, Keith D. and Emily Lewis. "Touchstones, Authorities, and Marian Anderson: The Making of 'I Have a Dream.'" *The Making of Martin Luther King and the Civil Rights Movement*. Ed. Brian Ward and Tony Badger. New York: Macmillan, 1996. 147–161.

Moody, Anne. *Coming of Age in Mississippi*. 1968. New York: Dell, 1976.

Olson, Lynne. *Freedom's Daughters: The Unsung Heroines of the Civil Rights Movement from 1830 to 1970*. New York: Scribner's, 2001.

Payne, Charles. *I've Got the Light of Freedom: The Organizing Tradition and the Mississippi Freedom Struggle*. Berkeley: U of California P, 1995.

Pfeffer, Paula. *A. Philip Randolph, Pioneer of the Civil Rights Movement*. Baton Rouge: Louisiana State UP, 1990.

Ransby, Barbara. *Ella Baker and the Black Freedom Movement*. Chapel Hill: UNC P, 2003.

Reed, Linda. "Fannie Lou Hamer: New Ideas for the Civil Rights Movement and American Democracy." *The Role of Ideas in the Civil Rights South*. Ed. Ted Ownby. Oxford: U of Mississippi P, 2002.

Robinson, JoAnn. *The Montgomery Bus Boycott and the Women Who Started It*. Ed. David Garrow. Knoxville: U of Tennessee P, 1987.

Sandage, Scott. "A Marble House Divided: The Lincoln Memorial, 1939–1963." *Journal of American History*, 80 (1993), 135–167.

Vander Lei, Elizabeth and Keith D. Miller. "Martin Luther King, Jr.'s 'I Have a Dream' in Context: Ceremonial Protest and African American Jeremiad." *College English* 62 (September 1999): 83–99.

Writing Textbooks in/for Times of Trauma

Lynn Z. Bloom

About suffering they were never wrong.
The Old Masters: how well they understood
Its human position; how it takes place
While someone else is eating or opening a window
or
    just walking dully along . . .
          —W. H. Auden, "Museé des Beaux Arts"

Anything can happen, the tallest things

Be overturned, those in high places daunted,
Those overlooked esteemed. Hooked-beak Fortune
Swoops, making the air gasp, tearing off
Crests for sport, letting them drop wherever.

Ground gives. The heaven's weight
Lifts up off Atlas like a kettle lid,
Capstones shift, nothing resettles right.
Telluric ash and fire-spores darken day.
          —Seamus Haney, "Horace and Thunder"
          (After Horace, Odes, 1, 34)

    —Jan. 18, 2002 *Times Literary Supplement*

SEPTEMBER 11, 2001:
WHERE WERE YOU, WHERE WERE WE?

SEPTEMBER 11, 2001, dawned, indeed like most of this most unusual autumn in New England, postcard perfect—a bright blue sky, with just a hint of briskness in the air. And there we were, dawdling over breakfast, windows open to the herb garden, savoring the day and the promise of a new year. For early September is always New Year's for academics, with the year to come shimmering on a bright canvas that we paint full of resolutions, plans, lists, and schedules—just an ordinary day when, as on every day, we were trying to impose order on our unruly corner of the universe. Yet as on every other day, this was a day to savor—just because it was there, and we were there to share it, and because it was my husband's birthday.

Then we heard the news. Then we heard the news again. And again, and again, for days that stretched into weeks and now into months, that day of days transformed in the twinkling of an eye to an unwitting watershed. The world was one way before September 11 and changed utterly thereafter. Only after the fact do I realize that the impressionistic watercolor of the Manhattan waterfront facing our bed, that I have looked at every morning for the past 25 years on first opening my eyes, is curiously up-to-date, though painted in 1955. Tall buildings, bright sugar cubes of reds and blues and whites provide a cityscape of blocks firm, but curiously fragile—as if you could pull out one from the bottom of the stack and they would all fall down. No twin towers. It is only as I write this essay that the publication date of "Musée des Beaux Arts" strikes home: 1940, during the bombing of Britain, by a poet who had written passionate witness to the Spanish Civil War and the beginnings of World War II in the Far East. Auden was no stranger to the suffering that takes place on an ordinary day, and now, neither were we—nor anyone else in the world. These personal reactions to "Where were you when. . . ." "What did you think at the time?" "What do you understand now?" invite dialogue, reflection, writing for oneself or an audience—as Heaney's "Horace and Thunder" reflects both. But whether private or public, these are in no way the last word. For 2001 was a year like no other, and though over a year has passed, that year is not over, and it may never be over. There is, to date, no termination, no closure.

We tell ourselves stories of cataclysmic events such as these to make sense of things that don't make sense, to bring order from chaos. Moreover, as Joan Didion says, "We tell ourselves stories in order to live." As time passes we are still trying to figure out what stories to tell, for the narratives of this fateful day and its anthrax-laced aftermath remain stories-in-progress, stories with complicated beginnings, muddled middles, and ambiguous trails that are not really endings seen through a glass dark with the rain of smoke and ash from the towers aflame in our imaginations, or smoldering still. These stories and the stories behind—and ahead—of them are the stories that I soon realized *The Essay Connection* my textbook-in-progress—would have to invite readers to tell, understand, and interpret, even as they continue to emerge and undergo continual revision, their meanings in flux.

TRANSFORMING A TEXTBOOK FOR A TRANSFORMED WORLD

I had been revising a textbook, seventh edition of *The Essay Connection*. "Shorten it a little," said my editor at Houghton Mifflin, in a desire to return the book, which had bulked up over time, to its earlier svelte shape. So I eliminated three chapters, and thought I was about through. That was before the Towers collapsed. Within the week, I realized that in a changed world, a collection of readings intended to stimulate students' reasoned discussion and critical thinking and writing had to respond to this cataclysmic event. As Elie Wiesel explains in "Why I Write" (included in all editions of *The Essay Connection* since its publication in 1988) his reasons for witnessing the Holocaust in everything he writes, "Not to transmit an experience is to betray it." I write, he says, "to help the dead vanquish death." I could ask the student readers of *The Essay Connection* to do no less—not because of morbid reasons, or a sentimental desire to memorialize a past that will never come again, but as an ethical response to a world they did not ask for but will nevertheless have to live in.

Although I knew I would be including readings on international terrorism suitable for use as a brief argumentative casebook, I realized it would be too soon to prepare the new chapter. I didn't want to assemble an instant book of knee-jerk reactions, written in the white heat of personal assault and national injury. It would take time for thoughtful commentary to appear, grounded in profound knowledge of Middle Eastern history, Islamic culture and religion, and international politics. Fortunately, I'd begun the revision a year in advance and had time to let the fallout settle—national as well as personal.

(Lack of) Knowledge

I also had time to learn more about what I was getting into—and to get scared, both by the subject and the extent of my ignorance. I was born, raised, and educated in the United States, where I have worked all my adult life as an English professor and writer, specializing in American literature and composition studies, focusing on American higher education. Although my research in creative nonfiction, essays, and American autobiography includes works by many ethnic groups from a range of cultural backgrounds, little of it is Islamic. When I write and teach in these genres I am comfortable, with the cushion of forty years' professional experience buttressed by a native's intimate lifetime knowledge of the language and cultural experience. I know what I know, and when I don't know something I know where to look for it and how to evaluate its intrinsic worth, integrity, and intellectual resonance. I know, almost intuitively by now, the canon, literary conventions, and the range of possibilities for breaking the mold in ways creative rather than simply weird.

Very little of this knowledge applies in direct ways to my new attempts to understand the world of Islam. I cannot claim expertise as a political scientist. My heritage is Christian; my husband's, Jewish. Although we have traveled extensively—including trips to Asia and the Middle East—and have friends from all over the world who have emigrated to the United States, my knowledge of the Islamic world's culture, religion(s), history, politics is—at its most euphemistic—superficial. How, then, could I even contemplate compiling a set of well-informed, accurate, up-to-date representative readings on the subject? How, as a textbook editor, could I know—or learn—enough to make the difficult, intelligent choices of materials and aids to reading and writing about them that would be crucial to such a chapter?

Ethical and Intellectual Responsibilities

In the moral universe of the academy, however, having had the right—and good—idea to devote significant space in the new *Essay Connection* to a discussion of the implications of world terrorism how could I *not* include this? No one expects moral issues to be easy, or understanding to be either immediate or complete. If we taught only what we know for sure, taking no risks and making no intellectual leaps or creative reaching for the stars, our classes would be static and stifling. Taking heart from Emerson's observation that "Knowledge is the knowing that we cannot know," I had no choice but to soldier on. My operative motto would be Thurber's observation that "It is better to ask some of the questions than to know all the answers"—and I would not mean it ironically, as he did in *Fables for Our Time*. Isn't this the attitude that enables all experienced teachers—and writers and textbook editors—to get through every bit of new work we do? It isn't chutzpah; it's hope that leads us to tackle totally unfamiliar subjects, I reasoned (well, maybe a little chutzpah)—but in a world so totally changed by cataclysm we have no choice but to plunge in and aim to keep our heads above water.

Nevertheless, I knew that to find suitable materials on international terrorism to use as a significant portion of a textbook I'd have to learn a lot, and fast. I'd have to admit—first to myself—the vast lacunae in my understanding of the subject, then figure out what I most needed to know, find reliable sources—expert, up-to-date, reinforced by a depth of background information. Because all sources emanate from the author's particular perspective on a particular culture, I'd also have to find representative authors whose biases offset one another. To do this I'd have to depend on the research skills I'd used—and sharpened—over the years, especially since the advent of the information explosion over the Internet. I'd also need some sense of where my prospective readers were coming from. What did the teachers and their first-year composition students know, think, and care about international terrorism? And in what ways did I want my readings to influence these readers? In the absence of material—which was probably not yet written—these specific questions were not easy to answer.

Generic Criteria for Selecting Material

However, because the generic considerations of selecting material remained consonant over any number of editions, I could use the following general guidelines in choosing the readings. The book's format dictated that I include four published essays by experts, preferably written with distinction, and a student essay, ditto. So vast and complicated was the topic, however, that I decided to expand the number. The material had to be teachable—that is, each piece had to be short enough to be discussed in one or two class sessions. It had to be self-contained, with sufficient information and background material to be understood by American teachers and students who, I assumed, would not be experts on the subject any more than I was. The fact that I was approaching the subject in relative innocence would enable me to see it as new students might, and serve as a reminder to address their concerns: what would they need to know and when would they need to know it?

Would there be students in class, or teachers, perhaps of Islamic background, whose background knowledge could be drawn on to help the others? Even though the topic was current, its contours changing with every day's developing news, the essays could not be so time-bound that they would become quickly out of date. How well would these essays lend themselves to the book's rhetorical concerns of critical thinking and thoughtful argumentation? Together, if not individually, would they contribute to a balanced argument, reflect and refract upon one another with illumination and intellectual integrity rather than with fusillades and fulminations? Or should these even be expected to provide a cultural balance, given the Western values and culture of myself and most of my readers?

CONTROVERSY IN CONTEXT: IMPLICATIONS OF WORLD TERRORISM AND WORLD PEACE, AN ARGUMENT CASEBOOK

Thematic Criteria for Selecting Material

I also knew even before the flood of materials on international terrorism reached the publications from which I draw most of the essays for *The Essay*

Connection—such as *Atlantic Monthly, Harper's, The New York Times Magazine,* and the *New Yorker*—some of the themes and values I wanted the discussion to incorporate. These included:

Definitions of war. The unconventional nature of the terroristic activities—the use of passenger planes as guided missiles—and the identification of these with a leader and a political-religious movement rather than with a country require rethinking—and redefining—the conventional concepts of war. By inference, new definitions of war would also entail new definitions of peace.

New language for new concepts. If the current political situation as the book goes to press isn't war, what is it? What should we call it? Whom—or what—do we call "the enemy"? allies? Is it appropriate to use such vague and general terms as "the forces of evil" to represent our antagonists? all antagonists?

Avoidance of polarizing language and attitudes. I did not want to encourage an "us vs. them" orientation to the subject, even though I would expect most teachers and students to share my own patriotic sentiments. Nor did I want to encourage racial profiling or other forms of racial, cultural, or ethnic stereotyping.

Consideration of ethical issues. All of the above concepts embed an ethical stance toward the issues embedded in the conflict, and the recognition that not all teachers or students would share these values. I wanted student readers to balance patriotism with humanitarianism, to balance the need for national security with respect for individuals' civil liberties, to weigh issues of security against issues of freedom. Even if their conclusions differed from the idealistic stance I hoped they'd take, these issues could not be ignored—proof positive that intellectual risk and controversy are possible in a free society.

Concerns for the future. I hoped the readings on terrorism would provide an abundance of issues and perspectives for students to discuss, argue over, and write about, and write again. I wanted them to emerge wiser but not sadder, thoughtful but not angry, and—rather than to expect to live forever under terrorist threats—and to be full of hope for a peaceful future. But would hopes for peace emerge from the literature on terrorism? Who could know?

READINGS ON INTERNATIONAL TERRORISM[1]

I waited as long as possible, until just before the manuscript went to the publisher in June 2002, to select the readings from a vast number that had accumulated since September 11—and then I revised it again in October when I was reading the copyedited manuscript. In contrast to the rest of the book, which consists entirely of essays, I decided to introduce the chapter with a poem written explicitly to commemorate the events of that fateful day—musing, meditative, inconclusive, Seamus Heaney's "Horace and Thunder"—a portion of which serves as an epigraph to this essay.

Six essays and a book chapter swam to the surface of this complex sea of print, from books on terrorism; Middle Eastern history, culture, and politics; editorial and op-ed pieces; magazine and online articles, long and short, highly specialized and somewhat simpler. I analyze below the pieces I have decided to use as of this writing, with one caveat. As my article goes to press, the Social Science Research Council will publish two companion volumes, *Understanding September 11,* and *Critical Views of September 11: Analyses from Around the World,* by international experts from a variety of disciplines. This will be the first American collection of diverse international scholarship to appear specifically on the topic of September 11, with all chapters specially commissioned after 9/11 to address such topics as "Islamic Radicalism," "Globalization," "New War/World Order?," "Terrorism and Democratic Virtues," and "The Intersection of Religion and Politics." Judging from the excellent materials on their website, *www.ssrc.org/sept11/toc11a.htm,* if an irresistible article or two appears, accessible to readers of *The Essay Connection,* I will push Houghton Mifflin to expand the book, once again. Never have I edited a book subject to such major revision right up to the publication date, but a new world requires adaptation.

I describe the current contents below as the beginning of a dialogue that students and teachers are invited to join, bringing to this colloquy other voices, from sources printed, online, and other media that continue the conversation and debate beyond the boundaries of this book. It would be tempting, as many writers and media commentators have done, to divide the world into "us"—the innocent, beleaguered victims of a horrific attack, and "them," the vile denizens of an evil empire who hate us all and will stop at nothing to destroy our free society, as Don DeLillo does in "In the Ruins of the Future," *Harper's* 2002. This is not a good way to conduct any argument, although this kind of thinking is often the basis for initiating and conducting a war, emanating from the halls of Congress, the Oval Office, branches of the military, with reverberations throughout the press and television, domestic and international.

Because the us vs. them view is so popular, it cannot be overlooked. Nevertheless, as the immediate impact of the events is somewhat mitigated by time, we realize that this is not the only perspective and that war is not the only alternative. Even if we can't change the past, or prevent the World Trade Center's destruction, we can interpret the present in ways that we hope will prepare for the future. Thus the essay opens with reflections by a New Yorker. In an eyewitness commentary on her experience of living ten blocks from "what used to be the World Trade Center towers," Laurie Fendrich, a painter and fine arts professor, writes a counter-narrative to combat media overkill, to interpret stories that "are polluted and demeaned by having been reduced to fodder for television, movie, and slick magazine entertainment." She looks, as people do in times of trauma, for guidance "to see if we can now act the way we ought to have been acting all along," and finds focus and stability in a reaffirmation of the core values of Western culture," which trendy postmodern theory has undervalued: "individual liberty, coupled with obligations to virtue, democracy coupled with responsibility, the requirement of courage, an acknowledgment—always tempered by reason—of duty, and an assertion of basic, not jingoistic, patriotism."

Those who examine the causes of international terrorism, as does Bernard Lewis ("What Went Wrong?" *Atlantic Monthly* Jan. 2002), are aware that there is no single interpretation and that all explanations are controversial. Even for those who concede the truth of Lewis's first premise, that by the twentieth century "Compared with Christendom, its rival for more than a millennium, the world of Islam had become poor, weak and ignorant," the reasons for this decline are in dispute. Because "it is usually easier and always more satisfying to blame others for one's misfortunes," Lewis claims that the Middle East could blame the thirteenth century Mongol invasions "for the destruction of both Muslim power and Islamic civilization"; the Arabs, Turks, and Persians could blame each other for "their loss of ancient glories," and the British and French for nineteenth-century depredations. Current scapegoats include America, and "the Jews." Self-blame includes attacks on Islam in general, or on fanatics, or "the relegation of women to an inferior position in Muslim society," thereby depriving "the Islamic world of the talents and energies of half its people." Because "Who did this to us?" leads only to "neurotic fantasies and conspiracy theories," concludes Lewis, the question "What did we do wrong?" leads naturally to the search for a solution. This is difficult because the condition of liberty in the Middle East is fragile and full of complications. Lewis's answer, that the peoples of the Middle East should establish a society where people have the freedom "to question and inquire and speak; freedom of the economy from corrupt and pervasive mismanagement; freedom of women from male oppression; freedom of citizens from tyranny," makes explicit the beliefs and values that undergird Fendrich's interpretation of the subject, as well.

However, "Why can't our antagonists be more like us?" is not the only way to look at the issue; critics such as Palestinian scholar Edward Said (not in *The Essay Connection*) strongly object to such solutions, which they interpret as the efforts of Westerners attempting to dominate an Eastern culture. "Theater of Terror" and "America as Enemy," excerpts *from Terror in the Mind of God* (University of California Press, 2000) present Mark Juregensmeyer's analysis of the "exaggerated violence" of terrorist attacks such as the 1993 World Trade Center bombing, eerily prescient of its 2001 successor. He explains them as "constructed events: they are mind-numbing, mesmerizing theater. At center stage are the acts themselves—stunning, abnormal, and out-rageous murders carried out in a way that graphically displays the awful power of violence—set within grand scenarios of conflict and proclamation." Such horrifically violent acts, "surpassing the wounds inflicted during warfare" because of their demonstrative "secondary impact . . . elicit feelings of revul-sion and anger in those who witness them." Indeed, claims Juergensmeyer, "terrorism is always part of a political strategy," performed not only to "fulfill political ends" but also to "have a direct impact on public policy."

"Thoughts in the Presence of Fear," by poet, essayist, and farmer Wendell Berry, offers 27 reflections on the aftermath of "the horrors of September 11," critically addressing the implications of the end of "the unquestioning tech-nological and economic optimism that ended on that day." In one stroke, he says, these terroristic activities should cause the "developed" nations to ques-tion—and revise—their policies that "had given to the 'free market' the status of a god," and sacrificed to it "their farmers, farmlands, and communities, their forests, wetlands, and prairies, their ecosystems and watersheds. They had accepted universal pollution and global warming as normal costs of doing business." In his commentary, each paragraph of which could be the basis for a policy statement, an argument, an essay, even a book, he thoughtfully explains why these values are wrong and makes the case for a peaceable, self-sufficient economy, based on "thrift and care, on saving and conserving, not on excess and waste." Berry's tone and language, though moderate, his agrarian, pacifistic, Christian views are bound to anger those who prefer swords to ploughshares as a means of settling international conflicts.

The possible solutions to dealing with terroristic acts, ranging from all-out war to racial profiling to severe restraints on the freedoms of speech, the press, assembly, worship, and travel—among others—are equally problematic. How are we, as individuals and a nation, to balance individual needs against the requirements of national security in a world that is never static but always in motion? In "The Information Wars," policy analyst Mary Graham identi-fies a number of the ways in which federal and state governments have, swiftly and silently, restricted public access to information since 9/11. For instance, the Environmental Protection Agency "withdrew from its website informa-tion about accidents, risks, and emergency plans at factories that handle dan-gerous chemicals." The U.S. Geological Survey "removed reports on water resources and asked libraries to destroy all copies of a CD-ROM that described the characteristics of reservoirs." Graham concludes that in the nominal interest of "national security," "temporary emergency actions have evolved into fundamental changes in the public's right to know," and that these restrictions are politically driven. They are a threat, she contends, not only to civil liberties but also to the health and welfare of everyone living in the United States. In support of Graham's view, in "The Futility of Homeland

Defense"(*Atlantic Monthly* Jan. 2002) David Carr contends that ours is "a big society designed to be open"—to commerce (two billion tons in 1999), mail (the U.S. Postal Service processes 680 million pieces of mail per day), immigrants and foreign visitors (some 350 million in 2000 alone)—and thus it is impossible to close. Homeland security may operate in limited venues, such as airports and the testing of postal workers for biological agents. But because "America will continue to be a place of tremendous economic dynamism and openness," our culture cannot be re-engineered to make it less porous: "The very small percentage of unwanted people and substances that arrive with all the people and things we do want is part of the cost of being America, Inc."

Terrorism has even hijacked the language used by millions of peaceful people. Susan Sontag's op-ed commentary in *The New York Times,* published on September 10, 2002, a year after the terrorist attacks, addresses the issue of "WAR? Real Battles and Empty Metaphors." Here Sontag, in contrast to her incendiary diatribe in *The New Yorker* immediately after the attack,[2] explores various meanings of war, as a figurative concept and as a literal activity—the language accompanying the politics as the United States "declares a war on terrorism . . . a multinational, largely clandestine network" of ill-defined, shadowy enemies." Sontag does not question "that we have a vicious, abhorrent enemy that opposes most of what I cherish—including democracy, pluralism, secularism, the equality of the sexes . . . and, well, fun," or "the obligation of the American government to protect the lives of its citizens." But she does question "the pseudo-declaration of pseudo-war" and the "dangerous, lobotomizing notion of endless war."

READINGS ON WORLD PEACE: NOBEL PRIZE SPEECHES

The Need for Peace—A Necessary Conclusion

My textbooks reflect my philosophy of life; I want students to be inspired by what they read, and not depressed or discouraged. I did not want students to regard the future with a mixture of terror, hopelessness, or resignation to a future of fear. Moreover, given the pro-Western bias of the terrorism materials, I had to locate writings that would reflect a world view. In an uncertain future, what could realistically ensure that *The Essay Connection* would end on a positive note?

As I pondered whether to include in the terrorism chapter—already too long—a section of Nelson Mandela's autobiography, *Long Walk to Freedom,* an inspiring account of his 25 years in harsh South African prisons as anti-Apartheid head of the African National Congress, and the enormous changes his moral example wrought, Kofi Annan was awarded the 2001 Nobel Peace Prize. He shared it jointly with the United Nations, on whose behalf he accepted the award, three months after the terrorist attacks on the World Trade Center and the Pentagon. As I read the stirring words of his acceptance speech, the solution became clear: I would include a chapter of Nobel Peace Prize speeches. Here is the way he began:

> Today, in Afghanistan, a girl will be born. Her mother will hold her and feed her, comfort her and care for her—just as any mother would anywhere in the world. In these most basic acts of human nature, humanity knows no divisions. But to be born a girl in today's Afghanistan is to begin life centuries away from the prosperity that one small part of humanity has achieved. It is to live under conditions that many of us in this hall would consider inhuman.
>
> I speak of a girl in Afghanistan, but I might equally well have mentioned a baby boy or girl in Sierra Leone. No one today is unaware of this divide between the world's rich and poor. No one today can claim ignorance of the cost that this divide imposes on the poor and dispossessed who are no less deserving of human dignity, fundamental freedoms, security, food and education than any of us. The cost, however, is not borne by them alone. Ultimately, it is borne by all of us—North and south, rich and poor, men and women of all races and religions.
>
> Today's real borders are not between nations, but between powerful and powerless, free and fettered, privileged and humiliated. Today, no walls can separate humanitarian or human rights crises in one part of the world from national security crises in another.

Fortunately, while the manuscript was being copyedited, Jimmy Carter was awarded the 2002 Nobel Peace Prize. On December 10 he will deliver the address; on December 11 we will receive the text from the Nobel website and add this to the book, just as it goes to the printer.

Indeed, the Nobel website, *www.nobel.se/peace/laureates,* had the texts of all the acceptance speeches I needed. Speech after speech reflected the fact that goodness, selflessness, adherence to high moral principles, as the lives and works of the Nobel Prize winners reveal, can emerge even in times of trauma—often, in responses to the challenges of trauma itself. Their talks, like their works, offered beacons of faith, hope, and good will. If, as Franklin Roosevelt said, "the only thing we have to fear is fear itself," a chapter of Nobel Peace Prize speeches would reinforce a value system that would help the audience to lead lives governed by principles and values that brought out the best rather than the worst of our common humanity. This was the message, implied and stated overtly, by every one of the Nobel Prize winners I decided to include.

As I wrote in the chapter introduction, "these Nobel winners form an international spectrum of the brave, the bold, the morally beautiful. Some of these Nobelists are people of high visibility and power—United Nations Secretary General Kofi Annan (Egypt); and national leaders Jimmy Carter (United States) Yitzak Rabin (Israel) (in fairness, I would also include his controversial opponent Yasser Arafat who shared the Peace Prize with Rabin and Shimon Peres in 1994) and Frederik Willem de Klerk (South Africa). Others are religious and political leaders who have suffered extensive privations for living their beliefs: the 14th Dalai Lama (Tibet), sentenced by the Chinese to lifetime exile as the embodiment of the Tibetan Buddhists; Nelson Mandela (South Africa); and Aung San Suu Kyi (Myanmar), Burmese pro-democracy leader confined by the military junta to house arrest for nearly eight years and thereby separated from her family (her husband died in England, forbidden to join her) even while she served as an international symbol of resistance to tyranny. Still others are people of humble origins whose advocacy of human rights and reconciliation catapulted them into international prominence—housewife turned peace activist, Betty Williams (Northern Ireland); and Guatemalan champion of Mayan rights and culture, Rigoberta Menchù. Activist humanitarian organizations are represented by Doctors Without Borders (Médecins Sans Frontières), whose members risk their own lives to travel to embattled parts of the world, providing medical aid to victims of genocide, massacre, rape, and other war crimes. "Ours is an ethic of refusal," explains James Orbinski. 'It will not allow any moral political failure or injustice to be sanitized or cleansed of its meaning.'"

All of these Nobel recipients, and others, like Martin Luther King, Jr. (whose "Letter from Birmingham Jail" is a canonical staple of *The Essay Connection*), are "'witnesses to the truth of injustice,' as Orbinski says, willing to lay their lives on the line—and to lose them, as Rabin and Dr. King have done—for a moral cause. Like their lives, their words in these inspiring speeches, can guide us to some answers. How we as individuals, family members, friends, and citizens can do our best not only to lead the good life but to make that life better for humankind is one of the aims of a liberal education and of this book."

IN CONCLUSION, THE INCONCLUSIVE . . .

I've concluded *The Essay Connection* with the following admonition, inevitable but necessary: Each of the issues embedded in this topic "is complicated, for matters of war and peace are never simple, never static, particularly when negotiated in an international arena. Most can be seen not just from two points of view, but from many perspectives embedded in the political, economic, religious, ethical, and cultural values of a great variety of individuals, cultures, and countries. In discussing any topics related to the subject you will need to consult additional, current sources, for you will be aiming to write papers informed by accurate information, terms clearly defined, that avoid blanket generalizations and simplistic conclusions."

To provide teaching material on the shifting sands of international politics involves, as we have seen, a leap of faith, a commitment to open-mindedness, and an abundance of good will—not just from the editor, but from the teachers who decide to teach the chapters on international terrorism and world peace, and from their students. I don't worry about the pieces becoming dated. These subjects, as our elected officials and the media remind us daily, are always with us. Even if the specific details change—and they will— the topics themselves are perennial; a publisher's website can point to supplements. I do worry that these chapters might be overlooked, whether from teachers' reluctance to tackle vast subjects represented in the small compass textbooks dictate, from fear of engaging in potentially incendiary subjects (but what subject of worth doesn't embed controversy?), or for other reasons. Novelty should never be a problem for textbook editors, but it always is, as I have argued in "The Essay Canon," because teachers tend to teach what they've taught before, and even if new material is extraordinarily appealing—or, in the case of the terrorism and peace chapters new, highly appealing *and* morally compelling—there is no way to force teachers to use it. Nevertheless, as a teacher and as a textbook editor, in addition to presenting these new chapters from sound intellectual, ethical, and pedagogical reasons, I have to proffer them as my form of witness to the events of September 11, 2001. As this essay goes to press there is no closure on the events of that fateful day; none of us is an island, as John Donne said, "entire of itself alone"; all of us affected by issues of international terrorism and peace (is there anyone in the world who is immune?) are interconnected in concern, remembrance, and suffering— general and personal.

"About suffering they were never wrong, / The Old Masters." While others were "eating or opening a window or just walking dully along," at 8:30 on that fateful morning our daughter-in-law Vicki was aboard a United flight destined for Los Angeles but stuck on the runway at JFK. As the plane finally began a slow taxiing out, around 9:00, it was ordered to stop, and five passengers in first class, growing ever more agitated, exploded at the flight attendant, "We must take off! We can tolerate no more delay!" They continued their cacophony, and when the plane finally returned to the gate, this quintet—yes, terrorists, said the F.B.I. in the investigation that followed— fled as soon as the doors were opened. "Anything," indeed, could "happen, the tallest things / Be overturned. . . . Capstones [could] shift, nothing resettle right." That it took Vicki two days to return home through traumatized roadways to our son Bard in Westchester is a happy anti-climax. Yet her experience is a vivid reminder that there are no guarantees that the rest of the lives of any of us, anywhere in the world, will be happily anti-climactic; our stories continue, under incessant revision. The perspectives offered in these chapters can help guard against personal solipsism, national narcissism, as we tell, revise, and continue to reinterpret the stories not only of those fateful days but of the days passing and to come.

NOTES

1. Some of the material in MSP 5–9 is adapted from my Introductions to Chapters 14 and 15 of *The Essay Connection*, 7th ed.

2. "The disconnect between last Tuesday's monstrous dose of reality and the self-righteous drivel and outright deceptions being peddled by public figures and television commentators is startling, depressing. The voices licensed to follow the event seem to have joined together in a campaign to infantilize the public. Where is the acknowledgment that this was not a 'cowardly' attack on 'civilization' or 'liberty' or 'humanity' or 'the free world' but an attack on the world's self-proclaimed superpower, undertaken as a consequence of specific American alliances and actions? How many citizens are aware of the ongoing American bombing of Iraq? And if the word 'cowardly' is to be used, it might be more aptly applied to those who kill from beyond the range of retaliation, high in the sky, than those willing to die themselves in order to kill others. In the matter of courage (a morally neutral virtue): whatever may be said of the perpetrators of Tuesday's slaughter, they were not cowards" (*The New Yorker*, 24 Sept., 2001).

WORKS CITED

Bloom, Lynn Z. "The Essay Canon." *College English* 61.4 (March 1999): 401–430.

Bloom, Lynn Z., ed. *The Essay Connection: Readings for Writers*. 7th ed. Boston: Houghton Mifflin, 2004.

Nobel Peace Prize website: <*www.nobel.se/peace/laureates*> Jan. 2003.

Social Science Research Council website: <*http://www.ssrc.org/sept11/toc11b.htm*>.

Sontag, Susan. [untitled] *The New Yorker* 24 Sept. 2001.

Loss and Letter Writing

Wendy Bishop and Amy L. Hodges

> The death that is the space between correspondents—a geographic space but also the space between signifier and the mirage of consensual meanings—haunts letter writers. . . .
>
> —William Merrill Decker

Dear Rafia,

Today in English our teacher asked us to write a meaningful letter to someone, and you came to mind. There are a lot of things I need and want to tell you but can't. It's always been really hard for me to tell you how I feel partly because I'm afraid of spilling my emotions to you and have you not take me seriously. I thought a letter would be easier.

I want to thank you for everything you've done for me. Believing in my potential when I was just a little kid—seeing past the attitude and spotting an individual who could be challenged. . . . Thank you for showing me the world, opening up my mind and widening my view of what is possible . . . [continues].

I love you always, Laura

*Mrs. Hodges: I'm not 100% I want to send this home just yet, I'm going to revise it a little more and I'm sure it will be more than just a page and a half (I had to squeeze it in a little).[1]

THE EPISTOLARY URGE

AS WRITERS, WE HAVE used letters to deal with love and longing, life and loss. We have learned from them. Letters are important to us and our personal valuing of this genre has informed our pedagogy. As teachers, we are drawn to literature for the way it can help individuals understand the events of their lives. Poet Lawrence Raab notes, "Most Americans don't read poetry, but many will turn to it at certain moments—marriages, for example or funerals . . ." and he believes poetry was so widely shared on the Internet in the fall of 2001 because "the presence of form does not deny the existence of chaos, but it asserts the possibility of order, and in this way is consoling" (10).

In the same way, writing provides consolation. It can help authors heal by leading their thoughts toward the possibility of order. While we too have found poetry-writing therapeutic, even more often we find letter-writing becomes our genre of choice during moments of challenge, complexity, or loss. We send letters on the same important occasions—marriages and funerals— but also use letters to note of changes in health, the demands of travel, the complications of personal relationships. As we use letters to investigate the conditions of daily life, we make meaning of our worlds via the written word.

One of us moves accumulated papers from college office to her home. Wedged between a file of evaluation materials and a student's writing portfolio, mislaid from a folder of memoir drafts, Wendy finds a letter, checks the faded postmark, extracts it from the envelope, becomes involved once more in a quarter-century-old conversation. Ghostly moment—irregular Royal typewriter, font like a fingerprint, cross-outs and retyped sections, hand corrections. He wanting to be a writer and worried about it. She, at that moment long ago, somewhere far away (in another country) wanting to be a writer, too. Speaking from the saved page, her correspondent says:

> . . . after pushing myself for three years to be a decent wordsmith I discover I have to wrestle with the very frightening possibility that I can't do it, in order to try to do it. I look over the poetry I did last year and find it wretched . . . the prose lumbers a little further. . . . It's another loop of course. I went through it all the last year and the year before and the year before that. The answer was always to keep trying . . .

Rereading the letter, she realizes she's older now than her correspondent was then, but Wendy knows that this discouraged writer published many books— novels, nonfiction, memoir—all after the distraught "old age" of 40 as captured in this archived instant. And didn't letter-writing help him through? They still correspond, by e-mail. About writing.

As two writing teachers, sharing stories like this one in order to examine the connections we find between loss and letter-writing, we considered the variety of letters—and epistolary sorts of correspondences—that we do and don't keep. We keep (or toss) business correspondence, keep (or destroy) break-up letters, and accumulate (and then weed out) stacks of birthday cards. We keep letters to document losses that we're not able to fully process at the time they occurred, and we write to share our triumphs over adversity, both large and small (think of the paperwork from a car accident, the reported death of a distant relative, the negative review of a fellowship application, the e-mail from a junior high friend who is searching the Internet in the hope of reconnecting). It's not simply that we're packrats. Instead, we're compiling a history, maintaining a memory-trail, undergoing a personal audit, and creating the necessary space for self-study, for reflection, for intellectual growth, which is sometimes built on the bedrock of emotional healing. Sharing experience through letter-writing moves us from passive suffering to active participation in healing.

Perhaps these many uses of letter-writing explain the popularity of and surge of communication on the Internet. Once letters were rare and saved for curiosity's sake, but now communication is common, more rapid, and includes e-mails sent by family and friends who now regularly use this media somewhere between phone and letter, talk and phone.

> Judging by anecdotal evidence, the efficiency of electronic exchange and the comparatively instant gratification of same-day, same-hour, same-minute replies lowers the threshold to epistolary activity, and more people are writing (or e-mailing) more people (who e-mail back) than they supposedly were at an earlier time. Such matters of perception are difficult to quantify. E-mail correspondence no doubt builds upon older traditions of letter-writing but differs from pre-electronic practice in significant ways. (Decker 236)

Although we're still deciding how much we value the art of e-mail, we're convinced that it offers an important entry into writing for many of our students, a needed meadow for private reflection amid the wilds of complicated public lives. And in our teaching, we often begin there and move back toward the tradition of letter-writing as well as forward—using letter genres, letter assignments—in order to help students find subjects and locations from which to launch engaged discussions. We realize that e-mails often aren't sites of careful and reflective writing but still we argue that varieties of informal letter exchanges can tap the pleasure and fluency our students have with this technology and then take them somewhere else, somewhere important, in their writing lives.

When do we seek to write letters (including e-mail letters) and to save them? When and how do they save us? Why are letters important? How do they become a space that haunts, that heals? Our experiences with letter-writing, personally and pedagogically, as a powerful genre for transforming and investigating loss, for ordering thought in times of chaos and confusion, leads us to advocating for more exploration and uses of the form for the writing classroom. Let us illustrate.

One of us first found letter-writing effective as an undergraduate when one of her writing teachers incorporated letter-writing into the curriculum. As

Amy began to write letters to her loved ones, to imagined people, and even to herself, she began to understand epistolary importance. Elaine Fredericksen contends that the language of letters is the closest language to natural speech (278), and one of Amy's letters in that undergraduate course began:

> Dear Dad,
>   Water was so important to us, to our family, and you may not realize this, but the times I remember most fondly from childhood are the times I spent with you on the water. Every year when we would search for scallops in the shallow water . . . I would look for the little gray shells, but I always watched your shadow and your net. You always found so many—I, so few. But I think it was during these times on the water that I first began to understand your true spirit. . . . So those scalloping trips were more than just searching for shells.

Amy noticed that her voice, and her classmates' voices, were familiar and comfortable when they wrote in letter format. She also noticed that her most promising topics and essays came from the letters she wrote that semester, discovering things about herself, even things she was reluctant to explore in formal essay-writing. Letter-writing proved more effective for her than journal-writing because she felt like she was writing to a "real" audience, even though sometimes that audience was herself.

As a new teacher, some years later, Amy adapted her positives experience with letter-writing to her own writing classroom. Having found power in the genre, she was excited about sharing that power with her students. She treasures the letter a student wrote during her first semester of teaching. In an assignment that invited classroom authors to address a person who helped shape their life story, this student composed a letter to her recently deceased mother:

> Dear Mama,
>   I am going through your things. Jen and Pam are taking nice fashionable clothes and purses. I open the top drawer in your armoire, and there it [handkerchief] is smiling at me, just like you did. I run my fingers along the stitching, and I am shaking. Your face is more comforting than a rainy day.
>   I just woke again from the dream where we have to pack your things, and the shadow on my wall gives me the most insecure feeling. All I can smell is toasted bread, and I once again think of your morning ritual—toast and coffee. I am constantly thinking of you, like right now. My attention is drawn to the floor, and to the left of my bed is the handkerchief I took. I bend down slowly and pick up the lace cloth with embroidered flowers. Bringing it to my nose, I breathe in deep. It smells like you. The phone just rang, and I drop the cloth.

Reading students' responses to this sort of assignment, Amy learned how letter-writing created a space where classroom authors could rehearse and revise, could investigate place and personas.

Because novice writers are often hesitant to begin writing, in fear that the student sitting to their right is a much better writer, ungraded letters are a very effective writing exercise. Students can experiment with unsent letters (to a former self or to someone they are no longer in touch with as a way of setting a record straight or commenting on and resolving past events) as well as with sent letters, which often address wider, more public audiences. First, to known audiences—family, local communities (between class sharing of letters, letters to the editor, letters of complaint). Second, to imagined audiences—the world at large. Letters as archive, time capsule, potential historical documents (open letters, modeled on examples like "Letter from a Birmingham Jail").

Both of us have found that classroom authors respond well to letters, because they produce a tangible result, which all writers appreciate and some writers need. Whether the letters are sent home or used as a way to begin an essay assignment, students tend to "get" these sorts of assignments, and they resist them less than assignments they see as being required primarily "for school" or "for the teacher." Lowered resistance often translates into rapid forward progress and community-building.

Still, we realize many teachers worry that asking for disclosure, even within the more traditionally disclosing sorts of genres like letter-writing, will lead them toward untenable roles, particularly that of therapist. In her study of abuse and eating disorder narratives, Michelle Payne argues against this fear and asks that "we as writing teachers, stop seeing emotion, pain, and trauma as threatening, anti-intellectual, and solipsistic, and instead begin to ask how we might, like therapists, feminist theorists, and philosophers, begin to recognize them as ways of knowing, not signs of dangerous pedagogies . . ." (30). It doesn't take a therapist to appreciate this letter from a struggling writer:

> Dear Cutie,
>   I'm writing this letter to tell you I miss you and what has been happening to me. It's been very lonely here since I don't have a roommate and I haven't really made many friends. I mean I do go play racquetball with this guy, Ron, everyday, but the rest of the time I've been pretty lonely. I know you're still mad at me for leaving and I know you don't want to talk to me and I understand, But Lorraine, I really would like to talk to you because I miss hearing your voice. Also, I am going to come down soon so I hope you will talk to me then and see me if you want. School hasn't been that hard. I got an A on my anthropology test but I still have to keep working on my writing for English because its not very good. It's very nice here and the people are nice too but I don't know if I can get used to this loneliness. I hope it doesn't last very long. I love you, Robby

A writing teacher can devise any number of initial assignments and drafting sequences that will tap issues of importance and interest to such a first-year writer, caught in the understandable throes of adjusting to life away from home. Some first-year students have the tools to help them process the new experiences of college life. Some have fewer tools. Letter-writing can provide a place where writing to know and writing to learn begin in earnest and perform excellent pedagogical work. Since we understand letters to be, primarily, an author-initiated genre, assigning letters transfers some of the burden *and* involvement of the writing assignment to that author. And because the genre is familiar, we find students readily take on (letter) writing roles.

The social aspect of letter-writing helps to differentiate it in the classroom setting from other sorts of school writing. Letters are immediate and dialogic, even if the letters are not sent to the intended recipients. Letters are thoroughly rhetorical, requiring an actual investigation of and response to the audience. Letters situate the personal writing assignment in a familiar and functional context: not writing to the teacher, but writing as classroom author to an audience of choice, the audience that needs to be addressed. Letters haunt us because they are catalogs of lived experience, they are spaces where—traditionally—writers express and share. Marion MacCurdy argues that students need the chance to tell their truths, the sort of truths, we feel, that surface usefully in letters:

> As Pennebaker and others have shown, most people are helped by speaking or writing to another of their experiences even if the 'other' is not a trained therapist (Christina Miller 75). Felman and Laub argue in their book *Testimony* that personal and cultural recovery from trauma requires a conversation between the victim and a witness, that indeed the witness is an utter necessity to complete the cycle of truth telling. If we shy away from offering our student the opportunity to tell their truths, we may be preventing them from learning what control they can have over their own lives. The more violent and threatening our culture becomes, the more we need to acknowledge the effects of trauma on our students. Those of us whose professional lives are defined by the classroom need to be aware that every pair of eyes facing us has probably borne witness to some difficult moments that can affect learning. (197)

Through letter-writing, students are able to discover, uncover, important issues about their writing voices and writing lives. Now certainly there are empty letters and there are letters full of meaning. It is possible to write a superficial one, but superficial writing can result from any classroom activity. Classroom letters are not a panacea but a possibility.

REFLECTION, WITNESS, TESTAMENT:
PRACTICAL PHILOSOPHY

We find reflection and healing to be the two great gifts of letter-writing. The baseline is conversation: talk captured and held out for regard. Lost voices made available for at least a partial listening, an emotional excavation.

When Wendy inherited her father's Victory mail from WWII, she found these exchanges captured a memorable version of her father; he spoke of the weather, collected souvenirs, made fun of Army life, worried aloud to her mother. To better understand these unknown parents, to reflect and connect, Wendy fashioned her father's V-mail into a found poem[2] discovering theirs was much like any war-time marriage, stressed deeply by the burdens of youth and national trauma. "V-Mail," begins:

> Passed by Base 083 Army Examiner
> Somewhere in Iceland
> 1940–1943

Today

> TWO YEARS AGO AT SIX IN THE MORNING I BROUGHT THE FIRST WORKING PARTY ASHORE IN ICELAND. WE WENT OVER THE SIDE OF THE TRANSPORT ON LANDING NETS AND USED LANDING OR HIGGENS BOATS TO COME ASHORE. IT WAS IN POURING RAIN AND WAS ONE OF THE MOST UNCOMFORTABLE DAYS I HAVE EVER PUT IN.
> TODAY IS CLEAR AND THE SUN IS SHINING BUT THE WIND IS COLD.
> TODAY IT IS RAINING LIKE THE DEVIL.
> TODAY IT IS SNOWING AND RAINING AT THE SAME TIME.
> IT IS RAINING PITCHFORKS TODAY.
> IT IS A VERY DEPRESSING DAY ANYWAY, DARK, AND RAINING, AND THE RAINIY SEASON IS HERE AGAIN SO WE WILL PROBABLY REVERT TO BEING DUCKS.
> TODAY I START MY THIRD YEAR IN ICELAND. I HAD HOPED TO HAVE A LETTER FROM YOU TODAY.

After hearing the poem at a public reading, veterans of three wars, WWII, Korea, and Vietnam, from that audience told her how the poem affected them. Wendy was surprised by their reaction until she read *Dear America: Letters Home from Vietnam* and found herself responding in kind to those messages, the striking voices of the boys of her youth. When men like these, returned from war, found their way to a poetry reading, and responded to "V-Mail," a circle was completed.

But many didn't return, and eventually, on a trip to Washington D.C., Wendy read their names inscribed on the Vietnam War memorial. Saw letters, more letters, wedged at the base of the wall, forming another private/public set of conversations. Release and reflection, healing and conversation. Connection, human to human. Again, a circle, that needs to witness and be witnessed.

Amy did not see the boys of her generation go off to the Vietnam War but still found these letters powerful enough to suggest a more specific classroom letter-writing assignment. When she first watched the documentary, *Dear America*, Amy, too, felt the words, the authors' fears and experiences intensely, as if she had stepped into a war zone. Moved by the boys' letters, she decided to share that power with her first-year writers, who were also away from home, in order to demonstrate the importance of shared experience.

Letter Writing Assignment
After viewing *Dear America*, I invite you to write a letter home like the soldiers in Vietnam we just viewed. You may choose to write about your day, your emotions, or your relationship with your family/friends back home. My only guideline for this letter-writing assignment is that you write a thoughtful and meaningful letter. Your letter should be at least one page single-spaced, and I hope you enjoy this assignment. You should bring your letter in a stamped envelope and an extra copy of the letter for me tomorrow at the beginning of class.

Leaving home to attend college, some of these young students—the same age as the U.S. soldiers in Vietnam—were prepared, but many were not.

Dear Mom,
   As I sit in my dorm, I try to explain to myself how it could be possible that time has gone so fast. . . . I've learned how to live on my own, take care of myself, and make rational and mature decisions. It has also made me come to the conclusion that it has been from your kind words and understanding personality that has brought me this far in life. I know I haven't told you this lately, but you have been the backbone of my entire life. Any rational decision I make is because of your teachings. You have been an amazing mother and more importantly, an amazing friend and teacher.
   You're probably asking yourself why I am sending you this letter in the mail, and not by e-mail or simply telling you over the phone. Well, today in English class, we watched a documentary called "Letters home from Vietnam." This video touched me and made me think a lot of stuff and life in general. It made me realize how lucky I really am. If this was the year 1964,

my life would be entirely different. I wouldn't be sitting in my clean and upgraded dorm room—I would most likely be sitting in a bunker with a gun as my best friend. So much has changed within the last 25 years. I can't even imagine graduating high school and being shipped off to go fight for my country. Those teens were so young. . . . Did you know there were 58,132 lives taken in that war?! Think about it—that is double the amount of people enrolled at Florida State University. Crazy, huh?! . . .

Love always, Ella

I witness: saying the self to others. Family to family. Lover to lover. Soldier to country. First person is also the voice of testament. The voice of record in world events. Viewers want to trust the war correspondent and look for the survivor's narrative in the aftermath of the natural disaster: hurricane, flood, earthquake. Ethnography, sociology, anthropology. Humans are natural categorizers, model builders, observers, deriving wisdom from the world around them. We're repulsed and riveted by Action News. We're moved and awed when human drama breaks out with all its multidimensional suffering: war, famine, loss, endurance, confusion, anger, revenge, despair, triumph, transcendence.

Letters allow for witness, as can be seen in the aftermath of the attack on the World Trade Center and the Pentagon. Cell phones: last conversations in the last air of innocence we now call "before 9/11." After, letters from school children. Notices, speaking the names of unfound relatives. And those who found themselves, the next day, writing e-mail testimony that circled the globe. As in this instance,

> After barely escaping from the 87th floor of the World Trade Center's north tower on Sept. 11, Adam Mayblum poured out his heart in an e-mail sent to family and friends.
>
> Less than 24 hours after he wrote his account of fleeing the burning tower and sent it to about 25 people, Mayblum received nearly 100 replies—most from people he had never met. And it kept building.
>
> Since then, more than 1,000 strangers from around the world have responded to his harrowing story. . . . Mayblum said he spent several hours writing his 2,100 word e-mail titled "The Price We Pay" as he sat at his suburban New Rochelle home on Sept. 12, still stunned from the experience. He knew it would help to put his thoughts into words, but he also wanted to let loved ones know he was safe. (Kugler)

Adam Mayblum's e-mail continues to receive response far after its date of composition. He stopped answering when the "letter" changed from conversation (after the first 500 replies) to artifact. In fact, many letter-writing manuals contend that letters are mainly written in today's technological society as a way to record events, words, or emotions—to preserve. May-blum continues to receive replies, and his e-mail is archived in a recent issue of the documentary journal *Doubletake,* personal words archived, trans-formed into a historical document.

Nationally, we save letters and we share them. American spiritual diaries to documents of independence. Collections compound. "Andrew Carroll founded the war letter-collecting Legacy Project when his Washington D.C. home burned down in 1990, taking his family letters with it. A "Dear Abby" announcement of the project led to 50,000 responses *(Publishers Weekly).* Let-ters, of course, help us recreate the lived life of a time. They also allow us to feel—to reach toward—the emotional tenor of those times.

Since September 11, 2001, there has been a marked resurgence of I-wit-ness writing. Children of New York City sent letters to firemen and ground zero workers. Middle-schoolers shared painted canvases of images that will live with them forever. Adults pasted pictures to the Internet and to street posts with words of memoriam and grief for lost loved ones. The healing process may take a lifetime, and we have all grieved and written together.

The events of September 11 did not spare our composition classrooms; in fact, prepared by her previous work with classroom letters, Amy turned to let-ters. On September 12, she decided to invite her students to write about the attacks of the previous day. At that time, Amy's class was working on a liter-acy history assignment, and she knew they could not continue the essay draft sequence without allowing her class the opportunity to pause and comment on the events. That day, 23 quiet first-year students looked back at her. No one moved in their seats or greeted her. Even the trees outside the window seemed to refuse to sway.

A teachable moment, yes, but a vulnerable one too. For teacher as well as for students. Amy set out a CD player and turned on Peter Gabriel's "I Grieve." She invited class members to choose a person to write to about the tragedy of the previous day. After the song played, still no one stirring, she assured them this letter could remain unsent if it were too personal or diffi-cult to send (although she had brought along envelopes and stamps for those who chose to send what they wrote; about half the class, as it turned out). To help these writers begin, Amy offered four writing prompts.

Explain where you were when you first heard the news of the attacks.

The following opening was taken from one student's letter to her father:

Dear Dad,
     September 11. You know it was my birthday yesterday, right? It all started out like a normal birthday. On my way to my 8:00 class, I saw two of my friends, and they had three helium balloons for me. But during class, I

realized this wasn't going to be a "normal" birthday. I heard people yelling outside, and my teacher went to see what was wrong. He came back in and told us a plane had hit the World Trade Center. And then I was so scared. I didn't know what to do or what was going to happen next. Most of all, I was worried about you, b/c I couldn't remember if you were in New York for work. I called your cell, but it wouldn't go through. I even thought you might be on one of those planes.

Explain how you feel now that 24 hours have passed.

Another student continued his letter to his brother with the following:

> On the way to school today, I noticed how empty the roads were. . . . I guess they just feel empty, or maybe I just feel empty. As I sat at a red light, I tried to comprehend what had just happened. I feel like the world is crashing all around me, and I don't feel safe. I wish I was home.

After students wrote of their initial reactions and feelings, Amy turned up the news radio on her small CD player/radio.

Describe the one news report, television image, or scene that haunts you most.

These descriptions were taken from two letters written during the exercise:

> The second plane crashing into the WTC will forever live in my mind. Everywhere I look, Justin, they are showing that image. Crash. Smoke. Fire. I keep reliving the scene over and over. It won't go away, and I've tried to make it go, believe me.

> The picture on the front page of the newspaper (I think it is *NY Times*) where people are holding hands and jumping from windows shakes me most. I don't want to look at the picture, but I can't take my eyes away. Do you think showing these images shows insensitivity or accessibility? I don't know, but I can't get those people holding hands out of my head for a second.

Share your experiences, your emotions, and/or your fears. Reflect on yesterday's events.

Emily's conclusion, like those of several other writers, exhibited her sense of grief and participation:

> People are still calling from their cell phones, Jen. Can you believe that? I guess they are trapped under the rubble, but I feel so sorry for them. Why would God allow innocent people to die? Why? Why? Why? Why? It's all

so mesmerizing. The TV keeps saying the same thing yet I can't take my eyes off of it. I sit paralyzed staring at the screen.

When I woke up this morning the sun was shining so bright, and I felt happy. Then I remembered, and I looked outside. All I saw were blank faces of kids walking to class. I heard a fighter jet, too. Sorry I don't know much what to say. I wanted to write to you when my teacher asked us to choose someone to write to, but the right words won't come. I love you. I'm glad you're okay . . . is that selfish? Anyway, I am. Love you, Emily

To link private and public, Amy suggested that all the letters be read aloud, hers included, in unison. The result was a moving linguistic chorus, words repeated but no single text dominated as public loss was given private voice.

Some students sent the letters home immediately following the class, others chose not to share their letters with anyone, even the teacher. That day, Amy was once again reminded of the power of letters, for these writings not only captured a moment in history but also served as an archive of what each student had experienced.

In his study of letter-writing practices, William Decker explains that "It is impossible, however, to read extensively in the literature of personal correspondence without becoming aware of the conditions of human isolation that generate such texts, and of the vulnerability, sorrow, folly, and crudity, as well as the invention, eloquence, and lyricism, that such conditions bring out" (6), and certainly that proved true in this teaching instance. The letters produced by Amy's classroom authors were not necessarily exemplary products but they were a crucial part of the process that would allow these writers to continue to reflect on the experience of personal and national loss and trauma in the weeks to follow. Letter-writing was the route to writing again.

PRACTICE INTO THEORY— WRITING LETTERS AND TEACHING WRITING

Letter forms range from the practical (aids to classroom communication like Web board, networked discussion papers, process memos, portfolio reflections) to the reflective (peer-to-peer interpretations of literary texts, letters to the author) to the more therapeutic (understanding and investigating issues of diversity, responding to trauma). Because letter forms are varied and most often viewed as practical, we don't want to overlook their real potential for altering our writing and our world(s). Certainly letters allow learners to reflect on personal experience, but they also serve a more complicated function by reinforcing an author's understanding that the personal is political and that the political is the personal care of each citizen. Letters allow for informal thinking, for practicing ideas, for trying out alternate opinions. And the practice of reflecting in the presence of a "real imagined" audience mirrors a number of life-long writing situations: the memo, the letter of complaint, the fundraising letter, the editorial.

As part of writing across the curriculum initiatives, many college instructors have instituted journal-writing as a place for the sort of reflective writings described in this essay. We see letter-writing as a similar sort of project with, perhaps, some added benefits. Letters can broaden a writer's audience repertoire. And when teachers write letters, with and to students, classroom dialogue takes off. Reflection takes center stage.

In writing classes where writers submit a portfolio at the end of the semester for evaluation, portfolio cover letters can encourage students to reflect on their writing progress. Both of us invite students to include personal letters of assessment in the final portfolios. In our writing courses, we ask each student to assess the body of the portfolio, making mention of each essay's progress and the revision cycle for that project. We ask each student to consider how he or she has changed as a writer over the semester. Portfolio letters are sometimes criticized for reading too much like form letters or for producing artificial words, but we both find that the portfolio letter, carefully assigned, provides an effective way for both the student and evaluator to record and reflect on the term's progress and in doing so producing a literacy testament.

We not only invite students to write letters to us, but we also often write letters to them. Wendy, for instance, responds to first essays of the term, en masse, posting the "Class Letter" on the course Web discussion board. When writing class letters, the teacher gains, becomes a pen-pal, a coach, a supportive voice, and has the chance to read a set of essays as if they were letters with the openness we all offer to friendly correspondents. Not students to be corrected but writers to be responded to. And not 30 responses but one thoughtful one, taking place anywhere that teacher feels comfortable sitting and working.

This type of practice is advocated by teachers like Elaine Fredrickson, Toby Fulwiler, Roger Ochse, Gregory Shafer, and Louise Todd Taylor who suggest class letter-writing encourages dialogue, rethinking, and rewriting, helps motivate writers and encourage collaborative activity, and allows writers to explore and affirm their identity even as they reach out to and connect with audience. Within a pedagogy of incremental risk, writers gain authority over their materials. Writers feel like shareholders in community discussions, and make invested responses to literature.

In our classes, each of us continues to investigate variations of letter-writing assignments for these and other reasons. The practice of writing letters to students and requiring that they write to each other and to us—done before online Web communities and now evolving in the templates of Blackboard, our university's online classroom support system—suggest this practice keeps us focused on the global issues of writing, helping classroom authors feel eager and ready to open up their texts to further revision. We know that writers should like their writing, become attached to their texts. We know that writing is hard work, each well-placed word seeming a precious stay against the distractions of dorm noise, job anxiety, the seduction of play (movies, parties, DVDs, sports, and visits to the local outdoors), and the sometimes incomprehensible drama of world events. So writers, once done, tend to push away from the screen and go away. A teacher's discussion, even if posted on the class website, might draw a writer to speculate about a next response. When saved in a letter dialogue, these words will allow a 19-year-old to look back on her class letters and remember the personal and the private events that shaped her freshman year:

> Dear Mom, and Dad, and Barbara,
>   . . . feel like I am finally on my way to being something great . . . I'm glad I have the chance to attend college and make something out of myself. I really do wish you all had the same opportunity that I did. But, needless to say, I will try and live to some of your dreams. At least the same ones that I have (ha . . . ha . . .). College is a great experience for me. I feel that it is making me more responsible and more aware of my surroundings. . . . Yesterday was my 19th Birthday! Yeah! I am so glad you (Mom/Dad) got the chance to come see me. I really was excited to see you both. I may not show it, but I really miss your company, and even the usual petty arguments at the house. . . . Love always, Karen

Being the first in her family to attend college, being part a generation marked by deeply shared national and international events will change this writer. Jeffrey Berman and Jonathan Schiff argue that "Whether one believes that writing leads to the discovery of truths by which to live or the construction of these truths, what is most important is that by writing about our life stories, we are able to compare them with others' and broaden our point of view. If knowledge is power, then there is no better way to empower ourselves than through reading and writing" (308–09).

We felt our commitment to letter-writing come into new focus in the last year. When a nation turns to reflection, we turn. When our students look for answers to questions they had not formerly thought to ask, we hope, as educators, to be in dialogue with them on that shared journey.

NOTES

1. All letters are excerpted, and samples are shared with authors' permissions and our thanks. Names have been changed.

2. A found poem is fashioned from the "found" text and that text alone; this one reproduces actual V-mail formatting: block capitals for Army censors. Imagine it typed on small blue rectangles of paper.

WORKS CITED

Berman, Jeffrey and Jonathan Schiff. "Writing About Suicide." In *Writing and Healing: Toward Informed Practice*. Ed. Charles M. Anderson and Marian M. MacCurdy. Urbana, IL: NCTE, 2000. 291–312.Carroll, Andrew, ed. *War Letters: Extraordinary Correspondence from American Wars*. NY: Scribner; 2001.

Decker, William Merrill. *Epistolary Practices: Letter Writing in America Before Telecommunications*. Chapel Hill, NC: U of North Carolina P, 1998.

Edelman, Bernard, ed. *Dear America: Letters Home from Vietnam*. NY: Norton, 2002.

Fredericksen, Elaine. "Letter Writing in the College Classroom." *Teaching English in the Two-Year College* 27.3 (Mar 2000): 278–84.

Kugler, Sara. "9/11 survivor e-mail touches hundreds." AP Dec. 26, 2001, 2:12 PM. *http://www.chron.com/cs/CDA/story.hts/side/1187061*.

Fulwiler, Toby. "Writing Back and Forth: Class Letters." *New Directions for Teaching and Learning* 69 (Spring 1997): 15–25.

MacCurdy, Marion M. "From Trauma to Writing: A Theoretical Model for Practical Use." In *Writing and Healing: Toward Informed Practice*. Ed. Charles M. Anderson and Marian M. MacCurdy. Urbana, IL: NCTE, 2000. 158–200.

Payne, Michelle. *Bodily Discourses: When Students Write About Abuse and Eating Disorders*. Portsmouth, NH: 2002.

Raab, Lawrence. "Poetry and Consolation." *The Writer's Chronicle* 35.3 (2002): 10–15.

Roger, Ochse. "The Pedagogy of Disclosure: Class Letters Fostering Partnerships between Instructors and Students." Paper presented at the 48th Annual Meeting of the Conference on College Composition and Communication. Phonex, AZ, March 12–15, 1997. ED408578.

Shafer, Gregory. "Using Letters for Process and Change in the basic Writing Class. *Teaching English in the Two Year College* 27.3 (Mar 2000): 285–92.

Taylor, Louise Todd. "Students Write Back: Letters in American Literature. *Teaching English in the Two-Year College* 19.3 (Oct. 1992): 201–05.

How Little We Knew

Spring 1970 at the University of Washington

Dana C. Elder

INTRODUCTION

TODAY I TEACH writing and classical (Western) rhetoric and chair an English department. I am far from the first-year college student I was in Seattle in the spring of 1970 when the national trauma was war in Vietnam and on American campuses. All of us alive at the time were traumatized by these forces, even those on the sidelines of the military reality and cultural upheaval impacting us, so these events resonate in the opening years of the new millennium. As I remember and supplement memory with photocopies of the campus newspaper, the *Daily*, I think that this should be an easy story to tell. It is not because it is a tale of the end of innocence impacting the lives and attitudes of college students and faculty colleagues today.

First, however, I struggle to paint a patina of the personal and historical context. My working assumption is that, to some readers, 1970 is prenatal and, therefore, pre-history. So I include some historical factoids and explanations, remembered or read, thinking how little they know, only to discover how little we (who were there) knew. In this traumatic time I was no more than a dilettante, an incidental observer usually and participant occasionally. I witnessed an attempt at social change on a massive scale. From a present perspective, it seems that what changed was not the society but the youthful optimism that believed large-scale change was possible.

The Context

Fall of 1969, I left a modest suburban home in Yakima to attend courses at the University of Washington in Seattle. I was 18, optimistic, innocent like all raised in small rural cities of the time, and completely convinced by the self-made-man mythos that success was determined by innate potential, hard work, good habits, and the "time and chance that happeneth to us all." Unquestionably, I was naïve (Elder). Many of the 18-year-olds I see today seem prematurely cynical by comparison, less likely to be shocked by or excited about anything.

Eighteen-year-olds in 1970 were shocked and excited by the war in Southeast Asia. Friends were there, "in-country," and others had returned in body bags, warranting the attention of even the least attentive. We had Richard Nixon in the White House (1969–1974), but the Tet Offensive of late January 1968 had damaged the patriotic confidence of those who had read the body-count rhetoric of the time as clear assurance of quick victory over an "inferior" foe; the rhetoric of "My county, love it or leave it" was rampant but in trouble. That year an average of 280 Americans were killed each week in Vietnam (Schlesinger 586).

The draft, a federal law requiring young men to serve in the U.S. military and begun during the Civil War (March 1863), was, therefore, a real threat. The Selective Service System required all 18-year-old males to register for possible conscription (this is still federal law) and to carry a document, a draft card, as evidence of compliance. Once registered, one could defer military service in several ways, but the most popular by far enabled one to pursue higher education. The choice seemed between college professors in frayed tweed sports coats with chalk and red pens or Southeast Asians in black pajamas with AK-47s and mortars. Many, mostly middle-class and white, young males chose the professors. When my parents were hesitant to subsidize my participation in this testosterone-laden immigration to an education, I threatened to enlist in the U.S. Army. World War II veterans, patriots, and Republicans themselves, still they relented, and I relocated and obtained a student deferment in the fall of 1969.

Effective January 1, 1970, however, the draft became The Lottery. Disturbingly, I was familiar with Shirley Jackson's 1948 short story with that same title. Before the lottery, 19-to-25-year-olds could be drafted, starting with the oldest and moving down year by year until the required manpower had been gleaned. The new law dictated a random drawing of 366 possible birth dates and then drafting conscripts in the order of drawn birthdays. The other changes were that 19-year-olds would be called first, and anyone whose deferment lapsed (as in flunking out of school) or expired (as in graduating) became 19 by law, regardless of actual age (*Keesing's* 23968). I would be 19 by natural and federal law in June—unless I paid attention.

(Perhaps because the draft is not in use today and because the United States is the world's only acknowledged military superpower, the students I serve assure me that the troubles in the Gulf and elsewhere will be over soon—before they themselves ever see the inside of a uniform. One student told me the war in Iraq was mostly really bad television—all action (or inaction) and no plot. I agreed only that there seemed no clear plot, but found the war shocking.)

Another shock for us in the spring of 1970 was the Sexual Revolution. One was surprised to learn that male dominance was not a birthright and ERA was a proposed amendment to the *U.S. Constitution* and not an acronym for "earned-run-average." ERA stood for "Equal Rights Amendment"—the idea that women deserved equal civil, economic, and legal rights. Sadly, this remains "a dream deferred," a strange and troubling deferment.

The feminists were advocating the ERA, women's control of their own destinies and bodies, economic parity with males doing similar work, opportunities to decide what should be done rather than only doing what they were told, honoring familial and even romantic relationships between "sisters," and the abolition of terms including "bitch," "lesbian," "maiden aunt," "spinster," "slash," "slut," and "cunt." The commodification of women and of us all was the target of these efforts. While these equality initiatives were advocated with a passion, science and its profitable marriage to capitalism had produced and marketed birth-control pills. One could "do it" and not be ethically, morally, nor soon legally married to the one with whom one did. We were learning.

Divorce was still expensive and emotionally, socially, and economically devastating to all involved, abortion was illegal, and sexually transmitted diseases (well before HIV and AIDs) were not rare. But we didn't know, so the oft-heard call to "Make love, not war" was well received and pursued with youthful vigor. Many who had no desire to see Southeast Asia eagerly volunteered to serve in the Sexual Revolution. The message had changed from "Don't do it" to "If you're going to, do it with friends." This was a radical change. We were also the first generation raised with television and rock-'n-roll, and there were drugs, mostly marihuana, which were findable and affordable. We were learning.

My current students seem to know everything that I learned in the spring of 1970 already: Institutionalized, officially-sanctioned discrimination against women is a problem of the past that has been fixed. Sex is just hormones and, therefore, no big deal. Divorce is so normal that it's expected. Pregnancies can be terminated. Yet the "free love" of the 1970s was and remains a theoretical construct, given that teen pregnancy, shotgun weddings, and women unexpectedly "in a family way" are not relics of the past. In a disturbing sense, the present single-parent phenomena is a legacy of this era.

SOME FACTS

Is social upheaval trauma? Yes, and the spring of 1970 was full of it. Some of this was "What's happening?" but much had to do with what had recently happened. 1968 challenged everyone's thinking. Martin Luther King, Jr., and Robert F. Kennedy were murdered. The Tet Offensive, mentioned above, signaled to many that, yes, perhaps we COULD lose a war. The Democratic National Convention that year in Chicago and the anti-war demonstrations there made "police brutality" a widely acknowledged redundancy, were followed by a lengthy trial that served to add martyrs to the anti-war cause, and ended finally in February of 1970 with the "System's" failure to make a substantive case against its chosen initiators of the conflagrations—the "Chicago Seven." Five of the seven were convicted of "crossing state lines with the intent of inciting a riot." "Intent" was the problem for many. Could intent be a crime, or did one actually have to DO something illegal? The "thought crimes" in Orwell's *1984* did come to mind.

In March of 1968 a village of South-Vietnamese civilians, My Lai, was exterminated by U.S. soldiers. Everybody. This was something we had never learned about before and seemed illegal. Attempts to conceal information about this slaughter resulted in Army charges against 14 officers in March of 1970. A hapless junior officer, Lieutenant Calley, received full credit for this malfeasance in a military court of law and on network television. There were those who doubted that a lieutenant decided U.S. military policy.

There were, in 1968, some 550,000 American service men and women in Vietnam. Over 200 million Americans watched them on television. Few families were disinterested. There were approximately 8,000,000 U.S. college students in 1970, and 35,000 of us were at the University of Washington.

WHO WE WERE

At the university that spring there were Black Panthers, young men in dark clothing and black berets who rarely spoke and, to my knowledge, never smiled. There were few. There were "Hippies"—long hair, bell-bottom pants, tie-dyed shirts, dresses, and tee-shirts, wearing love beads and smelling of incense and infrequent bathing—but not many. There were members of what was called "the radical left." They were said to be Communists, but when they spoke it was of violence and anarchy. They seemed unhappy, incredulous that so few chose to join them, and prone to shouting slogans. There were college athletes who tended to cluster in small groups based on ethnicity. There were people in Greek-letter organizations who drove expensive cars and seemed to be majoring in Party 101, but that's just an impression (I was never invited.). All of these taken together might have comprised 20% of the student population.

The following "other" groups are mentioned in the University of Washington *Daily* between January and June of 1970: the Black Student Union (BSU), the Seattle Liberation Front (SLF), the Student Mobilization Committee (SMC), the New Mobilization Committee (NMC), the Irresistible Force (IF), the Sundance Collective (SC), the Students for a Democratic Society (SDS)—with a faction called "Weathermen"—the National Student Association (NSA), the Christian World Liberation Front (CWLF), the Young Socialist Alliance (YSA), the Early Risers (ER), Students for Humor in Tactics (SHIT), the Strike Coalition (SC), the Students for Responsible Expression (SRE), the Women's Liberation group of Seattle (WLS), and the Black Panther Party (BPP). These are only some of the groups. Lists of demands—and demands became the rhetorical currency of student–group communications with campus administrators, city government, police, and the military—were publicly and proudly presented by one faction after another.

The largest group, however, was comprised of white, middle- and upper-middle-class students who had grown up in suburbia. Clean, well groomed, academically prepared, politically conservative, we saw college as a gateway to personal prosperity and family pride. While aware of the irony that it had put us in a privileged position, we learned to distrust and even hate what we called the Establishment. We became, to lesser or greater extents, alienated. We learned about racism, sexism, poverty, materialism, the "military-industrial complex" (Dwight D. Eisenhower's term), the bureaucratization of American life, the dangers of science and technology (including but not limited to "the Bomb"), pollution, and political and economic oppression. We learned that what we knew was little and much of it untrue. We blamed nearly everyone who was older than ourselves. We loved but could not talk to our parents. We had each other. We shared two tasks: ending the War and fixing all the wrongs in the world.

By contrast, the student organizations on the campus I serve now are small and focused on career development, faith, recreational preferences, or academic-discipline enrichment. Fair enough. The English Club, for example, just sponsored an amateur production of *Cat on a Hot Tin Roof*. It's hard to imagine these students marching, sitting-in, demonstrating, making demands, or shouting profanities at police officers or university administrators. Their agendas are shared but personal and familial, and they include getting a degree and building a career lucrative enough to have a life even while paying off massive student loans. Many of these students already have low-paying jobs and children of their own.

The Big Agenda Items

Very early on (before January 1970), the Black Student Union (BSU) had called for a boycott or suspension of the athletic competitions between the

University's Huskeys and Brigham Young University (BYU); the Mormons had a low hierarchical ceiling for African Americans. The BSU was also concerned about a nationally funded and federally endorsed program to kill, imprison, or frighten away surviving members of the Black Panther Party (BPP). The BSU continued to attack BYU and support the BPP. This made sense, and the Establishment offered no explanations.

All groups called for an end to military action in Southeast Asia, the draft, racism, pollution by corporate interests, police brutality, and the exploitation of women. Most joined the feminists asking for university-subsidized day care for students' children. Learners throughout the nation, regardless of age, ethnicity, gender, or geography were generally agreed on these "demands," but few shared the eagerness of some to employ violence when demands were, summarily, denied.

THE VIOLENCE

We were shocked, frequently, by the violence. The *Daily* published a half-page article, "Panthers and Police: A Scorecard," on January 8, 1970—a list of police actions against the Black Panther Party (BPP) during 1968 and 1969. It is a litany of searches without warrants, indictments without convictions, dismissed charges, and deaths by gunfire—both of Panthers and Police.

Locally, a demonstration at the Seattle Federal Courthouse protesting the trial of the Chicago Seven (reported as "eight" in the *Daily* on February 18, the day after) pitted 1,000 protesters against 300 police in what turned into, arguably, a riot. Seventy-nine people were arrested, including women and children. Windows were broken. Tear gas and nightsticks were employed. I was not there; I'd gone to class.

On March 3 a bomb exploded near the University District Post Office. Four suspects were charged the next day. Damage was estimated at $2,000 (*Daily*, March 5). This was not an isolated explosion: "In the past 16 months in the city of Seattle there have been, according to the police, some 62 different bombings. They have caused an estimated $400,000 to $700,000 damage" (*Daily*, April 28). Arson was also popular: "Over 100 arson fires were set in Seattle in March . . . resulting in over $200,000 damage, according to Seattle Fire Marshall Stephan MacPherson" (*Daily*, April 2). Several campus buildings were included in this figure.

Before mid-March there were Seattle Police (SP) and King County Sheriff Deputies (KCSD) joining the University Security Division (USD) on campus: "The exact number of policemen on campus . . . is 'classified information' according to a spokesman for the Seattle Police Department, which coordinated the affair" (*Daily*, March 13). There were also undercover Federal Bureau of Investigation (FBI) agents who had infiltrated many, if not all, "activist" groups. Many wondered, and still do, whether some of these served the Establishment as agents provacateurs. What if someone working for the FBI in the BSU and fanning the flames fueled by BYU was also in contact with the SP, KCSD, SLF, MC, and BPP, had TNT or other explosives (supplied by the FBI), and felt he or she needed a DOA or arrest to justify the money paid to him or her? Just a post-1970 thought.

The SP wore black leather jackets and white helmets with face shields. They sported duty belts complete with sidearms and nightsticks. The KCSD wore brown jumpsuits and white helmets with ample plastic faceguards, and they carried black sticks that were at least 30 inches long. These guys came out of busses, "on the double," and established military-looking perimeters that were very impressive. These were "tactical squads" or "riot police," and maybe not KCSD. I don't remember the campus security people, so perhaps they were plainclothed. All were young, fit, and frightened. There were no female officers.

COMING OF AGE

In late April Richard Milhouse Nixon, a U.S. President I respected because of the office rather than the man, made a choice that was probably sound for defeating a conventional enemy. He sent troops into Cambodia, after much rhetoric about "de-escalation" and "Vietnamization" of the war. We already knew there were U.S. troops in Laos, Vietnam, Japan, Korea, and Thailand. Everybody knew someone who'd been killed or a family so afflicted. We learned.

On Monday, May 4th, 1970, an estimated dozen Ohio National Guard (ONG) opened fire on students at Kent State University. Some protestors were surely throwing rocks and bottles at them and shouting unkind remarks. The Guardsmen's story of incoming "sniper fire" was never substantiated nor believed. Reportedly on orders, they fired 67 rounds in 13 seconds at unarmed students.

The weapons used, M-1 Garands (.30–06), are eight-shot, semi-automatic rifles delivering 150-grain full-metal-jacket (FMJ) bullets at over 2,700 feet per second (FPS). This is the rifle many of our fathers had used to win World War II.

Four students died. Nine were wounded. The photo by John Filo of Mary Ann Vecchio crouched over a dead student still haunts the American psyche (Hariman and Lucaites). It was in newspapers everywhere. America, and perhaps the world, was appalled. This was, and remains, too much.

The next day various student groups, unions, coalitions and committees agreed to strike the University of Washington. That morning I was one of an estimated 7,000 students gathered in front of the student-union building. We approved, by voice vote, four demands:

- a pledge by President Odegaard deploring the deaths of four Kent State University students Monday and a pledge by him never to call National Guard troops onto the University campus;
- an end to ROTC units on campus, and the turning of ROTC buildings into "memorial centers" for the four slain Kent State students;
- an end to University complicity with the war effort, including military recruiting and war-oriented research; and
- a severing of all ties immediately with Mormon-supported Brigham Young University.

University President Charles Odegaard spoke from approximately 1:00 to 1:15 that afternoon. Through a bullhorn, he read a telegram he had sent to President Nixon, the day before, asking him to explain his policies to all Americans. Odegaard largely dodged the students' demands but admitted that some university staff and faculty had already joined the strike. As the crowd grew louder, he retreated into a building already secured by some 50 uniformed police.

I thought the demonstration was over and returned to my apartment, but most marchers moved off campus and then west on 45th Avenue to Interstate 5. By 2:00 p.m., north- and south-bound lanes were blocked. There had been no damage to persons or property. Demonstrators marched south on I-5 until they met a small group of riot police near Roanoke. The marchers left the freeway and walked to the Federal Courthouse. There they heard several speakers before dispersing voluntarily (*Daily*, May 6th).

The next morning, Wednesday, May 6th, the Establishment was better prepared. Police arrived on campus in busloads by 10:30. By noon when the demonstration officially began, an estimated 10,000 students and supporters had gathered. We had come to march: "A split soon materialized between those who advocated very militant action on campus and those who wanted a peaceful march downtown" (*Daily*, May 7th). Several thousand demonstrators marched south across the Montlake Bridge. Chanting "1–2–3–4, We Don't Want Your Fucking War," "Power to the People," and other anti-Establishment mantras, we were joined by students from other schools and sympathizers. Capital Hill residents offered us water and encouragement. A group estimated at 15,000 arrived at the Seattle Municipal Building and heard a brief statement from Acting Mayor Charles M. Carroll. He was hard to hear and said little, as I recall.

Many protestors then headed towards the interstate in several groups. The police were ready. A series of clashes ensued. They "included Tactical Squad roadblocks, beatings, and gassings." Several protestor attempts to block the freeway were frustrated entirely or only briefly successful. A disorderly retreat was harassed by police roadblocks, clubs, and tear gas. (Tear gas causes eyes and lungs to burn and stomachs to empty themselves; while coughing, you throw-up on yourself and others because you can't see.) I was gassed. By then it seemed not law but punishment. We were taught a lesson, and we learned. Several marchers were arrested. No police were injured (*Daily*, May 7th). Nor was I, despite the gassing, but I saw protestors who were.

The next evening, the 7th, 40 men with nightsticks wandered the campus, randomly attacking people. They were initially called "vigilantes" by the press. On May 20, however, we read that they were "on-duty plainclothed policemen." Seattle's Acting Police Chief was reportedly concerned by "a lapse in judgment at the supervisory level" (*Daily*, May 20). In the middle of May, police at Jackson State (Mississippi) fired into student dormitories, killing two and injuring others. We were learning fear.

THE RETREAT CONTINUED

After May 7th there were more demonstrations and more campus buildings occupied by protestors, but most students returned to classes. Concerned about grades, many students called for "academic amnesty." A liberal grading system— for spring quarter only—was announced on May 29th (If you ask, you pass.). Some faculty were disciplined with loss of pay, and the contracts of others were not renewed because of their political activism. The U. of W. Board of Regents passed new rules for faculty conduct aimed at preventing such activism.

A combination of fear and frustration had broken the back of the "Movement." Most students geared up for summer classes, jobs, or vacations. The weather was good. Head Football Coach Jim Owens shared his concern that an incident involving Black athletes the previous fall, the BYU controversy, and the campus demonstrations would make it difficult to recruit "bluechip" athletes for the fall (*Daily*, June 3).

THEN AND NOW

In the early 1970s, we thought we'd lost both the military war in Southeast Asia and the social revolution on college campuses at home. In the process, college students, faculty, and staff had learned we could be shot, beaten, gassed, and criminalized for challenging the status quo, while those in power lied with impunity whenever it suited their interests. We learned to be quick to suspect and slow to trust. Yet the Establishment's tactics of killing, beating, gassing, and arresting middle-class college students did turn the tide of public opinion. While our service men and women (disproportionately minority, patriotic, and economically disenfranchised human beings) continued to win the battles in Vietnam, the War at Home was lost. "Vietnamization" of the conflict increased, and more and more troops came home. Most returned alive, but all were reshaped by the perils of war and the stigma of unsuccessful warriors.

Without the War to unite the many student groups with differing social-enhancement agendas, the critical mass of effectiveness, the voice, was lost. But we did not lose the lessons; how little we knew was changed forever. A brief review of our 1970 demands tells a tale:

- Today the "Justice System" does not, to the best of my knowledge, endorse planned programs of politically calculated brutality. "Profiling" remains a concern. Abuses remain, and new ones may emerge as law enforcers, in the name of Homeland Security, enjoy new powers to infiltrate private groups, tap phones, monitor e-mail, and target individuals who may or may not intend to do anything illegal. (In 1970 there was no e-mail, and invading people's privacy was illegal but done regularly and systematically.)
- Women's rights, including day care, are another sore spot, yet many campuses and workplaces have options for some parents. Most facilities, one suspects, are inadequately funded. The struggle cannot end without affordable and safe day care and true equality.
- The draft is on hiatus. Nixon's vision of an all-volunteer military did, indeed, come to pass. Still I think of him as the "crook" he denied being; he was, we learned, worse than a criminal. "Vietnamization" of the war? Smoke and mirrors. "Peace with honor?" Hardly. Watergate, in June of 1972, took his true measure. People were offended but not surprised. Nixon was smart but thought no one else was. His decisions and artful rhetoric killed and damaged people, often pointlessly. Now we hear talk of the need to have sufficient military strength to fight two or more wars, in different parts of the world, at the same time. The rhetoric sounds disturbingly familiar.
- University administrators are now responsive to issues of race, yet racial hatred flourishes in the new millennium. Over 30 years ago, however, there would not have been anyone Islamic worthy of our hatred (the Establishment then simply bought oil with weapons and money). U.S. imperialism is alive and well. Poverty, here and abroad, increases rather than abates. Right here and now, affordable healthcare hovers above far too many; there is no true equal access to education; and bureaucracy, Hollywood, and unabashed materialism rule many people's lives while pollution, which even Nixon recognized as a present and long-term threat to earthbound life, is still presented to citizens as the inevitable cost of progress and prosperity.

(IN)CONCLUSION

Are the fears so different today, our students less slow to suspect and more willing to trust? Too many of today's students seem not so much indifferent to social problems as convinced of their own inability to change things. Have they inherited our cynicism, our disillusionment, our hard lessons learned? I hope not, yet I acknowledge that there's reason for their believing in their own political impotence and that of the faculty members with whom they work. The people we now teach to write and participate critically in the world grew up surrounded by our "pre-history" concerns and others unimaginable in the spring of 1970. These all blend together to form a scenario of which Dante would be proud:

- The greatest of these is "overload." There is so much more each of us has to know, do, and fear—often without historical "safety nets" like traditional families, somehow lost in the "me generation" begun over three decades ago in the fertile miasma of the late 1960s and early 1970s.
- Meanwhile, the nuclear threat did not disappear with the (ongoing) dismantling of the Soviet Union, the Establishment, in part because of widespread rhetorics like "You do your thing, and I'll do mine," is no clear target for rebellion and social upheaval, and the self-made-person rhetoric, a powerful portion of the American mythos, is probably not worthy of trust. A new version of "My Country, love it, leave it, or stay out of it" still assaults our national consciousness. The Internet, born with the promise of equal access to information and education, is now the tool of rampant consumerism, credit scams, and pornography—in addition to its more positive features.
- Unlike those involved in the turmoil of the spring of 1970, anyone today who pays attention experiences the trauma and unearned fear of terrorism and knows that violence happens to people who do not deserve and have no reason to expect it—here and abroad.

All this and the age-old fears of not measuring up, shaming oneself or one's family, and/or failing in terms of promise or potential, remain firmly in place. These challenges and others seem to overwhelm the current generation. Still it surprises me when I'm brainstorming with students for topics for essays and some tell me there's nothing to write about. Nothing seems to really shock or excite them. The current open-ended war seems perfectly normal, for example, and "social injustice" is, for some, a vague buzz-term encountered in pop music played on the "Oldies" radio station or featured on tabloid television. Is the federal government more open, honest, and benevolent now than it was 30-some years ago, or is it just much better at appearing to be so? Certainly the national media now seems to serve as the White House's (the Establishment's) ally rather than its watchdog. Just another thought.

POSTSCRIPT

Maybe I'm just repeating the frustrations so frequently vented by mature teachers of writing upon younger generations that are often seen in written history. I do remember, in the spring quarter of 1970, a University of Washington teaching assistant's struggle and apparent frustration with my overloaded hormones, psyche, schedule, and naivete. She wanted to help students understand and address the twin challenges of writing essays and making the world a better place for themselves and for others. Now I teach writing and chair an English department, and the challenges we face as educators remain the same. If our current and erstwhile students are prematurely cynical, they learned their cynicism from us. Still there is a constructive response, and we must continue to help students and each other do this essential work today.

WORKS CITED

The Almanac of American History. Gen. Ed. Arthur M. Schlesinger, Jr. New York: Putnam, 1984.

Daily. (January–June 1970). Archives, Suzallo Library, University of Washington. Special thanks are due to the gracious librarians who generously lent the rolls of microfilm that made this project possible.

Elder, Dana C. "Different Climbs." *College English* 56.5 (September 1994): 568–70.

Hariman, Robert, and John Louis Lucaites. "Dissent and Emotional Management in a Liberal Democratic Society: The Kent State Iconic Photograph." *Rhetoric Society Quarterly* 31.3 (Summer 2001): 5–31.

Keesing's Contemporary Archives XVII (1969–1970). London: Keesing's, 1969–70.

"This rhetoric paper almost killed me!"

Reflections on My Experiences in Greece During the Revolution of 1974

Richard Leo Enos

INTRODUCTION AND DEDICATION

I have discovered that one of the commonplaces that has been both uttered (and muttered) by my students as they turn in their research papers is, "This rhetoric paper almost killed me!" The hyperbole of this mantra has been echoed by exhausted students for the 30 years that I have been a professor, but it has always and only been said to reflect an index of their midnight efforts and never has been intended to be taken literally. Yet, in my own case, and in one special instance, this utterance came far too close to being true. While studying rhetoric in Greece, I unwittingly stood in the middle of a dramatic scene that was nothing less than a passion play for the people of Greece: The Revolution of 1974. Although I have always stressed the relationship between political conditions and rhetoric in my classes, and have tried to take such exigencies into account in my research, the context has always been on a purely academic, speculative, and historical basis. The experience of this event not only sharpened my sensitivity to the political conditions that we all operate under, but also the relationship between the study of rhetoric and its social consequences.

I feel compelled to make certain and clear some qualifications at the very outset of this account. Despite the quip in my title, the Revolution of 1974 fortunately turned out to be both bloodless and quick. To my knowledge, no suffering occurred and, in fact, the change was widely welcomed. Lacking a violent clash of rival forces, some may not even consider the events that took place in July of 1974 as a "revolution" in the strict sense. Yet it was indeed a revolution, for it resulted in an immediate and dramatic political change. Of course, at the time we had no way of knowing that this revolution would end peacefully, probably because so many revolutions do not, and because knowledge of events are never fully understood by those who, at that moment, actively participate. With these caveats in mind, I wish to stress that this is my personal account, my reflection on those events, and the lessons that we can learn that bear on our discipline.

Second, and most importantly, I do not wish to infer that what I experienced at all resembles the sufferings that scholars have endured in other situations of much greater and unfortunate magnitude. My most poignant illustration is a distinguished professor who was a fixture in Greece and at The American School of Classical Studies at Athens for much of the twentieth century: Eugene Vanderpool. His daughter-in-law, Catherine deG. Vanderpool, who is the Executive Vice President of the American School of Classical Studies at Athens, helped me greatly to understand the true heroics of Eugene Vanderpool when I sought her help in providing information for this essay. Eugene Vanderpool, his wife Joan, and their four children had delayed leaving Greece at the outbreak of World War II. Captured by Nazi troops, Vanderpool was sent to a prisoner-of-war camp for several years while his wife and their children dutifully remained in Athens. During his time in camp, Vanderpool passed the hours teaching prisoners of war about Thucydides and that famous historian's account of the Peloponnesian War. (I suspect that the irony was not lost on his Nazi guards!) Joan was equally valiant, for while her husband spent years in prison, she not only cared for her children but also helped others by establishing a soup kitchen in an effort to relieve those suffering from the terrible famines that were widespread in war-torn Athens.

Toward the end of the war, Vanderpool was able to return to America in a prisoner-of-war exchange. As soon as the war ended, however, Vanderpool rejoined his family in Greece so that he could continue his Hellenic studies. Vanderpool remained in Greece for the rest of his life. When I heard him lecture in 1974, I saw him only as an aging, quiet, humble scholar whose bravery was never revealed or even mentioned. However, my program Director, Fordyce W. Mitchell, himself a wounded World War II veteran, told me that in tribute to his many contributions, Eugene Vanderpool was made an honorary citizen of Delphi. In the events that I discuss here, I came to appreciate the qualities that Vanderpool and Mitchell possessed, qualities that helped to make them not only distinguished educators, but also dedicated and passionate scholars. Either as a scholar or as a soldier, both risked his life for his beliefs and principles. This essay is dedicated to Eugene Vanderpool and

Fordyce W. Mitchell, who not only helped to teach me about the Hellenic world, but also taught me how important dedication in the face of adversity is to the academic life.

SCHOOLING UNDER A DICTATORSHIP

By May of 1974 I had completed my first year as an assistant professor at The University of Michigan. Not yet married, young, and free from any responsibilities, I decided to spend a portion of my first-year salary on enrolling in the Summer Program of the American School of Classical Studies at Athens. The prospect of studying in Greece was attractive for several reasons, not the least of which was that I had thought that I would be free from normal obligations and able to devoted myself wholeheartedly to the study of classical rhetoric in the very place where it originated. My wife has often chided me by saying that if I had been born in the Middle Ages, I would have been the ideal monk. At the time, I did think of this trip as a cloistered experience of sorts and did, in fact, envision a cerebral learning experience free from domestic constraints. I was, however, wrong in thinking that I would be removed from the daily affairs of life. What I experienced was quite the opposite. During my study in Greece, I witnessed the overthrow of the military dictatorship that had ruled Greece for years and the instantaneous reinstatement of democracy. In the process, I learned that life itself is the most dominant factor in our study and research, for I realized that the opportunity to study and do research exists not as a right but as a privilege, a sometimes unstable privilege that must be won, occasionally defended, and always treasured.

In America, we take the privilege of education for granted, but in my stay in Greece I came to realize how valuable our resources and opportunities are in this country. In short, every rhetorician knows that rhetoric must be understood in its environment if we are to advance any sort of sensitive understanding of the relationship between discourse and social context. What I learned during the Greek Revolution was that the same holds true for education. That is, education generally, like rhetoric specifically, can thrive only in certain contexts, and we must never take the fragility of these delicate conditions for granted. Cicero recognized this point in his rhetorical works when he observed that rhetoric did not create the Republic but—as a vital force within the Republic—rhetoric can serve as a normative and regulatory force to maintain the best features of the Republic (Enos). These observations became dramatically clear to me as I watched the political events in Greece unfold during the summer of 1974.

I must confess at the outset that I made my decision to study in Greece oblivious to the social and political constraints that had been in place since the dictatorship began in 1967. From my apolitical perspective, the opportunity to study at The American School of Classical Studies at Athens promised to be unique and exciting for several reasons. I was told that I was the first classical rhetorician to be admitted to the program in the School's (then) nearly 100-year history. The program promised not only to extend my knowledge of classical rhetoric by direct exposure to material evidence, but also to acquaint me with an array of different research methods. My graduate studies in classical rhetoric at Indiana University had provided me with a thorough exposure to the primary sources and secondary scholarship of ancient rhetoric. I felt, however, that the existing scholarship had not thoroughly covered the subject in two respects. First, I believed that there was a need to discover more primary material. The current existing sources had been passed down to us through the ages from a literary history but the archaeological discoveries of the last century had been left virtually unexamined. I felt that fieldwork would help to resolve this problem, for recent archaeological discoveries had laid bare artifacts that could tell us much about the history of rhetoric. Second, and as a corollary to the first point, I felt that the traditional research methods of our discipline were self-constrained. Much of the analysis was based solely upon the principles of either literary or rhetorical criticism, and empirical methods refined by such disciplines as archaeology and epigraphy could greatly extend our knowledge of classical rhetoric—if only these methods would be applied. In short, the Summer Program at The American School of Classical Studies at Athens promised not only to extend my knowledge of classical rhetoric and ancient Greek, but also to acquaint me with any array of different, sensitive research methods. I did know that my experience would be unique, but I had no idea that part of the scholarly "adventure" would involve witnessing the overthrow of the military dictatorship and the re-establishment of democracy in Greece. This essay recounts my experiences during those tumultuous events, reflects on values of scholarship in times of strife, and the direct and indirect benefits of the academic life of our discipline.

DEMOCRACY RETURNS TO GREECE

The three-inch headline on the July 24, 1974, edition of Athens' leading newspaper, *Apogeumatine,* contained only one word: *"Demokratia."* The simple but poignant "news" was that democracy had returned to Greece. This reinstatement of democracy was personified by the return of the exiled leader, Konstantinos Karamanles. Seven years earlier, in 1967, a group of right-wing generals, fearing that Greece would come under the control of leftist extremists and the ever-growing popularity of the Communist Party, brought about a successful coup. The reigning monarch, Constantine II, left Greece and, under the directives of the military leadership, Greece euphemistically became a "Presidential Republic." Many liberals were arrested or compelled to flee in exile. The military dictatorship established stringent rules, curtailed or removed several well-established "liberties," and the possibility of democracy was crushed. In the years that followed, countercoups failed. Despite international criticism, the military dictatorship persisted until a war with Turkey over Cyprus appeared imminent and the Greek armed forces were mobilized for action.

For several years, and some would argue since Antiquity, there has been an ongoing dispute over Cyprus and her Hellenic affiliation. Greece and Turkey have long had cultural roots in Cyprus and, in many ways, the tension between these two cultures escalated on the island to the extent that the possibility of war became imminent. Ironically, it was the Greek military's preparation for war against Turkey over Cyprus that directly led to the re-establishment of democracy in Greece and the securing of peace. Mobilized for possible action against Turkey over disputes regarding Cyprus, the soldiers had stood ready for battle over issues in the Aegean. When it became clear to all that war between Greece and Turkey was not imminent, the soldiers took the opportunity to "remove" their own generals from governmental control and reinstate democracy. Unable to secure control of Cyprus, the President, Lt. General Phaedon Gizikis, willingly returned the power to rule back to the Greek people. *"Demokratia"* had retuned to her birthplace. The seven-year dictatorship of military generals had, fittingly, been overthrown by the rank-in-file soldiers of Greece's army.

As a classical rhetorician, my observation of the political events mentioned above was filtered through the lens of the history of rhetoric. One of the first points that students learn when introduced to classical rhetoric is that rhetoric thrived in Athens because Athens was a democracy. After several decades of research I now know that this statement must be qualified. The study and practice of rhetoric did exist in several forms throughout Greece, and many of the city-states in which rhetoric flourished were nondemocratic. In fact, in perspective, the democracy of Athens within which rhetoric thrived was unrepresentative of the climate of many (if not most) of her rival Hellenic cities. That point qualified, it is also important to recognize that rhetoric was clearly a source of power in a democratic climate where the free flow of ideas and arguments doubtlessly contributes toward making the best judgments about questions of value, public policy, and social preference. Rhetoric and democracy have been inextricably, and often romantically, joined together not only by liberal-minded historians of rhetoric but also by the Greek people themselves. Realizing this historical prologue, it is understandable that the Greek people would be devastated by the usurping of their democracy. The loss of free expression under the military dictatorship struck at the heart of all that is Greek, both for her citizens and for those who study classical rhetoric.

As mentioned above, I began to realize how different my education in Greece would be from my American experiences when I first arrived for study in Athens during the summer of 1974. On June 15, soon after our arrival in Greece, James R. McCredie, the Director of The American School of Classical Studies in Athens, sent us a memo entitled, "Foreigners in Greece." In this statement Dr. McCredie outlined the rules, regulations, and protocol for citizens of foreign countries. For the most part, foreigners were granted unrestricted travel throughout Greece, except those individuals who came from Yugoslavia, Israel, and "Iron Curtin" countries. As guests of the Greek government, we were asked "to comply most carefully with the local regulations." Off the printed page, however, I was given further and more explicit directives by others. I was told that the Greek people do not wish to discuss the present government for fear of reprisals and that it was in our best interests as visitors not to discuss present political matters. This advice, however, was in direct opposition to the long-standing custom of politically-minded modern Greeks. In fact, the 1973 British *Blue Guide* to Greece explicitly mentions that while opposite to "English custom," it is absolutely common for modern Greeks to ask direct and even pointed questions about politics as a normal part of everyday conversation (52). In short, American and British travelers should not be taken aback and never offended by political conversation. Warned about this Greek political proclivity, I was shocked by the conspicuous absence of any discussion of current events. At the time, I did recognize that these procedures were different from the environment that I had enjoyed in America, but I took it as the norm and followed the guidelines. On a personal level, however, I became increasingly sensitive to how repressed many of the local Greek people were. By nature, outgoing, friendly and amicable, I felt a certain guardedness from local inhabitants during our conversations, feeling as if a pall hung over their heads. I freely admit that this observation comes only after reflection.

After the revolution I returned to the United States with the intent of improving my conversational ability in modern Greek. I had learned that knowledge of ancient Greek was essential but that knowing modern Greek was vital for fieldwork, where travel to rural sites often meant coming into contact with individuals who had no knowledge of English. In an effort to learn modern Greek to complement my ancient Greek, I had various Greek students who came to America to tutor me in modern Greek. To a person, each and every student-tutor has been politically sensitive and outspoken. Yet, reflecting back to 1974, I can now see how repressed and silenced the students in Greece were at the time. In this climate of military-ruled dictatorship, the study of rhetoric in democratic Athens was clearly an historical artifact and not a lived-out experience.

I also noticed that the government had direct and powerful control over educational sites. The Summer Program of The American School has two components to the curriculum. The first component is the presentation of information and observations. Students study, hear lectures by distinguished scholars, and give reports at various archaeological sites in and around Athens. The second component is travel. Interspersed throughout the summer study are excursions to various regions in Greece. Some of these trips involve travel to Crete, the Peloponnese, and various islands in the Cyclides. Such an educational experience is invaluable. Of course, it is the interaction of these two components that makes for a meaningful and unique educational experience. Students stand at the site of the Battle of Marathon, view the remains of the stadia and theatres where various literary and athletic contests were held, and see first-hand priceless artifacts at on-site museums.

All of these archaeological venues, however, are under the direct control and authority of Ephors or Regional Directors. The Ephors, in turn, operate through such governmental agencies as the Ministry of Science and Culture and the Greek Archaeological Service. These agencies must report and follow the directives of the Greek government. I witnessed both the power and the speed of authority first hand. I recall one occasion when we were to have studied at a part of the Athenian Agora that was currently under excavation. The Agora is known to those studying the history of rhetoric as the place where sophists, rhetoricians, and philosophers disputed, where Socrates had many of his dialogues, and where various epideictic orations were proclaimed at the Bema, or speaker's rostra. On our arrival that particular day, we were told by one of the archaeologists that study at this site was suspended because of the present "political situation." Eventually the site re-opened and we were allowed access, but that small experience drove home the point of how delicately balanced the situation for study was at the time.

In a country such as ours, where we take for granted not only the availability of information but also access to various sites, the constraints of governmental control are not taken seriously. I did hear many stories about the bravery of individuals, as mentioned earlier, but these stories were always in the context of World War II and seemed to me only "stories" of the past. I recall listening to Tete (one of my elderly tutors of modern Greek) tell me how a Nazi soldier broke her arm when she was a young girl during World War II. Our director, Fordyce W. Mitchell, who was a veteran of World War II, even told us stories of the Nazi invasion of Crete and pointed out machine gun nests and battle sites as we traveled across Greece. These stories of war in Greece resonated with stories from my own family. I even recall my Italian relatives telling me how one of our family members was tortured by the Fascists. The consequences of World War II went on for years after peace had been restored. In their book *Studies in Fifth-Century Attic Epigraphy,* Donald William Bradeen and Malcolm Francis McGregor mentioned, "for about a decade after 1939 Athens was inaccessible to epigraphists" (106). Yet, these accounts did not hit home to me until I directly experienced the Revolution of 1974. It is only when I saw education controlled and sometimes constrained, when I saw how rapidly sites of learning could be made "unavailable" for study, that I began to realize how nonchalantly we Americans take our education.

THE MOMENT OF EXPERIENCING
THE RHETORICAL SITUATION

While the small encounter at the Athenian Agora underscored the precarious status of study that we were under, the actual moment of the revolution, the literal rhetorical situation (if you will) drove the point home securely. In late July our study group, under the direction of Mitchell, was away from Athens and traveling through the various islands of the Cycladies. One of the principle islands of study is Delos. The island itself was excavated by the French Archaeological Society. Excluding members of the archaeological service, no one was permitted to stay on the island. Instead, we stayed at the nearby island of Mykonos. My notes reveal a thorough study of Delos. I was particularly impressed to learn that because Delos was the birthplace of Apollo, no one in Antiquity was allowed either to be born or to die on this sacred island. The sacredness of life would, however, be in stark contrast with what I experienced when we returned to Mykonos after spending the day on Delos.

In the days leading up to our travel to Delos we had learned that tension between Greece and Turkey was escalating and that the Greek military forces had been mobilized for war. One feature of preparing for imminent war was the control of all ships in the Aegean. The Greek government felt that it was necessary to have all ships available for possible duty, and this included the sorts of passenger ships that are normally used for tourist travel. When the directive came that our passenger ship was put on active duty, our study group was stranded on Mykonos. It is difficult to consider anyone being "stranded" on the island of Mykonos, for it is widely regarded as one of the most beautiful islands in the Aegean and a "jet set" site for all Europe. The elegant stability of this island, however, was in contrast to the uncertainty of our situation. It was during this time that I came to appreciate the leadership of our instructor, Fordyce W. Mitchell. Uncertain of our fate with Turkey, unclear about how the Greek dictatorship would respond, Mitch nonetheless continued to sustain our educational program, giving us all the important lesson of "carrying on" (as the British say) despite adversity. Mitch, as stated earlier, must have gathered this strength from his past. A wounded veteran of World War II, he would tell us stories of great scholars who so loved their discipline that they would risk imminent danger to pursue their studies and research. His favorite stories centered on his former teacher, Eugene Vanderpool.

Through such stories, and in such a difficult time, I gained a new awareness of the quiet courage of scholars who would research at great risk in order to pursue their scholarship. We in America take the environment for study for granted. We assume a natural peace and tranquil environment for study. I learned that the study of rhetoric should not be limited only to a stroll over to the library or a bucolic retreat to some lake cottage for the weekend. I learned that the price of discovery may well require tedious and difficult travel to remote locations, arduous fieldwork in the hot summer sun, and (as I was experiencing first-hand) the precarious political conditions that can leave the feeling that your very life is at risk.

When we learned that the risk of war with Turkey was reduced, we had thought that the "adventure" was over but, in fact, it was only entering a new phase. When the control of ships was lifted, we students were allowed to return to Athens on a freighter. I vividly recall feeling the exhilarating rush of freedom, but I expected a slow meandering return to Piraeus, the port city of Athens. I was used to slow passenger ships and sitting on the deck, feeling the breeze of the Aegean on my face. I was amazed at how rapidly we were returned to Athens. After we landed at Piraeus, we returned to the American School and learned that yet another development had occurred. The dictatorship had ended, and the exiled leader, Konstantinos Karamanles, would be returning to Greece. Democracy had returned to her birthplace.

Elated over the return of democracy, we students were given permission to leave the school grounds and join the jubilant Athenians in welcoming their democratic hero back to Greece. Naturally we went to Sindagma Square, the center of the city and the site of the Palace where, in 1843, the constitution was declared. On two occasions that evening I was within 20 yards of Mr. Karamanles as he openly walked through the streets of Athens, reuniting with his fellow citizens after years of exile. We were so taken by the moment of celebration that it was only later that we realized how dangerous that situation was for Americans.

While I am sure that all Americans rejoiced in the return of democracy to Greece, I believe that some of the Greek people had a somewhat different reaction and perception of our country. During the dictatorship, American had (doubtlessly) disapproved of the tyranny but had nonetheless done little or nothing to end the despotism. When I asked about the position of the United States, I came to realize, or at least was told, that Greece was a strategically critical site for NATO, and the United States did not wish to have her bases in Greece put at risk. As a result, I believe that it is fair to say that many Greeks were disappointed that the American government was not a force in restoring freedom to Greece but rather had acquiesced to the military dictatorship for pragmatic reasons. To the credit of the Athenians on that first night of freedom, the Athenians in Sindagma Square could have lashed out at Americans as a symbol of their disappointment with the U.S. government. Yet the Greek people showed an amazing ability to separate innocent foreigners from politics and allowed us to share in their joy.

This is perhaps a natural place to mention my own view of how Greeks regard higher education and scholars who visit their country. I realize that generalizations can often be hasty or unrepresentative, but let me say that I have made several subsequent trips to Greece since 1974 and continue to be amazed at the respect that all Greeks uniformly have for those who visit their country to study and do research. Even as a beginning assistant professor, I found that government officials, local residents, and officials at archaeological sites practice and live out a standard of courtesy that is (sadly) not readily evident in America. I also feel that the Greek people have a wonderful capacity to separate current international politics from individual visitors. In short, I have always felt both welcome and honored to study and to do research in Greece. I feel that this disposition was a factor in the Greek people allowing us to join in their celebration of freedom on that July evening of 1974.

MY RETURN IN 1977 OR "THERE AND BACK AGAIN"

I have returned to Greece with my wife and children many times since 1974, but I recall most clearly my return in 1977, for it was the first time that I had come back to Greece since the Revolution of 1974. In 1977 my wife, Jane Helppie, and I had only been married two years and had no children. I had received funding to do fieldwork at archaeological sites and museums throughout Greece in an effort to locate information that would expand our knowledge of classical rhetoric. While our home base was the American School of Classical Studies at Athens, we spent most of the time traveling. Because many ancient sites are on islands and in remote areas, my wife and I had two months of uninterrupted fieldwork that involved traveling throughout Greece. During this time of travel we had the opportunity to meet people from all walks of life and in many different regions of Greece. Although it had only been three years since the Revolution of 1974, I felt that a great deal had changed in Greece. The excellent facilities and the cooperative attitude of the American School of Classical Studies remained. The outgoing and friendly disposition of the Greek people—from the country shepherds to the highest government officials—also remained unaltered. Even the physical environment showed no real modification. What I do feel had changed was real but intangible. I felt a degree of joy and openness that was far different from the attitude that had existed three years earlier. While I fully realize that this may only be my perception and colored interpretation, I nonetheless am convinced to this day that the fabric of the cultural climate was positively altered by the political changes that had occurred.

As with any veteran schoolteacher I must ask myself the question, "What have I learned from this experience?" At the start of this essay I quipped that many students have uttered that fateful sentence, "This rhetoric paper almost killed me!" In 1974 the revolution that took place in Greece killed no one—but it easily could have resulted in death and carnage. At the conclusion of *The New Rhetoric: A Treatise on Argumentation,* Chaim Perelman and L. Olbrechts-Tyteca discuss the alternatives to rhetoric. The alternatives to "resolving" social problems, Perelman and Olbrechts-Tyteca observe, are not attractive: ambivalence or violence. That is, in an effort to resolve or cope with problems, individuals can become so apathetic that they will abide by any decision, or result to force in an effort to compel others into agreement. Through rhetoric, Perelman and Olbrechts-Tyteca observe, a reasoned decision can be reached that will result in adherence to a course of action through mutual agreement. It is somewhat ironic that I went to Greece to study rhetoric but instead literally saw rhetoric in action. The Greek people could easily have staged a violent revolution. Instead, however, agreement through discourse resulted in significant, prompt, and dramatic change without bloodshed. We have far too many examples of revolutions that have resulted in the massive loss of life not to be sensitive to how fortunate all of us were not to have suffered anything more than some slight inconveniences. In a literal sense, that rhetoric paper could have killed me. The fact that it did not, however, did not stop me from realizing how much we take for granted.

Specifically, I learned to appreciate the research that we take for granted. The opportunity and availability of sources and material for study is taken often as a right, but it is really a privilege. I also added to my realization that knowledge is valuable because I saw what could happen when it is denied. Finally, and most important to me, I gained a profound appreciation for those scholars who persisted in spite of obstacles and constraints that we barely could imagine. Through the work of these researchers, whose efforts often bordered on the heroic, I came to have a much deeper sense of, and appreciation for, the meaning of commitment to scholarship. Beginning assistant professors are prompted to think of scholarship as the activity that will earn them tenure. While the reality of that condition is too obvious for words, an experience such as the one I had in Greece in 1974 has given a deeper reality to the meaning of scholarly commitment than I could have imagined before I had set foot on Greek soil for the first time in 1974.

A Postscript

The previous rubrics of this essay represent the text as it was presented prior to our country's engagement in Iraq. Much has happened in the intervening time that is worthy of comment, but there is one point that struck me as especially poignant in light of my background and interest in historical research. An essay written by Kristin M. Romey in the May/June 2002 issue of *Archaeology* entitled, "The Race to Save Afghan Culture," discusses worldwide pleas by Afghans to help save their cultural treasures from destruction and looting. Recently, we have sadly witnessed the same plight in Baghdad, where priceless artifacts have been stolen and museums pillaged. While many would say that there are far greater issues to discuss than the destruction of a people's cultural heritage, it is nonetheless evident that years of painstaking efforts by scholars to preserve the cultural wealth of a people can disappear in moments. It is obvious to say that revolutions are termed "bloodless" and "without cost" only in retrospect, since the costs of life and heritage are tallied after the fact. What is not so obvious, but now dramatically illustrated by recent events in both Afghanistan and Iraq, is the need to guard and protect history from those who would steal and put up for sale to the highest bidder their very heritage for nothing more than personal gain or vengeance. The events of the last few months should reveal that history, and in that category we must include the history of rhetoric, is more than preserving "curiosities" for either the required reading of students or those who casually stroll through a museum. Our efforts at preserving, enriching, and understanding our history are nothing less than preserving our very culture and our identity. Historical lessons can be, like life itself, harsh teachers, yet the lessons are well worth learning if—to echo the sentiments of Greek playwrights—we are to realize any benefits out of tragedy.

Works Cited

Apogeumatine. Athens: July 24, 1974.

Bradeen, Donald William and Malcolm Francis McGregor. *Studies in Fifth-Century Attic Epigraphy.* Norman OK: U of Oklahoma P for the U of Cincinnati, 1973.

Enos, Richard Leo. *The Literate Mode of Cicero's Legal Rhetoric.* Carbondale IL: Southern Illinois UP, 1988.

"Greece." *The Columbia Encyclopedia.* Sixth edition (2001): <*www.bartleby.com/65/gr/Greece.html*>.

McCredie, James R. "Foreigners in Greece." Internal memo, American School of Classical Studies at Athens: June 15, 1974.

Perelman, Chaim, and L. Olbrechts-Tyteca. *The New Rhetoric: A Treatise on Argumentation.* Trans. By John Wilkinson and Purcell Weaver. Notre Dame, IN: U of Notre Dame P, 1969.

Romey, Kristin M. "The Race to Save Afghan Culture." *Archaeology* May/June 2002: 18–25.

Rossiter, Stuart (ed.). *Blue Guide: Greece.* Second edition. London: Ernest Benn Limited, 1973.

Vanderpool, Catherine deG. E-mail correspondence regarding the activities of Eugene Vanderpool during World War II. August 9, 2002.

Are You Now, or Have You Ever Been, an Academic?

Shane Borrowman and Edward M. White

We write this as a dialogue between two generations of scholars in English, both engaged in related dialogues with the present and the past. The reflections in this essay focus upon uncomfortable times for both of us, trying, usually without much success, to have some influence on—or to understand, or to be understood by—the world within and beyond academe during times of crisis and trauma.

> ac•a•dem•ic—theoretical or hypothetical; not practical, realistic, or directly useful [. . .] learned or scholarly but lacking in worldliness, common sense, or practicality.
>
> —OED

BORROWMAN: STUDENTS, TEACHERS, AND TRAUMA

I AM A MEMBER of the last generation to remember the Vietnam War, the generation that witnessed the fall of Saigon as children and the collapse of the Soviet empire as adults, the generation that came of age during the cold peace of the 1970s and 1980s when the U.S. and the USSR regularly tangled in the air over the Bering Straits and the Mediterranean Sea. Images of silent classrooms dot the landscape of my memory. Silent children sitting at round tables, listening as a crying teacher tried to explain a lost war and its lost warriors. Silent adolescents listening to a veteran of World War II explain the significance of places such as Panama, Grenada, and Libya. Silent adults in English 408: Composition Theory listening to a professor speak of United Nations' deadlines and war in the Persian Gulf. Silent students looking to me to explain terrorism and looming war as images of Ground Zero filled the screen of a television hanging in the corner. It simply never occurred to me that education was somehow separate from the "real" world, for trauma has always been a part of learning and teaching.

As teachers, we teach through our own traumas, the individual traumas of our students, and the shared traumas of the nation. As I write these words, a homemade sympathy card sits upon the crowded bookshelf behind me, a gift presented to me by a group of English 101 students during the summer that my paternal grandfather died. Names in my gradebook remind me of students past. Most of them are names without faces, students I would likely know on sight but whom I have otherwise forgotten; others I remember for the fine work they did—or went on to do. But some of them stick in my teaching mind for darker reasons: Lori E., who drove 20 miles after work to tell me she wouldn't be in class that night because her brother-in-law had broken his neck in a motorcycle accident; Erik D., whose daily hangovers finally convinced him to attend AA, which allowed him to finish his degree on schedule; Kelly R., who was raped in her dorm room at the beginning of the term and still completed the quarter. These students demonstrated absolute, unforgettable courage; like the other adults in their lives, I did what I could, and whatever I was asked, for these young people. But most of their trauma they dealt with alone. Any teacher could tell similar stories. During the summer of 2002, as the number of detainees at the U.S. base in Guantanamo Bay, Cuba, passed 600 and the War on Terror seemed to shift inexorably towards war with Iraq, I watched two students courageously face a kind of trauma I had, in my white, middle-class naiveté, never expected to encounter. Mohammed M. and Arfana L. were students in my English 101 class that summer, the first an Islamic student from the United Arab Emirates and the second a first-generation immigrant from Kashmir. Each of them, in different ways, spoke of his/her experiences in an America that had changed significantly since September of 2001. In *Slapstick*, Kurt Vonnegut writes of "the sudden American hatred for all things German which unsheathed itself when this country entered the First World War"; these students encountered the sudden American distrust of the Islamic world that rose with the fall of the Towers (7).

Mohammed is a traditional student, has studied English to near-native proficiency, and writes thoughtfully of the father-figure in his life (a lover of children and former ambassador from the UAE to Iraq). Like many ESL students, Mohammed spends much of his free time with a group of friends with whom he shares a culture and first language. And an ethnicity. In the months since September 11, Mohammed and his friends were kept under regular surveillance by the local police and repeatedly stopped for innocuous traffic infractions—such as turning a corner and moving immediately into the far lane without signaling. Tickets were always written in these encounters, which is not unusual. The questions asked by the police, however, were unusual. Mohammed was asked by multiple officers about his ties to Osama bin-Laden, asked if he has ever been to Afghanistan for training, asked to step out of his vehicle so that he—and it—could be searched thoroughly.

Mohammed's response to these events seemed as startling to me as the events themselves: He understood—and continues to understand—the anger and fear being projected onto him. "America was attacked," he stated during a class discussion as he repeated his stories of harassment to his peers, "and of course people would react this way." He was, and still is, grateful for the opportunities to pursue his education that America affords him.

As Mohammed spoke to the class, Arfana slowly and repeatedly nodded her head. Although she is a U.S. citizen by birth, Arfana's stories shared many common experiences with those of Mohammed. Before September 11, she had never left the United States and had never been stopped by the police for any reason. In the first two months after September 11, she calmly stated, she was stopped for traffic infractions seven times. She was never asked about her connections to any political group or about her travels outside of the United States, but her citizenship was always carefully verified before she was sent upon her way. Twice her vehicle was searched. Arfana's response to these incidents was nowhere near as understanding as that of Mohammed. She was angry at the sudden change in her status because, she surmised, of her skin color. She was angry about the intrusions into her life, the possibly illegal searches of her vehicle, and the careful questioning that always followed her assertion of citizenship.

Most Americans responded to such events as my students described—when they were publicized—with outrage, and officially they were certainly condemned by all levels of public government. But the experiences of these two students are not as unique as they should be, are not absolute aberrations in the working of the American machine. These students faced individual trauma inextricably bound to the shared trauma of September 11; their peers were outraged, as I was, yet all of us felt powerless in the face of larger issues, powerless when confronted by a national/international tragedy of such proportion that the rights of individual citizens eroded—or evaporated altogether, in some cases. A long time student of American history, married to a social historian, I found myself thinking of other American traumas—real and perceived—and the erosions of freedom coupled to them. I thought about the lectures I give my literature students about Arthur Miller and Elia Kazan—lectures about the firm refusal made by the former when he was called before the House Un-American Activities Committee and the anger still simmering around the latter after nearly five decades because he sat before the HUAC and named names. In particular, and in terms of my own formal and informal education, I found myself thinking of the Loyalty Oath I had been required to sign before I could be employed as a graduate student teaching associate at The University of Arizona, a document that is an artifact of the erosion of academic freedom that took place throughout the middle of the twentieth century. In this document, I swore before God to "support the Constitution of the United States and the Constitution and laws of the State of Arizona; [to] bear true faith and allegiance to the same, and defend them against all enemies, foreign and domestic. [. . .]" Thinking of Arfana and Mohammed, thinking of the ways in which my own education and work as an educator were bound to moments of shared trauma, thinking about how the world had changed since that day in September, I wondered what—or who—I had been forced to agree to fight in this document that reads more like induction paperwork into the military than a legal contract between an employer and employee. But I was powerless before this document; if I refused to sign it, I would not be allowed to teach, would lose my tuition waiver, would—in the end—not be able to pursue my PhD. I signed.

WHITE: THE FBI, DIFFERENCE, DISLOYALTY, AND POWER

In 1996, I was interviewed by a polite FBI agent who asked a long series of pointed questions about my teaching of English composition at Harvard in 1958. What had I taught? What had we discussed in class? What did I remember about the students? What did I remember about one student in particular? I had, it seems, been the instructor of Theodore Kaczinski, the Unabomber, whose anger at the forces of technology had led to a long series of seemingly-random mail bombings throughout the United States. I had—and have—no memory of Kaczinski, although I do remember others from that first-ever teaching experience, and the books I used in that course still sit upon a shelf in my office. But I do have another memory of being interviewed by the FBI, an interview with an even darker subtext than that in 1996.

Some 40 years ago, as Senator McCarthy, FBI Director J. Edgar Hoover, and the House Un-American Activities Committee trolled for Reds and other subversives, I was an assistant professor in Wellesley College's English department, enjoying my first full-time job in a supportive, even pastoral environment. When the tall, broad, almost square man in a dark suit appeared in my office, I was surprised to hear that he was a field agent for the FBI. What on earth did he—could he—want from me?

Nothing unusual, he said. One of my students had applied for the Peace Corps, and he was doing a routine background check. Was there anything special about Jill that I would like to tell him? Jill was one of 35 students in Survey of English Literature 1, a course moving at that time from Chaucer to Shakespeare. She sat in the back row, handed in adequate papers on the reading, and made occasional comments during class discussion. I was young, loyal, even patriotic, and I struggled hard to remember anything special about her so agent Gruff would not go away empty-handed. But all I could tell him was that she was prompt, diligent, pleasant enough, and capable. I was really pleased that she was idealistic enough to apply for the Peace Corps and said that she had my full endorsement.

Gruff sat still in the hard chair beside my desk waiting for more. Surely, he said, I must have more than that to report. I smiled and pointed out that I only knew Jill from class, where we were studying poetry written 400 years ago, and that he probably didn't want to know about her opinions on the Italian vs. the English sonnet form. It all seemed rather a joke to me. But he wasn't smiling. Has she, he went on, ever said anything to indicate she was, well, different?

I was puzzled. What was he getting at? Different from what?

"Look," he said, leaning towards me, "this is an all-girl school, and I need to know if she likes girls better than boys." I kept trying to keep things light, though the conversation was moving into darker areas. This was well before gay liberation brought homosexuality into the open, and we were treading on slippery ground. I smiled again and said that nothing she had said or done in class would lead me to suspect she was different. And then, riskily, I asked, "What would it matter if she had?"

Agent Gruff stood up and began to pace, though my tiny office cramped his style. He told me condescendingly that too many "pointy-head professors" didn't understand the risk to the nation posed by what he called "these homos." They could easily be blackmailed, since their "perversity" would always break out, and then none of our nation's secrets could be safe. I was stunned at his absolute conviction and kept trying to interrupt, but he was delivering a packaged sermon that went on for ten minutes or so. Was I aware, he said again and again, that it was the "homos" that let Hitler take over Germany and then gave away Austria? Was I aware that just one traitor in the Peace Corps could start all the dominoes falling? Was I aware that there were "homos" and traitors hiding everywhere in America, even on college faculties? Here I was supposed to be an educated man, yet I didn't know the first and most important fact about world history! Or did I have, he speculated, some other reason for pretending not to take seriously what he was telling me?

He paused and looked at me closely. "Now," he said, pronouncing his words pointedly, "do you see why I need all the information you can give me about this Jill?" Has she ever said anything disloyal in class? I saw this as a sudden shift, from sexuality to loyalty; Gruff clearly saw them as interchangeable. For him, homosexuality was disloyalty.

I had long ago stopped smiling. The man is crazy, I said to myself. Dangerous. I had to get him out of my office. I stood up. "I have nothing more to say to you," I said. "If I am going to report what my students say in class to the FBI, then they have the right to know that in advance."

For the first time, a glimmer of a smile came over the agent's face. "I want you to reconsider that," he said. "I'll be writing a report when I get back to the office, and I don't think you want me to report you as disloyal. The first thing we do to disloyal citizens is recommend a thorough audit of their tax returns. Think again."

We stood there looking at each other for some time that seemed very long but probably wasn't. I felt small and helpless in the face of this large square man and all the institutionalized power he represented. Finally he shrugged, said good day, and left.

I never did look to see if he had written me up, as he had threatened to do, even after the Freedom of Information Act gave me the right to check. I did write an account of the conversation, in case anything happened to me or Jill in consequence of it, and put it away in a file. Reading those notes four decades later, I recover the chill of that day. Maybe his superiors knew of his madness (or shared it so fully that they couldn't possibly investigate everyone who clearly needed it) and discounted what he said, and that's why there were no repercussions for me. Or maybe as the 1960s went on, FBI energies went so fully into infiltrating the anti-war and civil rights movements that one intransigent English professor wasn't worth anyone's time and effort. There are other groups for the FBI to infiltrate now.

As I heard FBI Director Robert Mueller assert early in 2002 that restrictions on agents' investigative powers were now removed, allowing them to more easily tap telephones and read e-mail, infiltrate religious and secular groups, and detain suspected terrorists (even those suspected on the flimsiest of pretexts), my run-in with Hoover's FBI came back to me full force, and sent me back to my own files. Ask anyone of my (emeritus) generation and you will hear similar tales: tapped telephone lines, interrogations, threats. The ever-present large square man in a dark suit asking insinuating questions about your students, your colleagues, your family. To be sure, we need protection from terrorists and we are at war; the FBI wants to protect us for our own good. But from what one hears, the culture of the FBI has not much changed, and we have almost as much to fear from it as from the alien forces out to do us harm.

BORROWMAN: ACADEMIA, ACADEMIC FREEDOM, AND DISTRUST

As our preceding narratives implicitly argue, in times of war or other peril, the university is no safe haven; rather, it is a location for suspicion. This is true both for students and their teachers, and has been so at least since Socrates stood trial—and suffered the ultimate penalty—for corrupting the youths of Athens. In American culture, the relationship between post-secondary institutions and the world around them is both strained and strange; the idea of a college education for any—or every—student is a powerful mojo by which politicians can conjure additional terms in office, but the reality of a college-educated individual has less appeal in some of those same circles. This distrust manifests itself in multiple forms at the post-secondary level, particularly in attacks on academic freedom. These attacks are even more dangerous now, yoked as they are, or can be, to issues of Homeland Security and all that that vague God term of self-defense can include. This issue has deep roots in American culture, roots that reach from the new millennium all the way back to censorship of Royalist publications and Loyalty Oaths required of teachers in all colonies during the American Revolution (Linfield ix, xiii, 10–13). While it is not my purpose here to give an exhaustive account of the assaults on individual freedoms, particularly academic freedom and the attendant right to free speech, in the United States during times of trauma (especially times of war), I examine two examples below, a case argued before the Supreme Court in 1967 regarding an individual's right to join the Communist Party and an indictment of higher education in general in the wake of September 11 by the American Council of Trustees and Alumni (ACTA) in a report titled "Defending Civilization: How Our Universities Are Failing America And What Can Be Done About It."

In 1967, in *United States vs. Robel,* the Supreme Court heard arguments regarding a situation where a member of the Communist Party continued to work in a shipyard designated a "defense facility" by the Secretary of Defense under the Subversive Activities Control Act. The case concerned, among other things, employment law, the Constitutional right of assembly, and the power of the government in relation to war and national defense. Expressing an attitude that would be reversed publicly by FBI Director Mueller and other government officials, if not in the legal system, in the months after September 11, the Court stated,

> [T]his concept of "national defense" cannot be deemed an end in itself, justi-fying any exercise of legislative power designed to promote such a goal. Implicit in the term "national defense" is the notion of defending those val-ues and ideals which set this Nation apart. For almost two centuries, our country has taken singular pride in the democratic ideals enshrined in its Constitution, and the most cherished of those ideals have found expression in the First Amendment. It would indeed be ironic if, in the name of national defense, we would sanction the subversion of one of those liberties—the free-dom of association—which makes the defense of the Nation worthwhile.

While the Court focuses here explicitly on only half of the First Amendment, it implicitly endorses not only the right to assemble but also the right to speak freely as well. But this freedom is uneasily extended to educators. The unease with which this freedom of speech is extended to those charged with educating students is clearly at the heart of ACTA's report on the failings of academe when responding to the events of September 2001.

"Defending Civilization" is a poorly argued and ill-conceived indictment of post-secondary education in general and of historians in particular. In this report, an artificial binary is posited: "Americans" vs. "academe." While "Americans across the country responded [to September 11] with anger, patriotism, and support of military intervention[, . . .] professors across the country sponsored teach-ins that typically ranged from moral equivocation to explicit condemnation of America" (1). Leaders from both major political parties are quoted as supporters of violent responses to violent acts, while anonymous students and professors are quoted out of context in support of ACTA's characterization of academia as a hotbed of subversion and equivocation. All of the quotations from academics are of a type (and there are many of them, more than nine pages of this 38-page document), suggesting that any thought about the then-current events that was not accompanied by anger, flag-waving, and declarations of knee-jerk patriotism were not only wrong but also very dangerous—as dangerous to the security of the nation as homosexuality or membership in the Communist Party had been a generation before.

The paradox at the heart of this report—and at the heart of this issue of academic freedom that it attacks—is that, even in these biased pages, academics are seen responding to a shared traumatic event *as* academics. Rather than joining "the President in calling evil by its rightful name," which the ACTA report firmly, simplistically, endorses, professors are indicted because "Some refused to make judgments. Many invoked tolerance and diversity as antidotes to evil. Some even pointed accusatory fingers, not at the terrorists, but at America itself" (1). The logic of the argument seems so superficial, so obstinately isolationist and willfully ignorant of America's role in the dynamics of world politics, that, as a teacher of writing, it is almost too baffling to elicit a response. But if evil is to be called by its rightful name, as the report argues, then ignorance must also be labeled and responses must be made.

And ACTA does make small gestures towards the larger issues of individual freedom that this report indicts. It is argued, for example, that "while professors should be passionately defended in their right to academic freedom, that does not exempt them from criticism" (4). The major criticism, it seems, is that courses in Western civilization have, since the 1960s, occupied an increasingly less-central role in post-secondary education, a charge that is only superficially supported in this report but that is dealt with more fully in the 2002 report "Restoring America's Legacy: The Challenge of Historical Literacy in the 21st Century" and the 2000 report "Losing America's Memory: Historical Illiteracy in the 21st Century." Worse, according to ACTA, is that "those surveys [in Western Civilization] have been supplanted by a smorgasbord of often narrow and trendy classes and incoherent requirements that do not convey the great heritage of human civilization" (5). But "human civilization" here refers to the heritage of the Western world and disallows study of non-Western traditions, especially if such an education results in "students at more than 146 campuses in 36 states [who] rallied to urge the country to avoid any military response" to September 11 (5).

Professors should, it seems, be allowed only enough academic freedom to hang themselves. For ACTA, academic freedom is the freedom to teach to the response-level of the masses. If 92% of Americans favor warfare as a response to September 11, then academia should—must—acquiesce (1). The logic of such an argument is staggering in its reductionism and eerily xenophobic. But it is also very American, and very understandable in its own context. It is the logic that led to my students, Arfana and Muhammed, being repeatedly stopped and questioned by the police about their citizenship and ties to terrorism, respectively. It is the twisted logic of anger in the face of an unknown and impossible-to-understand act of violence. It is a logic that expects—demands—that academics respond to the world around them not as academics but as swept-up members of a grieving culture.

WHITE: GRADING, TRAUMA, AND VIETNAM

I treasured my graduate student deferment from the draft during the Vietnam war, since going to fight was never an option. The alternatives were conscientious objector status or flight to Canada, both unattractive alternatives, but many of my friends found one or the other of them the only way to avoid implication in a war whose immorality was painfully obvious. When I started teaching at Wellesley, I was married with a child, which gained me a permanent deferment. My students, all young women, were protected from the draft by their gender. The war in Vietnam seemed as distant to my life as the country of Vietnam was distant from Wellesley College. But by the time I moved to California to help found a new university in San Bernardino, the war had become a gray shadow hovering over the country, and over my male students in particular. I had so far not only avoided the draft but also avoided thinking much about what role I would play in my students' lives in relation to the war. Teaching in a private elite women's college in New England provided an isolation from that issue that a working-class college and city in California did not afford. And I did not fully appreciate the moral ambiguity of my position. With the brief exception of my involvement with FBI agent Gruff, I had had it all too easy.

During the week classes opened at CSU San Bernardino, the local newspaper ran an editorial on the war, proclaiming that all who opposed it were traitors who should be expelled from the country, if not shot on the spot—a particularly virulent strain of America-Love-It-Or-Leave-It rhetoric. I dashed off a letter to the editor, arguing briefly that those opposing the war were patriotic Americans exercising their constitutional rights. The newspaper not only printed my letter but also ran an editorial about it and me, along with a front page teaser box for the exchange. As a corrupter of youth, the newspaper charged, I should be fired on the spot and run out of town on a rail. I don't have the paper before me, but as I remember the editorial it was headlined something like "Commies Invade New State College."

My new colleagues and administrators looked on me with baleful eyes for the next few days; we were supposed to make nice with the community, and I had, in seemingly Socratic form, splashed mud on the entire enterprise. Or had I? Wasn't the role of a university to raise the kinds of issues that I had so rashly let loose during my first week on the job? But my new institution had an enrollment-based budget, and outraging public pieties was no way to raise school spirit and lure students to our suspicious undertaking. But the barrage of bad news from the Far East pushed my little rebellion off the editorial pages, and my colleagues, most secretly in sympathy for my excesses, failed to bring the matter up again. I had, however, been put on notice about taking public stands on public issues.

During the Vietnam war, student grades meant more than they ever had before or possibly ever would again, although recent talk of war in Iraq has raised this specter again in the minds of students and teachers. To maintain a student deferment during Vietnam, a male student needed at least a C average, and the university was obliged to send grade reports directly to each student's draft board. Students doing failing work were genuinely at peril of losing their deferments, and they made sure to include that fact in their grade appeals. "If you give me that D," we would hear from an anguished young man, "you'll be sending me straight to Vietnam." And behind the anguish was an implied charge: "*You* haven't gone to fight, but you're perfectly willing to send me." By this time, early in 1966, nearly 200,000 American troops were stationed in Vietnam, and the body counts had risen so sharply that this was no idle matter; we might indeed be sending a young man to his death as penalty for a late term paper or a failure to understand the conflicts in *Mansfield Park* or *Fanny Hill*.

Some faculty members across the country felt the absurdity of this choice so strongly that they simply gave all students the grade of A, as a kind of protest against the war and its effects. The effects of that degradation of the meaning of course grades remain with us today, not only in grade inflation but also in a lingering suspicion of the very process of grading students that underlies academia. One faculty member at this time was brought up on charges of unprofessional behavior for giving a student an A in a spring term course despite the unpleasant fact that he had died during the previous fall term. Her defense was simple: "All grades are oppressive and meaningless, so I prefer not to be part of the system," she said. She was reprimanded and returned to the classroom. Giving all As was, at least, a consistent position, though I could not take it.

For me, the problem was different. It seemed to me then, as it still does now, that when we take on the job of teaching we also agree to evaluate honestly student performance. If we can't do that with integrity and discernment, we had best choose another profession. The students earn their grade, as we so often tell them; we don't give it. If the grades are misused, by the admissions office at another post-secondary institution, the government, or anyone else, that is really not our problem. Or our fault. I tried to make that argument with my students, the ones who did failing work and saw the jungles of Vietnam facing them as a result. It never worked. And I felt terrible making the argument and had trouble sleeping afterwards. And knowing that the San Bernardino *Sun-Telegram* would have approved my position on grading, at least, only made my discomfort worse.

BORROWMAN: ENGLISH STUDIES AND THE CHICKEN LITTLE REPORT

While the report discussed earlier is an indictment of academe in general and historians in particular, the perceived failings of English instructors have not escaped ACTA's attention. In a 1996 report titled "What English Majors Are Really Studying," the supposed shortcomings of English departments are laid bare. As the title of the report suggests, writing isn't the problem; instead, faculty in literature have, in specific ways, failed their students.

The problem, according to ACTA, is that Georgetown University, along with 13 of "twenty-two randomly selected colleges and universities" dropped Great Authors from the list of required courses for English majors. Instead, students are able to substitute such courses as "AIDS and Representation," "History and Theory of Sexuality," "Sexual Identity/Gender Studies," and courses in such subjects as Asian American or Chicano literature (3, 11, 12). While the departments under indictment had, generally, required courses in the great works of Western civilization, such requirements had slipped in favor of "trendy" courses. Worst of all, "The abandonment of Shakespeare requirements is not merely a trend; it is now the norm" (4). English majors—future English teachers—seem able to slip furtively through the halls of academe without ever reading a Shakespearean sonnet or play. Appendix A of this report lists the seemingly flawed requirements for English majors at 72 different institutions, alphabetically, from Amherst College to Yale University. To soften its claim, the authors of the report add, "It should be noted that, for the purposes of this study, English departments have been given the benefit of the doubt. We have assumed that at least some selections from the Great Authors are read in survey courses." But, the writers caution, "This may not actually be the case" (5).

At the heart of ACTA's concern is, as in the earlier report, a gross over-simplification: "Dropping Great Authors requirements might not be fatal if all other English courses were replete with excellent literature. [. . .] But, at many universities, new English courses focus less on great literature than on works selected precisely because they are not great." The list of the "not great" presented in Appendix B includes such questionable courses of study as Georgetown University's "Prison Literature," the University of Florida's "Women in Popular Culture," the University of Virginia's "Memory and America," and Haverford's "Postcolonial Women Writers" (23, 24, 25, 27). All of the courses are lumped together in broad categories; "Memory and America," for example, is listed along with ten other courses in the category of "Disappointing Content." The concern seems to rest not with Shakespeare's retreat from the list of required areas of study but rather with his being supplanted by literature that is, by definition, focused on texts that work in and on the world—in classes that "look more like sociology or political science than English literature." Worse, "Even the Age of Shakespeare is not immune from the emphasis on popular culture," for courses in "medieval and Renaissance literature [. . .] now focus less on literature and more on social conditions, sexual topics, and non-literary documents" (8). None of these courses of study (especially those that involve sex), according to the report, "are adequate substitutes for Shakespeare" (9).

The loss of Shakespeare outlined in this report matters, it seems, because for English majors not to study Shakespeare is comparable to "an M.D. without a course in anatomy. It is tantamount to fraud." And it matters to all of us because "This country cannot expect a generation raised on gangster films and sex studies to maintain its leadership in the world. Or even its unity as a nation" (10). Without Shakespeare, the nation will crumble. Students allowed to study in a "do-it-yourself" curriculum are wasting the time they should be spending "studying something deeper and more enduring" (9). Paradoxically, this Chicken Little report ends with praise for Hollywood: "Ironically, Hollywood is today doing more for cultural literacy than trendy English departments" (10). Irony is certainly present in this statement, but it is unintentional at best.

Like "Defending Civilization," "The Shakespeare File" is an indictment of a system with no attempt to understand it—or based in a terribly narrow, flawed understanding, an understanding of *academic* that rests in the definition that serves as the epigraph for this essay. It is an indictment based in a fundamental misunderstanding of both *academic* and *academic freedom* (an American term with its origins in the earliest years of the twentieth-century) and of those students and teachers who exercise it: "1. freedom of a teacher to discuss or investigate any controversial social, economic, or political problems without interference from officials, organized groups, etc. 2. freedom of a student to explore any field or hold any belief without interference from the teacher" *(OED)*. Academic freedom is based in the expectation that academics—including both professors and students—will ask questions that some groups may not even want to *have* asked, let alone answered. Including questions about gender, ethnicity, sexuality, and historical forces that lead/have led to war.

When I began this analysis many months ago, I expected to end with the point that reports such as "Defending Civilization" and "The Shakespeare File" are, in the end, far more troubling to academics than they are useful arguments that act upon the world of academe. I have seen no references to "The Shakespeare File" in mainstream media, and "Defending Civilization" received minimal coverage in the early weeks of its release. Both have been discussed widely at conferences and on academic listservs. My argument, before today, would have been that, while troubling, these reports are of limited significance. I can no longer argue this, no longer argue that these debates are merely academic, no longer argue without a feeling of unease—will I be defined, now, as disloyal?

As I write these words, the House of Representatives has sent House Resolution 3077, short-titled "International Studies in Higher Education Act of 2003," to the Senate. Among other things, this resolution, introduced on September 11, 2003, by Peter Hoekstra of Michigan, supports the creation of an advisory board to oversee higher education, particularly ensuring that the activities of these institutions "advance national interests, generate and disseminate information, and foster debate on American foreign policy from diverse perspectives" (HR 3077). Decisions about federal funding would clearly be linked to the "advice" generated by this committee. The language of the resolution is primarily innocuous and inoffensive, but the opening remarks by Congressman Phil Gingrey, opening debate on this resolution to the Subcommittee on Select Education, combined with the testimony of those who participated in the debate, are far darker and more troubling.

Closing his perfunctory, summative remarks about the purpose of the committee meeting, Gingrey states,

> Lastly, I am interested in opening the discussion and debate to learn more about the merits of and concern for federal support given to some of the international education programs that have been questioned in regard to their teachings, which have been associated with efforts to potentially undermine American foreign policy.

The alignment of this last point with statements such as those made in "Defending Civilization" is clear, and the testimony of Stanley Kurtz develops this argument in familiar ways. Kurtz defines post-colonialism as an unpatriotic field of study that is potentially dangerous to national security. He argues, "The core premise of post-colonial theory is that it is immoral for a scholar to put his knowledge of foreign languages and cultures at the service of American power." Connecting his arguments against post-colonialism's consistently one-sided, anti-American teachings to the events of September 11, Kurtz states that, "We know that transmissions from the September 11 highjackers went untranslated for want of Arabic speakers in our intelligence agencies." Given this, those teachers in post-secondary education responsible for the poverty of Arabic-speaking Americans, including the post-colonialists, "have all acted to undermine America's national security, and its foreign policy."

While reports such as "Defending Civilization" and its ilk seem to have limited impact on either the American academy or the American nation, testimony such as this from Kurtz is far more alarming. Before this resolution appeared in the House and moved to the Senate, the arguments about the academy's role in the post-September 11 world have been largely academic; now, instead of being academic, the debates are about the academy itself. The impact of "Defending Civilization" is minimal; the potential impact of HR 3077 is enormous, particularly for English studies, where debates about censorship and control of curriculum have long been part of the discourse.

WHITE: EXPERTISE AND OBSCENITY, ACADEME AND THE WORLD

I have twice spent a full day in court, as an expert witness; rather an odd task for an English professor, one might think. Each time involved a crisis situation of a sort: an obscenity prosecution of a classic novel during the 1960s, and then, 20 years or so later, a financial crisis at a community college involving dozens of possible layoffs. The first of those experiences confirmed my sense of the futility of academic involvement in the world of action, while the second suggested that under the right circumstances the special knowledge we bring to the world might have some impact after all.

One afternoon in the early 1960s I was holding office hours at Wellesley College, when the telephone rang. It was George Putnam, owner of one of the most distinguished trade houses in American publishing. Would I, he asked, be willing to go to court to testify in defense of an eighteenth-century novel under prosecution by the State of Massachusetts for obscenity? He had done his homework. He knew that I had written my dissertation on the work of Jane Austen and I was teaching courses in the novel. As we talked, I realized that this was no ordinary case. The attorney for Putnam's was Charles Rembar, well known for his defense of our right to read James Joyce's *Ulysses* and D. H. Lawrence's *Lady Chatterly's Lover*. Putnam and Rembar had chosen Massachusetts as the state in which to launch the book's defense because (despite the cliches about routine "banning in Boston") in that Commonwealth the state brings an action against the book in question, rather than against some hapless bookseller, as is common elsewhere. The book was John Cleland's *Memoirs of a Woman of Pleasure*, commonly known as *Fanny Hill*, a stylish and mildly erotic novel known to every student of English literature of the eighteenth century. I finally replied that I would find it an honor to join the list of faculty and literary critics lining up to defeat the proposed censorship of the book. Putnam asked me to think more about it and to call him back. You are, he warned me, the only English professor from a New England women's college to agree to testify; there may be repercussions I had not considered. I did notify the college president of my intention to testify. Margaret Clapp said I was acting in a grand tradition and she would only ask that I make if very clear that I was speaking for myself and not the college.

The hearing was held in Massachusetts Superior Court, before a single judge, a chunky man with a deep Boston accent and an Irish name. "We'll lose here," Rembar told us early on, looking keenly at the judge, "so our job is to establish the evidence we'll need on appeal." The prosecuting attorney was not District Attorney Edward Brooke, whose political ambitions led him as far away from this case as he could get, but rather a young assistant DA who looked scared and tried to cover it up by bluster. His basic tactic was to keep the academics and critics from testifying. The entire morning was taken up by the legal question, were we expert (and hence disinterested) witnesses or were we interested parties and hence not admissible? I couldn't quite follow the legal language, but found the argument fascinating. Rembar argued that we were experts in the same way a physician is an expert in a medical case; that is, our professional training and experience qualified us to make literary judgments. The DA argued that a literary critic, and, even worse, an English professor, is so committed to reading that he (curiously from the present perspective, no women were involved) cannot come to a disinterested opinion on obscenity. A decision in this case must be made by the community, and we most certainly were not representative of the community.

In the middle of the morning, the judge ruled for the state. Rembar objected strongly, pointing to the witnesses ready to testify. The judge then allowed us to testify, but with a legal proviso that what we said was not to be considered in the judgment—a curious twist that satisfied Rembar, since all he really wanted was to get our testimony on the record. The DA then called his one and only witness, the rector of a Catholic boys' school, who said, repeatedly, that the book was just a compilation of filth. Rembar was exceedingly delicate with the rector, asking him only two or three questions. Most significantly, Rembar asked him if he could recount the plot of the novel or its themes. Just a compilation of filth, said the rector. Rembar got more specific, asking if there was any connection between Fanny Hill's first lover and her last one—a trick question, since they were the same person and at the end of the book she marries him. "No connection," said the rector, "It's just a compilation of filth." Rembar allowed himself a hint of a smile and dismissed the witness.

Over lunch, we academics attacked our lawyer for failing to crucify the rector, who obviously had not really read the book. Rembar was cool. "I got what I needed from him," he told us. Then he asked, "Did any of you notice what the rector looked like?" We agreed that he was a squat Irishman with a strong Boston accent. "First rule of questioning," Rembar said. "You never attack a witness who looks just like the judge."

The afternoon was spent on the testimony of the experts, an interesting seminar on the book and its place in English literary history. After each witness, the hapless DA raised questions that demonstrated his utter incapacity to talk about literature. At one point he asked the distinguished chair of the Williams College English department something about what he pronounced as "the hero-whine" of the book. "Young man," the professor said to him, "have you yourself ever actually read a book?" "I ask the questions here, professor," shouted the flustered DA. "No further questions." I had my testimony written out, all ready to go, when to my astonishment I heard Rembar say, "No further witnesses." Later I protested, saying I had a severe case of testimony interruptus. He said that he would have called me if he needed more ammunition, but he had plenty already. And, he went on, he was worried about the press and the women's college issue. So my testimony went in with the rest, but only in writing, and the United States Supreme Court, which overturned the convictions of the book by the Massachusetts courts by a 5 to 4 vote, agreed with the young DA and tossed out all of our testimony as by interested parties, not expert witnesses. A sad legal judgment, this, and a sad commentary about the role of the highly educated in time of crisis: we may be heard, but not really listened to.

My other experience in court, in the late 1980s, led to a more optimistic conclusion, no doubt because the substance of the case had to do with qualifications to teach at the college level. This time the voice on the other end of the telephone line was that of an attorney for a community college district in California. A financial crisis was forcing the district to cut faculty jobs and, after much discussion, the administrators had decided that they would protect the academic core of the liberal arts and let go the many teachers of peripheral matters, such as social dancing, macramé, and personal finance management. But that was not as easy as it seemed. Many of the teachers of these peripheral courses had been employed for years, some of them for decades, while numbers of the best teachers in the academic core—particularly those in English—were relatively new hires. The faculty union was suing the district to protect the jobs of senior employees, arguing for the traditional last-hired/first-fired policy in many union contracts.

"Wait a minute," I interrupted, "surely the union can't be arguing that a teacher of macramé is qualified to teach college English."

"But they are making exactly that argument," came the reply. "And with some grounds. Many of those teachers have an old K-14 teaching credential so they are by definition qualified to teach *anything* we offer."

I had never heard of such a teaching credential, abandoned many years ago when the community colleges moved from an extension of high school to genuine college status. But now I saw the problem.

"You want me to testify that someone teaching college English needs to know something about the field, don't you?" I said. "I think I can do that. But I need to hear from the chair of the English department before I agree to say that in court."

Five minutes after the conversation ended, the chair of the community college English department called. He began by telling me that if it became known that he was making the call, he would deny that it had ever occurred. "Our department is a major supporter of the union," he went on. "But it's our own union that is killing us, and we need you to come in to protect us from it. They want us to fire a dozen of our newest and best teachers and replace them with an elderly bunch of people who have never even studied the field."

The English department had tried mightily, he said, to change the union's position, but without success. The whole department was grateful that the administration had the energy and integrity to fight for quality of instruction, but nobody could come out and say so. "So please help us out, save our people, and be careful not to implicate us in your testimony."

I spent six hours on the witness stand the following week, in a hearing before an administrative court judge. The union attorney was a tough, sarcastic, old-timer, fired up to protect the jobs of old and loyal employees; he had no concern for such niceties as graduate degrees or the reputation of the college he was prosecuting. Deep down, I sympathized with his mission; I've been a union member for many decades and firmly believe in the importance and value of unions for workers, even intellectual workers. But his approach was demeaning to the college and to what it means to teach English at the college level, so I knew I had to argue him down as well as I could.

He had isolated a group of courses from the college catalog that he though anyone could teach. After reading the course description, he would turn to me and, with sarcasm, ask me if I thought a teacher needed five years of graduate school to teach it. Here's a sample.

"English 052, Spelling. Now, professor, you aren't really going to pretend that we need a highly trained scholar to teach spelling, are you?"

Now, I knew nothing of what went on in this spelling course, but that freed me to give the best possible answer. "A college course in spelling has to be much more than passing out lists of spelling demons," I replied. "It has to deal with *why* words are spelled the way they are. That means the teacher needs to know about Latin and Greek roots of words, the movement of Anglo Saxon under the Norman conquest, the great vowel shift, the ways in which words were pronounced in Chaucer's day, in Shakespeare's day, and—"

"Oh, come now, professor," the lawyer interrupted. "For a spelling class, for heaven's sake?"

"OK," I continued. "Then suppose you tell the court just why there is a *gh* in the word *though*."

I had him there. He paused, for just a few seconds, but enough to allow the judge to smile. Then, in an echo from the *Fanny Hill* case, he blustered. "I ask the questions here. Let's turn to this next course: English 048, English Grammar."

And so it went, for course after course. If I do say so myself, he was way out of his league. Not that I was smarter than he was, but I knew the field and he didn't, so he kept stumbling into traps I could close him in. By the time the day was over, the district and its lawyers were jubilant, and indeed they did win the case. I treasure the experience as the one occasion in which my academic training seemed to make a difference in the world outside my campus. But, lest I seem too triumphant, I must note that all results took place on some other campus, not the world outside academe.

CONCLUSIONS: THE NEVER-ENDING TRAUMA OF THE TWENTY-FIRST CENTURY

The attacks on New York and Washington of September 11, 2001, have launched us into a state of war with terrorism that appears to have no end. U.S. troops continue to die in liberated Iraq and Afghanistan, and tensions continue to grow between the United States and both its traditional enemies and allies. At this writing, as 40,000 more National Guard members are told to prepare for deployment abroad, this looks like the dominant fact of life in the new millennium. Instead of a clear enemy in a fixed location, there are now an endless supply of enemies everywhere, all bent, U.S. citizens are told, on America's destruction. The echoes of Cold War rhetoric are eerily familiar. Instead of an enemy that may be defeated on the field, there is the prospect of a continual state of war both within and outside America's borders. And there is every reason to believe that the future will be punctuated from time to time with serious acts of violence.

This is a recipe for an Orwellian condition, like that of the eternal war in the novel *1984*. That war was maintained as a way of keeping the population under control and its rulers in power, and it hardly mattered who the enemy was. The mere existence of the war was more important than any grounding reality. Academically free teaching and learning had disappeared in Winston Smith's world, as had privacy and the elements of humanism. Only cynics are currently predicting that kind of result in the United States, but there is no question that every institution in the country will be under a different kind of scrutiny in the future. But the ranks of the cynics grow daily, and the position they take seems increasingly less cynical. In academe, as in Orwell's London, the clocks are now striking 13.

The incidents we have recounted in this essay seemed at the time to be exceptions to the smooth and free running of our lives. Only in retrospect do they link with each other, as a possible guide to what the future may hold. That is, we may be facing trauma as a permanent state, rather than an occasional anomaly. We may have always faced trauma in this way, in fact—trauma as an ongoing condition—without fully realizing it. We may have always been teaching during times of trauma, and the debates about the meaning of these traumas may never have been academic.

WORKS CITED

"Defending Civilization: How Our Universities Are Failing America and What Can Be Done About It." American Council of Trustees and Alumni. Nov. 2001. <*http://www.goacta.org/*>

Gingrey, Phil. "Opening Statement for Congressman Phil Gingrey." June 19, 2003. <*http://edworkforce.house.gov/hearings/108th/sed/titlevi61903/osgingrey.htm*> November 6, 2003.

HR 3077. October 21, 2003. <*http://thomas.loc.gov/cgi-bin/query/C?c108:./temp/~c1080AEvwE*> November 6, 2003.

Kurtz, Stanley. "Statement of Stanley Kurtz." June 19, 2003. <*http://edworkforce.house.gov/hearings/108th/sed/titlevi61903/kurtz.htm*> November 6, 2003.

Linfield, Michael. *Freedom Under Fire: U.S. Civil Liberties in Times of War.* Boston: South End, 1990.

"The Shakespeare File: What English Majors Are Really Studying." American Council of Trustees and Alumni. Dec. 1996. <*http://www.goacta.org/*>

United States v. Robel, 389 U.S. 258. U.S. Supreme Court. 1967. <*http://laws.findlaw.com/us/389/258.html*>

Vonnegut, Kurt. *Slapstick, or Lonesome No More.* New York: Dell, 1976.

"We have common cause against the night"[1]

Voices from the WPA-l, September 11–12, 2001

Editor's Note: The messages that follow appeared on the writing program adminis-trators' listserv, based at Arizona State University East and directed by David Schwalm and Barry Maid—with more than 1,000 members. The posts are pre-sented with only minor format editing (or with content editing done at the original author's request). Because individual authors are identified in the headers, closing identifiers have been deleted from messages (except when the closing seemed espe-cially important to the content of the email itself). Messages comprised entirely (or primarily) of pasted copyrighted material have been deleted.

Unlike the previous essays in this collection, which reflect on professional and peda-gogical responses to trauma at a time long past the original event, these posts pro-vide a running response to the events of September 11, 2001, by a diverse commu-nity of scholars in rhetoric and composition, including faculty and students; they demonstrate, in no uncertainty, the commitment the members of this field have to students, to teaching, to one another, and to the common good. The personal connec-tions demonstrated here—between list members themselves and between list mem-bers and the tragedy that they describe—is moving. As I write these words, more than two years after September 11, 2001, these posts still bring tears to my eyes.

The primary thread in this discussion begins, it seems, in the middle of a conversation.

Date: Tue, 11 Sep 2001 08:46:13
From: Bonnie KYBURZ
Subject: terrorism

So, for those of us who have been all morning working w/ email and otherwise avoiding the news, you might want to check it out.

I think I'm going home.

Date: Tue, 11 Sep 2001 11:00:46
From: Debra Combs
Subject: Re: terrorism

For those of us who can't go home, and can't get any information because of busy cites, could some one quickly report? I'm from New York, and I can't get much of nothin'.

Date: Tue, 11 Sep 2001 11:04:43
From: "Donna N. Sewell"
Subject: Re: terrorism

Deb,

Two planes have crashed into the World Trade Center—both towers have now fallen. Also, there's been an explosion at the Pentagon (another plane crash). Evacuations are occurring in some governmental buildings.

NPR is covering the stories if you access to a radio.

Date: Tue, 11 Sep 2001 09:06:23
From: Bonnie KYBURZ
Subject: Re: terrorism

Apparently, 4 planes have been hijacked and deliberately crashed. Two into the World Trade Center Towers (both subsequently collapsed), one into the Pentagon, and another crashed in Penn but was headed for D.C.

These were commercial airliners w/ passengers. Some talk of PLO involvement.

That's what I know, in brief.

Date: Tue, 11 Sep 2001 11:06:40
From: "Clyde A. Moneyhun"
Subject: Re: terrorism

For folks having trouble getting news, I'm watching CNN right now:

Two airplanes have hit the World Trade Towers, at least one a highjacked commercial airliner, about 30 minutes apart. They both immediately burst into flames and have now collapsed.

Another airplane crashed into the Pentagon, where a portion of the building has also collapsed.

Date: Tue, 11 Sep 2001 10:23:13
From: Traci Gardner
Subject: Re: terrorism

And a plane from Chicago to DC was crashed in Somerset County, Pennsylvania—where my great uncle lives.

Fortunately he became terribly ill about a month ago, and my parents have them at their home in Virginia. I never ever thought I'd need to begin a sentence with "Fortunately my uncle became terribly ill."

Date: Tue, 11 Sep 2001 10:07:25
From: bruce_leland
Subject: Re: terrorism

Apparently all the Web news sites are overloaded, making radio and tv the only way to get the news. Two planes crashed into the two towers of the World Trade Center this morning. Just a few minutes ago both towers collapsed. Lower Manhatten is covered with smoke.

There was also an explosion at the Pentagon, and the building has been evaculated. They just announced that another plane just crashed in Pennsylvania, but whether that was connected to the other attacks hasn't been confirmed.

No one has claimed responsibility yet.

Date: Tue, 11 Sep 2001 11:03:04
From: JMullin
Subject: Re: terrorism

It's been hard to get news stations on line here; our university is streaming cnn at *http://video.utoledo.edu/*

Date: Tue, 11 Sep 2001 10:15:26
From: C J Jeney
Subject: Re: terrorism

Now (said the American) we know how large-scale terrorism feels. And it feels worse than I could have imagined.

Ever.

Date: Tue, 11 Sep 2001 11:20:01
From: Lauren Fitzgerald
Subject: Re: terrorism

I've been watching live local coverage from home, in the Northern tip of Manhattan. Looks like the entire wall street area is covered in smoke and debris. The most chilling thought: 40,000 people work in the world trade center each day; the work day had just started, but those folks get to work early . . .

This is horrifying. I've now got to go to work (I can walk, luckily, since most of the ssubways are shut down) and try to convince [the] administration to cancel classes.

Date: Tue, 11 Sep 2001 11:31:11
From: Jena Burges
Subject: Re: terrorism

Also, the FAA has grounded all domestic as well as international flights now. All international flights that were en route to D.C. have been rerouted to Canada.

Date: Tue, 11 Sep 2001 11:53:13
From: Kurt Bouman
Subject: Re: terrorism

Somerset County, PA, is everywhere: a place so isolated, so local, that no one could possibly think of attacking it. Somerset County is where many of our students are from; I'm about 45 minutes or an hour away, and they've closed the north–south route through here. The University of Pittsburgh has just closed, and my campus closes in 8 minutes.

We thought we were safe here in lil' ole western PA.

I'm being chased out now. See y'all online.

Date: Tue, 11 Sep 2001 12:25:09
From: Chet Pryor
Subject: Re: terrorism

They've just shut our campus down and told us to bug out—perhaps because we're directly under the flight path to Washington-Dulles, which is on the other side of the Potomac. But, if anything *really* interesting happens around here, I'll inform the list.

Date: Tue, 11 Sep 2001 09:34:14
From: Gordon Thomas
Subject: Responses to Terrorism

I'd like to hear how people are responding to these plane crashes in their Writing Programs.

Has your university closed?

Has it been suggested that you cancel class (as our chair as done) simply because it is hard to imagine anyone paying much attention to anything else?

For those of you who will be teaching for the first time again tomorrow, how do you imagine what you will do in class? (It's hard to believe that it will be business as usual.)

I meet all the new TAs this afternoon for our regular meeting about what will soon happen in Engl 101 starting tomorrow, and I'd like to have some sense of what everyone else thinks is called for.

This is an unprecedented event; historically, it's very significant. Perhaps it's worth asking student to write about what has happened in the past few hours. Clearly we will know more tomorrow. And I suspect that students who may not yet be aware of the depth of the consequences will have more awareness by tomorrow.

Does asking students to write or even discuss these events unduly inflame their emotions and make later teaching more difficult?

I'm particularly concerned with what WPAs might say to instructors working in their programs. What suggestions might we make?

Date: Tue, 11 Sep 2001 12:48:18
From: Marcia Ribble
Subject: Re: terrorism

My kids are scared silly. They are talking about this as equivalent to the bombing of Pearl Harbor, about "having to go," about whether they'll reinstitute the draft. Some of the kids in dorms are weeping because they have family in or close to the scenes of the crashes. And this is in pretty mostly hopefully safe Appalachian KY. We talked about this being one of those you will remember for years where you were and what you were doing when you heard kinds of days. Remember that our kids haven't lived through WWII, Korea, Vietnam, etc. They are in enormous shock over this.

We need to work to make sure all of our kids are and remain OK.

Date: Tue, 11 Sep 2001 11:53:37
From: Carol Rutz
Subject: Re: Responses to Terrorism

Gordon, I just talked with my son, who is an MA student at George Mason U and also an ensign in the Navy. He says that while this is the kind of worst-case scenario everyone has feared, that caution and calm are the best responses. Try to help people with their concerns about loss of life, fears for relatives and friends, etc., but resist jumping to conclusions about "the enemy" or "another Pearl Harbor," etc. There will be a place for anger, but now, clarity and calm are needed.

He'll know in a day or so whether his orders have changed, and the same is true of many, many young people in uniform. They'll do well. We must support them.

Date: Tue, 11 Sep 2001 11:53:30
From: "Martha A. Townsend"
Subject: Re: Responses to Terrorism

Gordon,

Out here in Missouri, no one has suggested we shut down. But our provost has sent an email memo authorizing faculty to cancel classes if they wish or to devote class time to discussing the incidents. Our Board of Curators has cancelled its meeting in NYC this weekend, and the College of Arts & Science has cancelled this Saturday's "Mizzou on Broadway" performance of three one-act plays in NYC.

Date: Tue, 11 Sep 2001 11:56:40
From: Gerald Nelms
Subject: Looking ahead

I sent this message to my faculty and grad student colleagues this morning. I'm told it might be appropriate for faculty elsewhere. Worth consideration, I guess.

Everyone,

Given the sobering events of this morning, I think we need to begin thinking about the consequences of this for our students and us. I don't claim to have any great insights, only past experience. Those of you who have additional insights, I'd be grateful to hear from you.

First, some/many of our students are going to talk about—that is, to express their feelings about—these events. One of the great strengths of English classes, especially writing classes, is that, as Lad Tobin has discussed, they provide a space for such personal expression that students may not find much elsewhere in the academy. We may want to consider giving over a class period or two to these discussions. Also, we might want to provide students with the opportunity to write in a personal manner about their responses to these events. Some of our students will not want to talk in public but will need to express their feelings. Thus, writing. We know that writing can be therapeutic. There may also be students who will want to talk to us individually in conferences. It might be good to let them vent, cry, whatever. We're not psychologists, but we are teachers. We can respond as teachers—that is, I never try to analyze or counsel, only talk.

Second, we have a number of Middle Eastern faculty and students and others here in southern Illinois. We need to be sensitive to their feelings and to any hasty generalizations by American students about them. It might be worth discussing with students the variety of ethnicities and ideologies in the Middle East. And we need to encourage our students to understand that they have a right to be angry, but they also need to be sensitive to the fact that, while entirely unacceptable as a political act, such violence can be understandable—again, not acceptable—from certain points of view [my opinion]. In other words, we need to try to calm racial, ethnic, etc., prejudices.

Third, because these events are acts of war, some of our students in the Reserves may be called up for military duty. The University will, no doubt, send down information on how to deal with these students. Hopefully, that information will come sooner rather than later. Just in case, here are my own personal guidelines: I first ask the student nicely to provide papers or some other evidence indicating that the student has indeed been called up. I then talk to the student about what he or she needs to do before they leave school and how to complete the course at some point in the future. I strongly suggest giving these students lots of leeway in completing their coursework. After all, these students are going to be angry, frightened, really, really stressed.

Let's take care of ourselves, too. Not a bad time to connect with loved ones and family members. The world has changed.

Date: Tue, 11 Sep 2001 12:49:29
From: "Core, Deborah"
Subject: Re: Responses to Terrorism

I was a TA at Marshall University in 1970 when a plane crash killed the whole football team. Classes were cancelled for a while (don't recall how long), and then when we re-convened we just let the classes talk for a class period. Seems to me that letting them talk is more appropriate at this point than asking them to write, to the extent that writing is private and students need the communal at this point.

Date: Tue, 11 Sep 2001 13:01:30
From: Marcia Ribble
Subject: Re: Responses to Terrorism

Gordon,

The students are talking about it anyway. We probably all need lots of TLC and debriefing. Posttraumatic stress syndrome is likely for many of us nationwide, especially as the additional trauma of closed universities and college campuses hits home along with fears about what has happened to relatives and friends and whether they might be at risk now. Talking helps, as does trying to keep things in perspective, though it's difficult to do with this much horror involved. I know it isn't the pc thing to say, but praying, however one does that, might help.

Date: Tue, 11 Sep 2001 12:02:03
From: Gilchrist White
Subject: Re: Responses to terrorism

Thanks, Carol for your words of reassurance. I have a son in the army . . . can't
get in touch with him.

Date: Tue, 11 Sep 2001 12:14:18
From: "J.L. McClure"
Subject: Re: Responses to Terrorism

This happened about an hour before my 2–hour class this morning. The TV
was on in the room when I got there and we spent an hour watching until the
second tower collapsed. It was horrific, and most of my students were clearly
moved. It was clear there was no way of continuing class, so I let them go, as
did several other teachers. One concern I have (and I hope I'm not alone) is
how our Middle East students will be treated and how they will react over the
next few days. Obviously, we won't know probably for some time who committed this act, but it's no surprise that the immediate speculation is to assume
it's Islamic terrorists.

Date: Tue, 11 Sep 2001 11:19:03
From: Nick Carbone
Subject: Re: Responses to Terrorism

Several colleges in Massachusetts, especially in the Boston area, are closing.
UMass Amherst closed; Bently, Simmons, UMass Boston and other city colleges and U.'s. I don't know when they'll be re-opening. Amtrak is closed, but
local subways/commuter rails are running, and waiving fares. I know too there
will be calls for blood donations.

I left work early to be home when my daughter gets home from school. Some
high rises in Boston have been evacuated. Our building—75 Arlington St.—
has not been, but many of us have left work.

We have an office in New York, and many of us regularly commute by rail and
shuttle to Boston. Luckily, no one was flying in today, though our colleagues
in the New York office who did go into work and don't live in the city will be
going home w/ colleagues who do live in the city.

Date: Tue, 11 Sep 2001 13:21:21
From: Erika Lindemann
Subject: Re: Responses to Terrorism

At the University of North Carolina at Chapel Hill, classes are meeting as usual today, though most of us are using the time to help students talk (and write) about what's on their minds. Tomorrow classes will be suspended from noon until two so that students and faculty who wish to meet in the main quad can "gather in mourning and recognition for all that we have lost as a nation and as individuals."

Date: Tue, 11 Sep 2001 13:26:00
From: Sid Dobrin
Subject: Re: Responses to Terrorism

The University of Florida has been closed "until further notice." My brother at Florida Atlantic University, Davie Campus, tells me that faculty there were told to go home and that all Colleges/Universities in the Florida system have been closed.

I hope y'all have heard McCain and a few other Republican senators/congressmen who have blamed spending on education and social programs for taking away from resources to prevent such an attack. We are watching our concept of civil rights vanish.

Date: Tue, 11 Sep 2001 13:27:13
From: "Robert A. Russell"
Subject: Re: Responses to Terrorism

Our university closed at noon today. I'm surprised (and actually quite moved) by the emotional force of my students' and staff members response to this. I was shocked, but I guess I didn't expect my undergrads to be quite so shaken.

I don't see how any class or group could get much done today, considering the circumstances.

Date: Tue, 11 Sep 2001 10:41:45
From: Gordon Thomas
Subject: Re: Responses to Terrorism

I have formulated the following exercise as a suggestion to the instructors in our program, especially the first-year TAs, for what to do in classes starting tomorrow:

Writing Exercise Concerning the Events of September 11, 2001, for classes meeting on September 12–14:

Start by just having a general discussion for a few moments about the events of Tuesday, September 11, 2001. Try to get the students to contextualize the event historically (many news commentators are now saying that the only thing that this compares to is the attack on Pearl Harbor and the Oklahoma City bombing, these comparisons may be controversial, but they are already being made).

Be prepared for the possibility of some students expressing great anger or fear (or both). It is quite possible that some students may say things that they don't really mean. Do your best not to inflame such feelings, and keep in mind that it does help some people to talk about this at the time. The best attitude for you to take is to be nonjudgmental about their responses unless someone says something that is overtly hostile to international students, Moslem students in particular. If that happens, you might go directly to the question below about the initial responses to the Oklahoma bombing.

After this short oral discussion, ask them to take out paper and write freely in answer to the following questions.

Give them the questions one at a time. Have them write for approximately five or ten minutes on each question. Write with the students. Keep your eye on how they are writing. When it appears that many of them have finished, have them stop and go on to the next question. (You may think of your own questions as well.)

Try to gauge the mood of the class. You may not want to have your class write about all these questions. After 10 or 15 minutes of writing, have them stop and share what they have written with other students. (They can either read what they have written or simply talk about it for a few minutes.)

What were you doing on Tuesday when you heard the news about the plane crashes? Where were you? What were your first thoughts upon hearing this news?

Who did you first talk to about these terrorist activities? What did people say? Did they speculate on who might be responsible? What did you think of those responses? (Did they make sense to you? Did they seem unfounded?)

Now that some time has passed since you first heard the news, write down some of the pieces of information that you have learned since the initial news. Just list the information, not how you feel about it (yet).

Describe how your initial response changed as you learned more about what had happened.

What is the primary feeling that you have concerning these events? Why do you feel that way?

What do you think the response of the U.S. government will be to these events? How do you feel about that potential response?

In the hours and days immediately following the bombing of the Oklahoma bombing, many people thought immediately that it must be a terrorist attack by Arabs or Palestinians. Many people of Arab descent or who were Muslim were immediately suspect. It later developed that the attackers were white Americans and the attack had little or nothing to do with America's activities outside the U.S. What does this initial
response to that event suggest about how we might think of Tuesday's attacks?

When the students have finished writing, ask them to put their writing away and keep it until later in the semester. Explain that you won't be collecting or reading their work. Tell them that they may want to save this writing as a personal record of what has happened.

I haven't distributed this yet. Any suggestions or comments would be welcome.

Date: Tue, 11 Sep 2001 13:45:45
From: "Donna N. Sewell"
Subject: helping students cope

I have class tonight at 5 p.m.—a writing class.

I'm wondering how people are leading discussions about today's events—just talking about what they know and how they feel?

At least one student can't come; she's on alert for the Fire and Rescue Squad.

I just don't know what to expect. We talk about our students not having lived through such a thing, but some of us teachers haven't either. I'm just worried about what to expect.

Date: Tue, 11 Sep 2001 13:41:21
From: "Dr. Lance Rivers"
Subject: Re: Response to Terrorism

Lake Superior State University has cancelled all classes for the day, and will hold a candlelight vigil tonight. With the International Peace Bridge (no comments, please, about the irony:) closing and opening erratically today, many of our Canadian students are finding it difficult to make it to classes, hence the cancellation. (Our hospital is on alert status, as are the Soo Locks.) Offices remain open, but I'm going home.

Date: Tue, 11 Sep 2001 13:38:07–0400
From: Marsha Holmes
Subject: Re: Responses to Terrorism

Dear Colleagues,

Here in a very little town in western North Carolina (Western Carolina University in Cullowhee), the English Department chair has suggested that we excuse any student who is too overwhelmed to attend class today but not to cancel classes since that would, as he put it, help the aggressors achieve their goal of disrupting our lives. The university has set up "Information Central" with television coverage being aired in the student union. One student organization has already scheduled a prayer session to be held this evening. As WPA, I haven't even thought about contacting instructors about how or why they might proceed in the rest of classes today or tomorrow. Your note reminds me that I should think about how to help others who are, like me, reeling in shock.

In my second wave of reactions upon hearing the news, I said, "Well, I must be a through-and-through composition teacher. My first thought is to have our students write about what they are experiencing." I wondered if the suggestion would seem trite to some students. I wonder what prompts or invitations to write would be more or less helpful—? I just checked the newsgroups (list-servs) for my two sections of first-year composition. They are already talking/writing there . . .

I often lurk and have very, very rarely posted. Today's another reason I am grateful for WPA-L. I will hold you and yours in the light (as a wanta-be Quaker is likely to do).

Date: Tue, 11 Sep 2001 13:58:13
From: "Donna N. Sewell"
Subject: Re: Responses to Terrorism

Gordon,

Below is a list of questions that integrate some questions you raised as well as some I was thinking of.

I'm not sure yet how I'll use them—to prompt discussion or to let students write in their notebooks. I know the list is overwhelming. I won't keep all the questions on the list.

1. Where were you when you heard the news about the attacks on the World Trade Center? How did you hear? What were your first thoughts upon hearing this news? How did you react?

2. Where were you when you heard about the attack on the Pentagon? How did you hear? What were your first thoughts upon hearing this news? How did you react?

3. Where were you when you heard about the plane crash in Pennsylvania? How did you hear? What were your first thoughts upon hearing this news? How did you react?

4. Who did you first talk to about these terrorist activities? What did people say? Did they speculate on who might be responsible? What did you think of those responses? (Did they make sense to you? Did they seem unfounded?)

5. Do you have family in New York or Washington? Are you worried about the safety of family members and friends? Have you been able to contact those you need to?

6. Did you watch any of television coverage? Did you see any of the pictures posted on the web? How did you react to those images? Can you shake them?

7. How do you feel? Sad? Angry? Surprised? Worried? What can you do to help yourself feel better?

8. What can you do to help others? What are you going to do?

9. What support do you need from others? From your family? From VSU? From your friends?

10. What rumors have you heard that have been proven false?

11. What do you want to know? What will you never understand?

12. Have you read this scenario (or any simiilar scenarios) in books? See it portrayed on film? How was that scenario resolved? Can we learn anything from the fictional portrayal?

13. What do you think the response of the U.S. government will be to these events? How do you feel about that potential response?

Date: Tue, 11 Sep 2001 13:53:25
From: Jennifer Morrison
Subject: Re: Responses to Terrorism

I'm also looking for suggestions on how best to address this tragedy with students, and I appreciate the suggestions that have already been posted, and I'll be forwarding your other suggestions to my local colleagues.

Gordon, in reading your prompts below, a couple of them hailed me. I was inclined to write about my reaction when I first found out, in order to gain a handle on what I was feeling and in order to preserve it for reflection afterward. (I didn't because I couldn't collect myself enough.) But now I'm worried about intellectualizing this tragedy or turning it into fodder for powerful writing assignments. I think I would make writing optional, and I would respond to students' writing if they chose to share it with me. I will definitely open the floor to discussion, and I might use some of your prompts, if they seem appropriate.

Date: Tue, 11 Sep 2001 14:34:37–0600
From: Corri Wells
Subject: Re: Responses to Terrorism

I teach at William Paterson University in New Jersey on a hill a few miles across the Hudson in view of Manhattan. Just outside my office door (on the second floor), one can see the New York skyline. Despite the fact that many of our teachers live in Manhattan and cannot get to the campus to teach today, our school has not closed. I do not understand this decision, but I cannot respond to it emotionally because I have not heard from my husband in Manhattan for several hours, and though he is probably just fine, my mind is there. He works for NBC TV in Rockefeller Center, which we have heard by way of other television stations here, was also evacuated, as a precaution. I have more Muslim students this semester, for whatever reasons, than I have had in ten years. I agree with all those who have spoken about the dangers of reactionary stereotyping of our Middle Eastern and other Islamic students. Probably it would do good to refer students to the movie _Snow on Cedars_. Many of them may have seen that. For those who haven't, it sympathetically portrays the internment in the United States of Japanese Americans during World War II. I certainly don't want any ethnic insensitivity in my own classes. The "hunt down and punish" rhetoric we are hearing from our country's president is disheartening to me. I do not think this kind of bloodshed will end until "justice" and revenge cease to be automatic responses. Seems to me that bloodshed begets bloodshed.

Date: Tue, 11 Sep 2001 14:12:26
From: Clyde Moneyhun
Subject: Re: Responses to Terrorism

About 95% of our students live here (on campus or in this little college town), so the campus is remaining open to take care of them. The school has made counseling available at the biggest student union building, and the Red Cross has also set up a blood bank there for donations. A lot of people, I hear, are either cancelling classes or giving them over to discussions of the events. My wife directs a small Honors tutoring program, and she just e-mailed all of the tutors to open our home to them in case they want a place to go.

Date: Tue, 11 Sep 2001 14:21:18
From: "Therese M. Zawacki"
Subject: terrorism

I should have added to my last post that in the midst of the shock and disbelief at our institution, so close to Washington, D.C., it helped me to retreat to writing about "business as usual." We are closing our campus at 4:30, but I think the administration also might be thinking that students will need the sense of some kind of order in the midst of chaos. I don't know how many students will be in my 3:00 class this afternoon and I don't know how calm I will be. I just know that writing my last post gave me some moments of calm, some reassurance that everything had not changed in my world.

Date: Tue, 11 Sep 2001 14:23:57
From: "Ammirati, Theresa P. (Dean of College Office)"
Subject: Re: Responses to Terrorism

we're having a prayer service this afternoon, counselors are in the health services building, chaplains at the chapel, deans walking around campus stopping in at dorms where the tvs are going non-stop. The student life office is getting names of students who may be directly affected (we have a large population of NYC area students, many of whom have friends and relatives who work in the financial district, as well as a fairly large population from DC). Faculty are holding classes or not, depending on personal inclination, but obviously, no work is getting done—

Date: Tue, 11 Sep 2001 14:02:48
From: "Heilman, Christine"
Subject: Re: Responses to Terrorism

The response at my Catholic college in Cincinnati (College of Mount St. Joseph), Ohio was not to cancel classes or shut down the college. Instead we held a prayer service in the chapel at noon and also announced that we have counselors available to small groups and individual students in the health/wellness center and the women's center. Our monthly faculty meeting began at 12:30 p.m. with a moment of silence. Our college president told us that the small groups would help the students the most but that shutting down the college would leave them without our support. I know that tomorrow in my writing class I may use Gordon's suggestions—the reactions to this for students will resonate for some time.

Our downtown Cincinnati federal building has been evacuated since those are often the targets. Before I began my college teaching, I was a federal government worker in Atlanta, Georgia in the 1970s. Once, the building where I worked was shut down because a veteran with a gun took hostages on the first floor where the VA was housed. So I know that government workers are prepared for violence against them and realize that they represent the country no matter what their jobs may be. The agency I worked for was recruiting Peace Corps and VISTA volunteers at the time our building was under siege—but our mission didn't keep the violence from happening.

Date: Tue, 11 Sep 2001 13:55:30
From: Lauren Fitzgerald
Subject: Re: helping students cope

Hi Donna—

I'm wondering the same thing, esp. given that I teach *in* Manhattan. A plane flew overhead 20 minutes ago and everyone's hearts stopped; apparently "just" a military plane. A colleague was looking out the window after the planes hit world trade and saw the towers collapse (even 12 miles away you can—or could—see them). Another colleague walked 5 miles between our two undergrad campuses because there is neither public nor university transportation. We can smell the smoke up here.

The city is covered in a gentle bubble of white cloud. We're all on the verge of tears and hysterics.

So what do I say, particularly in a class on Gothic literature? I'm thinking about contemplating the connections between "terror" and "terrorism."

Date: Tue, 11 Sep 2001 13:21:47
From: David Jolliffe
Subject: Re: Responses to Terrorism

DePaul University closed this morning at 10:30. Our downtown campus, itself comprising four high-rise buildings, is one block away from the Dirksen Federal Building and across the street from the Immigration and Naturalization Service. We are in for some very scary times, my friends.

Date: Tue, 11 Sep 2001 12:47:30
From: Raul Sanchez
Subject: Responses to Terrorism

Colleagues:

All of us understand the therapeutic/pedagogic benefits of writing about traumatic events and the importance of critical reflection on difficult issues. So, with no disrespect intended, I have to say that the assignment offered below sounds like a very bad and rather inappropriate idea *at the moment*. It's a question of timing, as I see it, for a couple of reasons.

First, I don't see how you could assign what's below without a) fanning the flames of xenophobia, b) painting yourself (and your profession) as being apologists for terrorism. Even if we are writing teachers, we're not in control of discourse, especially not in times of turmoil.

Second, I think it's disrespectful and maybe even a little ghoulish to have thousands of innocent dead people become grist for a writing assignment so soon after the fact of their deaths. The teaching machine isn't starved for material.

If we're talking about using writing as therapy, then I think we're talking about the work of therapists, i.e., people who are trained professionally to help people cope with trauma.

If we're talking about using writing as a way to process an issue that's intellectually, emotionally, and culturally complex, then I think we need to allow for some time and distance to go by if we really mean to have serious matters addressed in serious and nuanced ways. This won't happen tomorrow or the day after.

Again, I don't mean for my disagreement to be contentious or disrespectful. I realize it's a delicate time, which means that, more than ever, words need to be chosen and used (and received) with extra care.

Date: Tue, 11 Sep 2001 14:19:40
From: Keith Rhodes
Subject: Re: Responses to Terrorism

Y'know, I'm just doing what was on the schedule and asking my students and student assistant tutors to do the same. I'm not doing it especially well, nor am I expecting anyone else to be in top form; and I'm not even going to notice the "overwhelmed" absences. But the normal side of life is still there, can even be a bit of solace.

Date: Tue, 11 Sep 2001 14:39:18
From: Chet Pryor
Subject: Re: terrorism

Now we've got fighter jets flying back and forth, crisscrossing the area (I'm now at home in Rockville, Maryland, 15 miles WNW of DC). People are in the supermarkets buying bottled water, bread, and milk just as if a snow storm were coming.

And I guess my Saturday night through Monday trip to LA is out now. Or maybe I can switch over to Southwest Airlines—terrorist don't seem to like Southwest.:-(Chet

---

Date: Tue, 11 Sep 2001 14:55:45
From: Elizabeth Hodges
Subject: Re: Responses to Terrorism

Gordon—This is an interesting approach and I thank you for sharing it, but I have been thinking the last few hours about how to proceed tomorrow in a rather diverse and somewhat international class with six Middle-Eastern men. I sort of can see how some of the questions you pose as writing prompts for discussion could really erupt into something difficult to handle? I say that with the intuition of 25 years plus in the classroom. It is probably interesting how our plans for addressing this crisis in their classes and helping our composition program faculty do, particularly the inexperienced teachers, might vary regionally.

Date: Tue, 11 Sep 2001 11:56:53
From: Gail Stygall
Subject: Re: Responses to terrorism

My thoughts and prayers are with all of you in NYC. My very dear step-daughter lives in lower Manhattan. Of course we can't get through.

Date: Tue, 11 Sep 2001 15:38:22
From: Anne Beaufort
Subject: Re: Responses to Terrorism

Gordon

Thanks for this posting, which I think is appropriate and helpful. I plan to pass it along to our writing faculty.

Here at Stony Brook, the mood is grim. Classes have been cancelled as of noon. About half of our faculty and half of our students are commuters from NYC. Some are stranded here, unable to get home due to the public transportation shutdowns.

Writing teachers who did teach this morning had a difficult task.

Date: Tue, 11 Sep 2001 14:31:27
From: "Marsha L. Millikin"
Subject: Re: Responses to Terrorism

Our university has not closed yet but I did get a bit misty-eyed when when one of my students was called out of class and required to report to active duty. I don't know what branch of the service she is in. One of the instructors cancelled his class but it was an individual decision since all of the infor was coming in after the initial bombing of the towers in NY. We talked about it in my 11 a.m. class and then went on to a workshop on thesis statements. Did my best at business as usual and so did my students. We'll have to see what tomorrow brings.

Date: Tue, 11 Sep 2001 12:33:02
From: Joseph Eng
Subject: Re: Responses to Terrorism

J.L.'s reminder is very important. Our president said something similar this morning as he announced the tragedy and called for sensitivity and prayers.

Our TA workshops will take place a week from now and I'll certainly let them talk and write and discuss the sensitivity part of class life. While I don't recall having middle eastern students as TAs, some of their students are. As instructors of writing we need to be prepared for a changing discourse in the class after today.

Date: Tue, 11 Sep 2001 16:32:08
From: Debra Combs
Subject: Re: terrorism

Thanks to all for getting me some information. Eric, on one of these lists, said something like "shit, we're at war." Yeah, I think we are . . . and maybe we have been for a while. . . .

Date: Tue, 11 Sep 2001 14:52:11
From: Nick Carbone
Subject: Re: Responses to Terrorism

Raul,

I can see your take, but find the opposite reaction. The assignment's a suggestion, a starting point, a way to think about what I'll do in class tomorrow.
It's not a mandate. I know today's events will come up in class, and we might
talk about it and might write about it. So much will depend upon the mood
in the morning.

I see the assignment—and maybe that's just the wrong word, but it's what's in
use—as one suggestion for a way to cope in the context of what we do.

Date: Tue, 11 Sep 2001 12:36:07
From: Patricia Donahue
Subject: Re: Responses to Terrorism

I'm in California on sabbatical, but my friends at Lafayette College, which is
in eastern PA, about 60 miles from NYC, told me that classes have been cancelled. Many of our students have parents who work at the WTC.

Date: Tue, 11 Sep 2001 17:13:58
Subject: Re: Responses to Terrorism

[My institution] also didn't close, for reasons that escape me (they apparently had nothing to do, for instance, with taking a stand, or anything like
that). But our students closed it down anyway, for at least part of the afternoon, to pray together for 45 minutes on our little urban campus. [. . .] It
was really powerful to see over 100 guys praying together outside the writing center window today; a potent counter-image to the collapsing world
trade buildings.

I'm exhausted.

Date: Tue, 11 Sep 2001 15:20:57
From: Bonnie KYBURZ
Subject: Re: helping students cope

Lauren,

I'm simply shocked that you are teaching in Manhattan today. In a way, I'm awed by it in terms of a kind of admiration. At the same time, I can't believe there was any real expectation that you *would* or *should* show up.

When you describe the plane passing overhead, I myself feel fear. You must be made of steel!

Either way, do stay well.

peace,

bonnie

Date: Tue, 11 Sep 2001 15:25:40
From: Bonnie KYBURZ
Subject: Re: Responses to Terrorism

At first, when I read Gordon's prompts, I was shocked at the suggestion that we should create assignments—especially so soon—out of today's unthinkable events.

So, on the one hand, I strongly agree with Raul . On the other hand, I appreciate the questions (along with Donna's) for my own, personal use. Because you see, I'm simply in shock. Literally feeling ill. And maybe if I commit to some activity, I'll feel a bit more sane than I currently do.

I also think these are good questions for classroom consideration—LATER.

Date: Tue, 11 Sep 2001 16:54:31
From: Annie Olson
Subject: Re: responses to terrorism

Today's posts about helping students cope were thought provoking as I prepared for class. My students are overwhelmed by a wide range of issues, and we needed to spend time talking about them. They are concerned about children who have lost parents and what will happen when the kids go home today. They are concerned about front-line medical workers and fireman who are picking up the pieces—literally. They know that their world has irrevocably changed and are feeling it deeply, despite the fact that we're far from the big city here in northeast Texas.

Our university, Christian and smaller than most (about 3,000 students if you include our satellite programs but only about 1200 on the campus) suspended activities this morning for a campus-wide prayer time on the mall. About 700 people out there joining hands praying together. Powerfully moving. Lots of tears and deeply felt emotion.

I think that writing about it will be an important step, but for know we seem to need just to talk and pray.

Date: Tue, 11 Sep 2001 15:13:47
From: Gordon Thomas
Subject: Re: Responses to Terrorism

From the varied responses concerning my suggestions for a writing activity, I can see that one's local circumstances will make a big difference. Our students at Idaho are a long way from New York or Washington, but they will want to talk about this tomorrow (and today) in class. The central area of our student commons now is packed students watching the big-screen TV; some of them are obviously upset. But the student body is relatively homogenous compared to other campuses.

I can understand some of Raul Sanchez's concerns too, and I worry a bit about "fanning the flames of xenophobia." But these xenophobic reactions will occur anyway; I don't think this writing activity makes it worse or better. I don't see how this would make the teacher an apologist for terrorism.

If one simply wanted to have the student's produce an "interesting" paper on this subject by, say, next Tuesday, I can see why that might be viewed as exploitative or even "ghoulish." But this is not an assignment; it's just an activity, something to do the day after. Notice that I suggest that the students not hand their writing in; they just keep it.

I agree completely that to use writing to explore issues that are "intellectually, emotionally, and culturally complex," we need to ask people to write about it later. But that is exactly the point of this exercise. Notice that I'm suggesting that students note down their initial reactions and then reflect a bit about those reactions. They then write about the initial impressions, details, etc., they compare it to how they're thinking now (just a day or two after the attacks), and (here's the important part), they PUT THAT WRITING AWAY.

Whether they take it out again depends on what the teacher wants to do later. I think it would be interesting and instructive for them to consider writing something about this AGAIN in a couple months, after they've had time to think about it, to learn more facts, and to change. That LATER assignment can make use of this earlier writing, which even in its best form will probably be a kind of over-reaction, a simplification, or even just plain wrong. But I don't think they need to wait that long to record an intitial reaction. The writing that they might do tomorrow is, for the most part, private.

Is this a therapeutic exercise? Well, maybe, but it's pretty mild. I don't think teachers have any business offering complex diagnoses of how the students are thinking or feeling. I am certainly trying to suggest that this activity might substitute for counseling or something more specific that an individual student might need. To agree with the idea that teachers are not couselors and writing class should not be viewed as therapy does not mean that we can never engage in an activity that might have a therapuetic outcome for some people.

I do think that it could appear rather cold-hearted ("ghoulish" might be too strong) to simply carry on class as usual. What is any of us doing tomorrow or Thursday that is so important that it couldn't wait a day or two?

Date: Tue, 11 Sep 2001 18:28:41
From: "Dr. Bob Holderer"
Subject: Re: Responses to Terrorism

In addition to being the WPA on my campus, I also serve as international student advisor for incoming freshmen and transfers. At about 11:30 I got a "summons" from the Provost to addend a memorial service to be held about an hour later and be prepared to speak to those present. What in the world does one say?

Fortunately, I did not have to get in front of a packed house of shocked students, but I did stay around to talk with a mob of international students who are obviously shaken up about this. My big worry is that there will be a backlash on the part of our American students. While I don't teach any ESL sections this semester, I have already been invited to come to the three classes we have on campus to help lead class discussions. Hopefully, the students will do most of the talking because I'm not quite sure what the right thing is to say, especially to our Muslim population.

Date: Tue, 11 Sep 2001 17:51:29
From: Jami Carlacio
Subject: Re: Responses to Terrorism

Dear Gordon, and Nick, et al.:

Thank you for your suggestions for handling this tragedy in our classes today. My first thought was to ask students to do some personal writing on it (they didn't share it per se, but three did print their writing and give it to me to read) and then to discuss it as a class.

We had a valuable discussion and no one was silenced during this time; in fact, more people spoke up and wanted to express their confusion, shock, and distress even as we wonder what the ramifications are for our small town in middle America. As a class, we came up with some suggestions for changing the things we can, locally, and here's some of what they came up with:

- give blood
- donate to the Red Cross (money or time)
- walk or bike instead of drive
- car pool
- pray and come together as a community (join prayer vigils)
- put ourselves in the shoes of those less fortunate than we are (wherever they may be)

Students seemed to need to make some sense of this now, but they surely also know they will need to continue to make sense of it.

Thanks again for your ideas.

———————————

Date: Tue, 11 Sep 2001 18:46:39
From: "Welch, Karen A."
Subject: Re: Responses to Terrorism

Our campus did not close today; our chancellor encouraged us to simply be around for students to talk to, to hold classes if we could, and to guide discussions however we saw fit.

But tonight we will hear the first speaker of our fall semester forum series: Helen Caldicott, a 1985 nobel Peace Prize winner and 20-year advocate of citizen action to remedy nuclear and environmental crises. Her topic—set way last year—is "George W. Bush and the Threat of Nuclear War." Our campus has scheduled a candlelight vigil to follow her talk and discussion.

And tomorrow we'll try to start healing . . .

———————————

Date: Tue, 11 Sep 2001 21:53:24
From: cj
Subject: Re: Responses to Terrorism

I cannot presume to counsel or provide therapy for my students. It's not my job, I'm not qualified, and I'm probably more upset than they are . . . they have the beautiful callousness of youth to prevent them from becoming the kind of quaking puddle that I am when faced with this kind of event.

So I just turned on the LCD projector, tuned into CNN, and let my Web Authoring students watch it. Most of them stayed. We invited the FYC class next door to come in and watch with us. I did paper work, made copies, checked some html code I wanted them to look at next time—anything to keep from having to look at the pictures. I wasn't ready.

But then it was time for the literature class . . . they did not want to talk about crushed buildings or crashed planes. They all came to class, even though they didn't have to, and they all stayed, even though I told them they could go if they wanted to. One asked politely if she could answer her cell phone—her brother's national guard unit was on standby. He called during class, to tell her he was shipping out soon.

Together we made it through a sedate and pleasant discussion of scansion, syntax, diction—dactyls and anapests, and some e e cummings ("Me up at does") and then we read "Let me not to the marriage of true minds. . . ."

Such impediments. I could not teach, only be a human among humans, we clung so pathetically to our intellect and our grammars of wit, and hoped that when the hour was up, the door would open, the bad dream would be gone, and that Raeann's cell phone would un-ring.

Date: Tue, 11 Sep 2001 22:34:27
From: Brenda Tuberville
Subject: Responses to Terrorism

Here in the southeast corner of Texas, classes were held as usual, except for small groups of students and teachers alike standing in hallways, sharing their thoughts and fears, sharing any late-breaking news they may have to give.

I wondered seriously about cancelling my one class tonight: they're predominantly high school "co-enrollment" students, and I didn't know how all of this would affect them. The strongest reaction I got, however, was from a non-traditional female student, who came into class visibly shaken. "I don't know if I'm gonna get through this," she said, starting to weep. "I've already seen enough heartache for one lifetime. I don't know if I can stand much more."

One sadly ironic twist to all of this: one of the closings in the L.A. area was the Museum for Tolerance. How sad that a building and organization dedicated to understanding has to be closed because of acts of blind hatred.

Date: Wed, 12 Sep 2001 08:43:09
From: R Yagelski
Subject: Re: Responses to Terrorism

Like so many other campuses, the response here at SUNY-Albany was to cancel classes and, later, organize a vigil. Initially, our Provost urged faculty members to hold classes and be available to students. That was late morning. But as events unfolded, it became clear that no attempt to carry on with normal activities could work at this campus, where the majority of our students are from "downstate" (NYC and surrounding area). I walked through the student center around 11:00 on my way to a meeting to see several hundred students gathered around a few TV monitors watching the horrifying images in silence while dozens of others paced frantically as they tried to reach loved ones on their cell phones. As you might imagine, just about everyone on this campus has either a direct or indirect connection to NY City, and eventually the administration became concerned about students trying to get to the city, which by noon was effectively closed down. Classes were cancelled just after noon, but faculty were urged to stay on campus and be available to their students as best they could. I kept hearing the word "surreal" all day, and although it's one of those terms that TV news has turned into a cliche, I could think of no better word to describe the way things felt on this campus yesterday.

Perhaps the most surreal aspect of the day for me was a meeting, set up only about two weeks ago, between faculty members and administrators of our School of Ed. and a high-level delegation of education officials and researchers from the People's Republic of China that is visiting the U.S. as part of a large nationwide education initiative they have just embarked on. We all sat in a big conference room, talking about education in our respective countries through an interpreter, while the campus emptied out around us and periodic announcements came over the PA system informing us that the governor had closed all state offices. The Chinese delegation stayed in NYC on Monday night and drove up to Albany on Tuesday morning, having left NYC a few hours before the first plane crashed into the World Trade Center. We were told later that had we not been able to schedule our meeting with them for Tuesday morning, they were planning to visit the World Trade Center instead. Once our meeting ended, the task was to find somewhere for them to stay, since going back to NYC was not an option.

It sounds feeble, but I send my sincerest wishes for peace to everyone and my sympathies to all those who lost loved ones yesterday. Like so many others, I'm feeling rather small and vulnerable and worried about our students, many of whom must have spent a horrible night wondering about their families in NYC.

Date: Wed, 12 Sep 2001 10:13:18–0400
From: Libby Miles
Subject: Re: Responses to Terrorism

In light of all the horribleness of yesterday, I was thankful for people who made me particularly proud:

- my 101 students, all of whom came to my morning class to make sense of what was happening—not from the "beautiful callousness of youth" as one colleague has put it, but rather from a need for community, connection, and continuity. We discussed what was happening as it was happening, and found ways to keep going with our assignment while being mindful and respectful of the larger world events.
- my 301 students, all of whom came to class because they didn't really know where else to go but knew they needed to go somewhere seemingly safe and structured. The class focus has been on community service and sustainability, and these students easily made the link between the morning's events and the matter of sustainability on our planet. It was a moving class discussion, and we ended the period by walking across campus to a photo exhibit on sustainability in North America. Soon, they will propose the community service projects our whole class will embrace, and several students have disaster relief projects in mind.
- our university president, who made the call *not* to cancel classes in order to encourage the very sense of community my students seemed to need. In his announcements, he encouraged those of us who could stay on campus to do so, while acknowledging that others (students, faculty, and staff) would need to attend to their families and other loved ones.
- my graduate students in the Writing Center, who made the appropriate choice to close the door and attend to their families (many in the Boston area). With me in class, somebody else had to make the call—and did.
- our multi-cultural center, which became a gathering place in the late afternoon. The president, provost, and our dean spoke again of our important role in keeping ourselves going so our students would have the support they need. Later, they sponsored a vigil.
- the director of our child development center, who issued a letter to parents encouraging appropriate choices we could make on behalf of our small children. She suggested specific language choices for talking about the tragedies, and emphasized the 3–5-year-old view of the world: the need for personal safety and the security of those they love. Her letter was an important reminder for us to meet all of our students—regardless of age—where they are in their development, and to provide what is appropriate. It's not callousness; it's developmentally appropriate practice.
- Raul's remarkable post to WPA-L. With sensitivity and grace, Raul voiced my concerns much better than I would have been able to.

Here in Rhode Island, snuggled between New York and Boston, populated by students from Manhattan and New Jersey, we made it through yesterday. Some people, many people, now know their families and friends are safe; a few know people who were on those 4 planes; some simply don't know yet and are still waiting. We made it through yesterday, but today and tomorrow and the next day seem more challenging. The need for community, continuity, and connection is so much more acute now.

Wishing peace for all,
Libby

Date: Wed, 12 Sep 2001 05:04:12
From: Kurt Bouman
Subject: Re: Responses to Terrorism

> Editor's Note: This message originally appeared out-of-sequence in the
> archives of the wpa-l, between two posts from 11 September 2001. SB

My class met today on schedule (well, before the university was closed). I didn't consider at all cancelling my class; like some others on the list, I wanted to be able to offer a sense of normalcy and continuity. Still, the news was fresh at 11:00 AM eastern time, and I had no intention of continuing any kind of instruction today. I saw my class time as a space to answer questions students have, and to try to reassure them that they are pretty safe here (a sentiment somewhat undercut by the plane crashing in Somerset County, quite close by).

I talked from my heart, and from my head: after all, they see me as a resource for them, and I needed—wanted, too—to occupy that role as well. Students asked questions and shared concerns about national security, economic distress, international terrorism, and other similar topics. I am unprepared to offer definitive answers to many questions like these, but I cautioned against jumping to conclusions about where this might have come from, and I answered what questions I could as directly as possible.

Class was fine, and I think it helped. I know it helped me. We didn't do any writing—didn't even talk about assignments or anything related to the class. But we came together as a community experiencing shock and distress. And it was okay.

NOTE

1. Bradbury, Ray. *Something Wicked This Way Comes*. New York: Avon, 1962.

Contributors

WENDY BISHOP, Kellogg W. Hunt Professor of English at Florida State University, teaches composition, rhetoric, poetry and essay writing. A former writing center director and writing program administrator, she studies writing classrooms, writes assignments with her students, and shares her evolving techniques in textbooks like *Thirteen Ways of Looking for a Poem*, *The Subject Is Writing*, *Metro*, and *Reading into Writing, A Guide to Composing*. She lives in Tallahassee and Alligator Point, Florida, with her husband Dean and children Morgan and Tait.

LYNN Z. BLOOM, Board of Trustees Distinguished Professor and Aetna Chair of Writing at the University of Connecticut, is completing *The Essay Canon* (Wisconsin Press, 2005)—a canon whose research informs her recent textbooks—including *The Arlington Reader* (2003) and *The Essay Connection* (7th ed., 2004), which is the focus of the essay in this book. Her creative nonfiction ranges from "Teaching College English as a Woman" (1992) and "Living to Tell the Tale: The Complicated Ethics of Creative Nonfiction" (2003), both in *College English*, to "Writing and Cooking, Cooking" in *Pilaf, Pozole, and Pad Thai* and *Chronicle of Higher Education* (2001). Other research interests include auto/biography (*Doctor Spock: Biography of a Conservative Radical*, 1972; *Forbidden Diary*, 1980, 2000) and composition studies, in such works as *Composition Studies as a Creative Art* (1998) and *Composition Studies in the New Millennium* (2003).

SHANE BORROWMAN is the former Director of Composition at Gonzaga University, where he teaches business and professional writing, introductory composition and literature courses, and advanced courses in both fiction and dramatic literature. His most recent work has appeared in *Writing with Elbow*, *Alternative Rhetorics*, *Rhetoric Review*, and *Composition Studies in the New Millennium: Rereading the Past, Rewriting the Future*.

DAPHNE DESSER is an assistant professor at the University of Hawaii, where she teaches graduate and undergraduate courses in twentieth century rhetoric, legal rhetoric, argumentative writing, and writing and difference. Most of her academic work explores various aspects of identity construction and negotiation in writing; she has published in such journals as *Rhetoric Review, Journal of Electronic Publishing, Composition Forum,* and *Women in Judaism* and has chapters in *The Politics of Writing in the Two-Year College* and *The Writing Program Administrator's Resource.* She also enjoys creative writing and has published poetry, fiction, and creative non-fiction.

DANA C. ELDER is proud to work with talented students and colleagues at Eastern Washington University in Cheney and Spokane. He teaches classical rhetoric and ethics, and composition theory and praxis. A seasoned educator, he has published articles, personal essays, poems, and textbooks. His "Expanding the Role of Personal Writing in the Composition Classroom" received the *Teaching English in the Two-Year College* Best Article of the Year Award for 2000. He believes teachers and writers serve the greater good.

RICHARD LEO ENOS is Professor and Holder of the Lillian Radford Chair of Rhetoric and Composition at Texas Christian University. His research concentration is in classical rhetoric with an emphasis in the relationship between oral and written discourse. He is a Past President of the Rhetoric Society of America and former Editor of *Advances in the History of Rhetoric.*

THERESA ENOS is Professor of English and Director of the Rhetoric, Composition, and the Teaching of English Graduate program at The University of Arizona. Founder and editor of *Rhetoric Review,* she teaches both graduate and undergraduate courses in writing and rhetoric. Her research interests include the history and theory of rhetoric and the intellectual work and politics of rhetoric and composition studies. She has edited or coedited ten books and has numerous chapters and essays published on rhetorical theory and issues in writing. She is the author of *Gender Roles and Faculty Lives in Rhetoric and Composition.*

MAUREEN DALY GOGGIN is Associate Professor of Rhetoric in the English Department at Arizona State University, where she teaches courses in the history and theories of rhetoric and in writing. She is author of *Authoring a Discipline: Scholarly Journals and the Post-World War II Emergence of Rhetoric and Composition* and editor of *Inventing a Discipline: Rhetoric Scholarship in Honor of Richard E. Young.* Her publications on the history of rhetoric and composition as well as on visual and material rhetoric appear in *Rhetoric Review, Rhetoric Society Quarterly, Composition Studies,* and various edited collections.

PETER GOGGIN is Assistant Professor of Rhetoric in the English Department at Arizona State University where he teaches courses in rhetoric, theories of literacy, and in writing. His scholarship includes theorizing literacy and technology as well as inquiry into public literacy and the environment, especially as these relate to international policies and debate on environmental remediation.

AMY L. HODGES is a Ph.D. student in Rhetoric and Composition at Florida State University, where she teaches courses in first-year writing, advanced composition, and literature. She is presently researching a writing and healing pedagogy for first-year writing, and she is very interested in the connection between writing and therapy.

JOSEPH JONES has taught in the public schools of Arizona for 19 years. He holds a Ph.D. in Rhetoric, Composition, and the Teaching of English from The University of Arizona. His research interests include histories and theories of composition, the relationship between college and secondary education, and writing's possibilities for personal and social transformation.

RICHARD MARBACK is Director of Composition at Wayne State University. He has published on the history of rhetoric, rhetorical theory, and the teaching of writing in such journals as *CCC, Composition Studies, JAC,* and *Rhetoric Review.* His current research is on language rights and language policy in Canada, South Africa, and the United States.

KEITH D. MILLER is the author of *Voice of Deliverance: The Language of Martin Luther King, Jr., and Its Sources* and of many scholarly essays on the rhetoric of King and the songs of the civil rights movement. With Theresa Enos, he recently co-edited *Beyond Postprocess and Postmodernism: The Spaciousness of Rhetoric.* He is currently the Associate Chair of the Department of English at Arizona State University, where he previously served as Writing Program Administrator.

RYAN MUCKERHEIDE is a graduate student specializing in Medieval Literature at Arizona State University. He maintains an active interest in military and aviation history. He continues to revise and update his "Terrorism 102" course and encourages anyone who currently has or is interested in developing such a course to contact him.

PATRICIA MURPHY earned Bachelor's degrees in English and French literature from Miami University and an MFA in Poetry from Arizona State University. She currently teaches writing at Arizona State, where she serves as Faculty Mentor to adjunct writing teachers. Her poems have appeared in numerous journals, including *The Iowa Review, Quarterly West,* and *American*

Poetry Review. She has received awards from the Associated Writing Programs and the Academy of American Poets. Her most recent manuscript, *Sun Damage,* examines the intersections between culture and capitalism in the desert southwest.

DARIN PAYNE is an Assistant Professor of English at the University of Hawai'i, specializing in Rhetoric and Composition. Much of his scholarship is focused on technology and its impact on literacy, student subject formation, and the intellectual work of composition studies. His research has been published in national and international presses, appearing in a variety of anthologies and journals, including *Preparing College Teachers of Writing* and *The Writing Program Administrator's Resource: A Guide to Reflective Institutional Practice,* as well as *JAC: A Journal of Composition Theory* and *Rhetoric Review.* He is at work on a book, tentatively titled *Mediating Education: Technologies, Writing Instruction, and Cultural Reproduction in the Virtual Classroom.*

LONNI PEARCE is a graduate student and teacher of writing at The University of Arizona. Her scholarly interests include the rhetoric and history of U.S. consumer culture, rhetorics of time and technology, and theories of dialectic. She is currently working on her dissertation, a rhetorical analysis of the dialectical relationship between representations of consumption and citizenship in marketing and public relations texts produced by socially responsible companies.

DUANE ROEN, Professor of English, currently directs the Center for Learning and Teaching Excellence at Arizona State University, where he previously served as writing program administrator. In addition to directing the Writing Program at Syracuse University, he served as Coordinator of Graduate Studies in English at the University of Arizona, where he also worked as Director of Rhetoric, Composition, and the Teaching of English from 1988 to 1992. In addition to his five previous books and many chapters, articles, and conference papers, NCTE has recently published *Strategies for Teaching First-Year Composition* (with Veronica Pantoja, Lauren Yena, Susan K. Miller, and Eric Waggoner).

KENNETH R. VORNDRAN teaches writing and creative writing at Pima Community College in Tucson, Arizona. His essays, poetry, and fiction have appeared in various magazines including *HOPE, Mothering,* and *Sandscript.* Ken is currently working on a Ph.D. in Rhetoric, Composition, and the Teaching of English at The University of Arizona.

KATHLEEN WEINKAUF graduated from the University of Wisconsin—La Crosse, where she earned a BA in English. Currently an MA candidate at Arizona State University, she is studying Ethnic American Literature. She looks forward to earning a Ph.D. This is her first publication.

EDWARD M. WHITE is an adjunct professor of English at The University of Arizona and professor emeritus of English at California State University, San Bernardino, where he served prolonged periods as English department chair and coordinator of the upper-division university writing program. His *Teaching and Assessing Writing* (1985) has been called "required reading" for the profession; a revised edition in 1994 received an MLA award "for outstanding research." He is author of more than 60 articles and book chapters on literature and the teaching of writing and has written, edited, or coedited ten books, including *Composition in the Twenty-First Century* (1996), *Developing Successful College Writing Programs* (1989), *Assessment of Writing* (1996), *Composition Studies in the New Millennium* (2003), and *Assigning, Responding, Evaluating* (1999).

Index